The English tone of voice

The English tone of voice

Essays in intonation, prosody and paralanguage

David Crystal

Reader in Linguistic Science, University of Reading

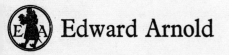 Edward Arnold

Printed in Great Britain by
Western Printing Services Ltd
Bristol

Contents

Introduction

The phrase 'tone of voice' makes a succinct and perspicuous title, but by itself it is inadequate as a precise specification of the various fields of inquiry with which this volume is concerned. Technical equivalents could be 'non-segmental' or 'suprasegmental phonology', terms which have the merit of relating easily to an established domain of linguistics, but which are unfortunately rather negative in character. More positively, it is possible to isolate distinct areas of emphasis from within this general field, thus bringing into use such terms as 'intonation', 'rhythm', 'prosodic features' and 'paralanguage', and this is the orientation of the present collection of studies. Each chapter focuses on a particular range of vocal effect, and concentrates on elucidating the problems of linguistic analysis central to that range: Chapters 1, 4 and 7 look mainly at intonation; Chapters 2 and 3 at paralanguage; and Chapters 5, 6 and 8 at the functional study of the whole range of prosodic and paralinguistic features. It will be evident from the cross-references between chapters, however, that there are no sharp functional boundary-lines to be drawn. One of the underlying arguments of this book, in fact, is that non-segmental phonology does constitute a coherent field of research, within which the different categories of vocal effect need to be formally and functionally related. Too little empirical work has been done for any well-grounded 'theory of non-segmental phonology' to emerge as yet, and certain crucial theoretical notions—such as the concept of 'graded contrastivity' (see Chapter 2)—have yet to be properly investigated. But it is nonetheless towards such a theory that the essays in this book hope to make some contribution.

From another point of view, this book aims to take a stage further the approach to the analysis of non-segmental phonology first described in detail in *Prosodic systems and intonation in English* (1969). I hope in particular to have made good two of the most general limitations of that book.[1] Firstly, it is acknowledged that the relationship between prosodic features and other levels of linguistic analysis—especially grammar—was given a patchy treatment. In its concern for phonologically-detailed description, there was less emphasis than there should have been on how this description would accommodate itself to the requirements of a general linguistic theory, whether generative (as insisted upon by Hubers 1971) or otherwise. Chapter 1 of the present book therefore tries to take this into account, and Chapters 2, 3 and 4 also raise theoretical issues which the earlier book did not treat adequately. Secondly,

1 Reviews of this book include Hubers (1971), Lindström (1973), Lipka (1973), Markel (1970), O'Connor (1970), Weinberg (1970) and Wodarz-Magdics (1973). There is a general discussion of the approach in Lyons 1972.

there was a superficial treatment given to the various 'applied' areas of study where non-segmental analysis could be used to good effect. The sociolinguistic and stylistic fields were most obviously neglected; and Chapters 5, 6 and 7 of the present volume comprise a discussion of the role of non-segmental features in these respects. Chapter 8 reviews the relationship of these features to language acquisition, another topic not dealt with in *Prosodic systems and intonation in English*.

Despite the dramatic increase in interest in these matters in recent years—witness the Conference on Intonology at Prague in 1970, or such collections as Bolinger (1972a) and Léon (1970)—there are however still many aspects of non-segmental phonology which have hardly begun to be studied. Particularly neglected is the relationship of this research to psycholinguistic procedures, for example in relation to work on memory, recall and attention (Smith and Goodenough 1971, Leonard 1973), to ethological studies (Blurton-Jones 1972, Hinde 1972), or to foreign-language teaching (Crystal and Davy 1975). The notion of social stereotype, referred to in Chapters 2, 4 and 5, is much in need of study in non-segmental terms, as is the whole question of the relative roles of linguistic and non-linguistic vocal effect in sociolinguistic and semiotic work (Giles 1970, Robinson 1972, etc.). And everyone is still walking extremely warily around the edge of the semantics cage. I have therefore tried to treat as comprehensively as possible the fields which have attracted most research, in the hope that by suggesting fairly definite boundaries for the present state of knowledge, I may incline some readers to begin tackling topics from within the no-man's-land beyond. I make no apology for the bibliographical detail included, accordingly.

The papers on which this book is based were all written between 1969 and 1973, and have appeared in journals or conference proceedings. The first half of Chapter 1 was given at the Second International Conference of Nordic and General Linguistics, Umea, in June 1973, and appears in the Proceedings, edited by K.-H. Dahlstedt; the section on tone was written for the Festschrift for Dwight Bolinger, edited by Sangster and Van Schooneveld (The Hague, 1975). For the present volume, sections on tonicity and comparative implications have been added. Chapter 2 was written in 1970 for inclusion in the Current Trends in Linguistics Series, Volume 12, *Linguistics and the adjacent arts and sciences* (The Hague). Chapter 3 was given to the Sixth International Conference of Ethnographers and Anthropologists, Chicago 1973, and appears in Volume 1 of the Proceedings. Chapter 4 was written for Volume 1 of the *Journal of the International Phonetic Association* (1971: 17–28). Chapter 5 was given to a conference of the Association of Social Anthropologists on 'Language and Society' in 1969, and appears in the Proceedings (see Ardener 1971: 185–206). Chapter 6 was given to a section meeting on the Sociolinguistics of Religion at the 1972 Georgetown Round Table Conference, published as a separate volume, edited by W. Samarin (New York). Chapter 7 was given to a meeting of the Philological Society in May 1971. Part of Chapter 8 was given at the Second International Congress of Applied Linguistics, Cambridge 1969, later published in *Lingua* 32 (1973: 1–45); part was given to a conference on 'Prosodic Feature Analysis' in Toronto in 1969 (see Léon 1970: 78–89); and part was given to the First International Symposium on Child Language Acquisition, held at Florence in 1972, appearing in the Proceedings, edited by W. Raffler Engel. For the present volume, points of overlap between these papers have been removed, and there have been a number of minor changes, in the interests of stylistic consistency. Apart from this, the only alterations to the original texts are the addition of references which bring the papers more up to date, with associated discussion. The Bibliography, in addition to containing the references used in the chapters, also includes publications on non-segmental phonology that have appeared between 1969 and 1974.

I
Prosodic features and linguistic theory

Background

My starting-point is the assertion that prosodic features in general, and intonation in particular, have until very recently never held a prominent place in discussions of linguistic theory. Two simple reasons account for this: on the one hand, intonation analysts have on the whole not involved themselves with general questions of theory; and on the other hand, theoretical models have on the whole been oriented towards other things than prosody. Neither of these points is intended to be derogatory: they simply reflect the alternative pre-occupations of earlier generations of scholars. Within the European tradition of intonation studies, for example, the priorities were dictated by demands for materials capable of being used in the context of foreign-language teaching. There was an over-concentration on points of phonetic detail, and on the means of intonational transcription, and negligible attention paid to the criteria for establishing phonological categories. There were numerous *ad hoc* comments about the grammatical function of particular intonation patterns, but no systematic attempt to investigate the relationship between intonation and other aspects of language structure, especially syntax. The range of data which was taken into account was extremely restricted—usually the intonation of written language read aloud—and judgments about frequency of use or semantic interpretation were largely impressionistic. The pedagogical orientation for the work was not a compatible framework for theoretical inquiry, and the methodological difficulties involved in the collection and analysis of intonational data made systematic investigations impracticable, until the development of appropriate instrumentation. Whenever theoretical claims were made, therefore, they tended to be vague or oversimple—for instance, that intonation was an affective phenomenon, or that for every tone there was a basic meaning. The European tradition produced many descriptive insights into intonation, but whatever theoretical position underlay the work of such scholars as Passy, Palmer, Jones and Armstrong, it remained largely implicit. The American tradition of studies before Chomsky was quite different in its general orientation, but again, what was produced was primarily a descriptive framework and a set of methodological directives, with little by way of an explicit theory within which prosodic observations could be interrelated and predicted.

These points have been made before,[1] and bear witness to the general neglect of theoretical considerations by students of intonation. They can be paralleled by the neglect, amounting at times to total ignorance, of prosodic

1 A general discussion, with full bibliography, is to be found in Crystal 1969a: Ch. 2 and 253ff.

features by linguists working within the 'mainstream' of their discipline. Segmental phonology, morphology and syntax have each received a respectable measure of attention in post-Saussurean linguistics, but despite the pleas of Pike, Trager, Bolinger and others, the dominant attitude in the 1950s was still to see intonation as on the edges of language, referring to it in descriptive or theoretical inquiry only when absolutely necessary, or reducing parts of it to units of the same kind as segmental phonemes.[2] Early work in generative grammar generally maintained the structuralist emphasis, either by ignoring intonation altogether, or by dismissing it as mere performance. And even more recently, there has been a reluctance to deal with intonation at all other than to see it as an extension of word-level stress phonology (as in *The sound pattern of English*, discussed further below). It is this reluctance which current trends in linguistics are beginning to erode.

In the past ten years, views of intonation have radically altered. The intonation analysts have been affected by the general stimulus of the Chomskyan approach to search for general explanations of particular events, and the theoreticians have been impressed by a confluence of ideas about prosodic features from a number of distinct branches of the subject which suggests that such general explanations are both possible and relevant. Prosodic features seem nowadays to hold an importance for the explanation of linguistic behaviour not previously realized. This was first recognized in the various educationally-, anthropologically- and sociologically-oriented studies in the mid-1960s, out of which developed, *inter alia*, concepts of communicative competence and the ethnography of communication (see Gumperz and Hymes 1972). The ethnographic approach was in principle concerned with the microscopic analysis of the data of social interaction, to establish what features in the act of speaking had the function of signalling the various social assumptions, relationships and categories found in different types of situation. Early on it became clear that conventional analysis in terms of the segmental phonology, syntax and vocabulary of sentences was leaving out a great deal that was significant, and closer attention came to be paid to prosodic phenomena. A recent paper on classroom interaction shows this emphasis, suggesting 'that the prosodic component encompassing stress, pitch and timing along with speech features usually termed paralinguistic is . . . part of an optional set of communicative strategies that can be used alternatively with syntactic, lexical or phonological variables' (Gumperz and Herasimchuk 1972: 111–12). The key role of non-verbal factors (under which term is subsumed both linguistic features such as intonation and non-linguistic features such as voice-quality) is a main theme of Robinson (1972). This book takes the view that 'patterns of stress and intonation [and other non-segmental patterns, as the author makes clear elsewhere] are best treated as essential rather than peripheral features of the language' (187), and in his review of social psychological research into linguistic behaviour, it is remarkable

2 Early criticism of segmental reductionism came from Haas (1957: 159), Bazell (1954: 133) and Bolinger (1949, 1951, 1958). The arguments have nowhere been answered.

how many quite distinct lines of research conclude that the understanding of these patterns is a key to the problem being investigated: not only the marking of emotional states, but the marking of personality, social identity, role relationships, social class, the regulation of encounters, and much more (see further, Chapters 5 and 6 below). For example, an investigation by Seligman, Tucker and Lambert (1970) indicates that the prosodic characteristics of children's voices unconsciously affect teachers' evaluations of their intelligence and capabilities. The social and psychological significance of non-segmental features is also accepted and illustrated, along with visual (kinesic) and other communicative modalities, in recent work on semiotics: for example the identifying function of prosody in schizophrenia is argued by Ostwald in Sebeok, Hayes and Bateson (1964), and there is a general review of the significance of paralanguage in the paper by Mahl and Schulze in that volume. More recently, the whole field of non-verbal communication has been studied in a Royal Society study group (see Hinde 1972), and due attention to the importance of prosody and paralanguage is paid there by Lyons, Argyle and others.

The second trend towards the recognition of the centrality of intonation and related features is in language-acquisition studies. There are now a number of reports which show that prosodic contrasts are used as part of a child's production long before the development of segmental phonological contrasts, and thus before identifiable 'first words'. Prosodic features are used grammatically, to identify sentence-boundaries and sentence functions ('wanting', 'identifying', etc.), and this process appears productively from around six to seven months, and receptively much earlier (for a review of research, especially on production, see Chapter 8; for a discussion largely on reception, see Kaplan 1970). The specification of early semantic categories in terms of the prosodic and paralinguistic features which expound them is the direction in which the study of early language development is tending to move, and this of course has been reinforced by current developments in linguistic theory and description.

Recent developments here have increasingly recognized intonation. We may begin with the most recent reference grammar for English (Quirk *et al.* 1972), which is the first to give a separate section to intonation, and which illustrates throughout the role of prosodic factors in distinguishing grammatical patterns within sentences and in the connectivity of sentences and sentence parts. A number of their descriptive points will be referred to below. It is important to note that this grammar was based upon a particularly large sample of data, within which the area of spontaneous conversation was given considerable coverage. Their observations about the role of intonation are thus a major development from the statements of the pedagogical studies referred to above. A second and more far-reaching development was the recent attempt of some generative grammarians to take account of these phenomena within the frame of reference of the standard model of generative grammar. This debate, largely published in *Language* 47 and 48, was of value in that it set a seal of approval on intonational studies, and brought them more within the purview of linguistic theory, as then understood; but it can be argued that it failed to provide an adequate account of intonation, and that it took account of but a very restricted range of data, and ignored the way in which the assumptions of an *Aspects*-type model of generative grammar pre-set the direction of the argument, making it impossible to give appropriate discussion to certain significant questions.

The generative debate

The starting-point of the generative discussion was the Nuclear Stress Rule (NSR) as formulated by Chomsky and Halle (1968: 17ff.), whereby primary stress is assigned to the rightmost primary-stressed vowel within a major constituent (NP, VP, S), weakening all others. It is a cyclic rule which applies after all the rules which determine the stress of individual lexical items, and results in the traditionally 'neutral' intonation for an English sentence, the last constituent being stressed. This rule is assumed to apply to surface structures, operating as part of the phonological cycle and applying to the various constituent bracketings, starting with the most deeply-embedded constituent. Chomsky and Halle themselves recognised that there are classes of exceptions to this rule, referring to an example they found in Newman (1946)—though it had worried Sweet and Palmer long before—wherein the ambiguity of *He has plans to leave* (= he intends to leave/he has documents to leave) is claimed to be resolvable by contrastive tonic placement, and to an example of contrastive stress in cases of syntactic parallelism (e.g. *He wanted to study electrical rather than civil engineering*).[3]

Bresnan (1971) took up the question of these types of exception. She referred to other well-known examples of cases where the final constituent is unstressed, namely sentences with final anaphoric pronouns (e.g. *Helen teaches it*), final indefinite pronouns (*The boy brought some*), and repeated items (*John knows a woman who excels at karate, and he avoids the woman*), and then concentrated on four types of syntactically complex constructions which do not conform to the NSR: (a) *George has plans to leave*; (b) *Mary liked the pro'posal that George left* (vs. . . . *proposal that George 'leave*); (c) *John asked what Helen had 'written* (vs. *John asked what 'books Helen had written*); (d) *George found someone he'd like you to 'meet* (vs. *George found some 'friends he'd like you to meet*). Her hypothesis was that these cases are all predictable from the NSR, without any special modifications, assuming that the NSR is ordered after all the syntactic transformations on each transformational cycle. This claim was counter to the basic assumption in Chomsky and Halle (1968: 15) that '[prosodic] contours are determined in some manner by the surface structure of the utterance', for Bresnan was arguing that the contours are determined by the underlying sentence structure. She claimed that evidence for this was provided from the above examples, whereby the stress patterns found were argued as reflecting

3 What does not seem to have been noticed is that tonic shifting does *not* resolve the ambiguity of this sentence: tonic on 'plans' certainly means 'documents', but tonic on 'leave' can mean that 'plans' can be interpreted as *either* 'intentions' *or* 'documents', depending on context. It is a pity that a better example could not have been found for the discussion.

those of the simple sentences embedded within them in deep structure. In other words, a basic stress pattern is preserved throughout the syntactic derivation.

In her article, Bresnan placed a great emphasis on the consequences her claim had for generative linguistic theory, in particular that her ordering hypothesis provided evidence for a lexicalist view of language (as it reinforced the view that all lexical insertion occurs on or before the first transformational cycle). It was unfortunate, in a way, that this emphasis was made, as it attracted a discussion of various general issues which was premature, in view of the absence of any clarification of certain rather more basic matters in her article. Lakoff (1972), for instance, took up the question of the lexicalist hypothesis and related matters, and attacked Bresnan on a mixture of observational and logical grounds; his own analysis was to see the NSR as a global rule which applied in the phonological cycle. Berman and Szamosi (1972) argued that her hypothesis could be rejected on observational grounds, that it made too many incorrect predictions and missed certain generalizations. In particular, they argued that there were many important cases where surface structure was essential for the determination of sentence stress (308–10). Their stronger argument was that the NSR as such is unworkable, because there are too many cases where primary stress assignment depends on factors other than structure—especially semantic factors. There was a reply by Bresnan (1972), some further discussion by Stockwell (1972), and an important contribution by Bolinger (1972b), which I shall discuss separately below.

My present aim is not to enter into a detailed consideration of the various arguments just referred to: I leave this to those who wish to work within the framework of assumptions used by that approach to generative grammar. My purpose is to use this debate as a taking-off point for a discussion of the merits of an alternative approach. The debate usefully focused attention on the detail of some relatively neglected facts of prosodic distribution; but it suffered from a failure to realize that many of the difficulties it got into, and much of the dispute, was due to the set of theoretical assumptions within which the analysts chose to work. It is only natural, of course, once one has opted for a particular theoretical approach, to try to make that work at all costs. But intonation, and prosody in general, is a rather different kind of phenomenon from anything generative grammar had attempted to cope with previously, and the above debate showed very clearly the problem generative grammarians had to face—the problem of having to graft onto a well-developed syntactically-oriented model a phenomenon whose importance the model in its early processes of construction totally ignored, and whose study depends on assumptions incompatible with that model.

The most illuminating attack is to query the fundamental assumption of the generative approach, that intonational phenomena are predictable from syntax. This is the line taken by Bolinger (1972b). This article attacks the basic assumption, which is taken for granted in the whole of the above debate, that the location of sentence accents can be explained by reference to syntax. He agrees that stress is explicable in this way, and goes on to point out that much of the confusion is due to a failure to distinguish word- and sentence-level phonology, stress belonging to the lexicon, and accent to the utterance. He argues that placement of accent is primarily conditioned by the speaker's view of how to distribute the semantic weight of his sentence, for which it is necessary to take account of the entire context (linguistic and situational). 'The error of attributing to syntax what belongs to semantics comes from concentrating on the commonplace' (634). Highly predictable patterns (e.g. '*work to do,* '*clothes to wear*) will have the verbs unaccented; less predictable patterns will not (e.g. *clothes to* '*launder*). His article concentrates on demonstrating that sentences whose accentual pattern is said to be dependent on (predictable from) syntax can have this pattern readily altered by varying contextual factors. Tonicity is to be seen, in his view, in terms of the distribution of new information in a structure, directly reflecting the speaker's intent, and essentially independent of the syntax. Talking about prosody in a contextual vacuum (641) will inevitably produce innumerable disagreements about the 'empirical facts', and the citing of 'special rules' to handle apparent problems (as the generative debate displays, e.g. Bresnan 1972: 333n.). His conclusion involves a rephrasing of the NSR: instead of claiming that the main accent normally goes on the last stressable constituent, he states:

> The intonational reality is, rather, that the speaker will put the main accent as far to the right as he dares, when assertive pressure is high; and he frequently [*sc.* e.g. in excitedly emphatic speech, cf. 643] dares to put it on a syllable (almost but not quite always one containing a full vowel) farther to the right than the recognized lexical stress. . . . The distribution of sentence accents is not determined by syntactic structure but by semantic and emotional highlighting.[4] Syntax is relevant indirectly in that some structures are more likely to be highlighted than others. But a description along these lines can only be in statistical terms. Accents should not be mashed down to the level of stresses, which are lexical abstractions. In their zeal to reverse Trager-Smith phonology, transformationalists have fallen into the same trap. Whether one tries to set up prosodic rules for syntax or syntactic rules for prosody, the result is the same: two domains are confused which should be kept apart. (644)

This approach seems quite correct, but it should be noted that it applies only to accent placement (or tonicity), which was almost the entire subject-matter of the generative debate. It would be misleading to suggest that this or any other conclusion can be generalized to other aspects of intonational patterning, such as tone-unit distribution or type of nuclear tone (see below, p. 15): a semantic explanation may be satisfactory for one aspect of intonation, but other explanations may be required elsewhere. The problem of intonation's functional complexity is in fact well recognized in the literature—as a signal of grammatical structure, of emotional expression, of semantic organization, of social role (for an illustration of the interplay of these factors, see the description of 'softening' phrases—*you know, I mean,* etc.—in Crystal and Davy 1975).

4 Cf. the reluctant conclusion of Berman and Szamosi (1972: 313) who, after finding that optional stress placements must be taken into account, say: 'It seems that the grammar has to be able to assign both stress contours, and to designate either one as normal, in accordance with principles which are at least in part semantic.'

It is not necessary to go any further into a sub-classification of these functions in order to see that any theory which assumes that *one* of them is primary or basic for the whole of intonation is going to have difficulty justifying this decision, apart from appealing in advance to such vague, *a priori* notions as simplicity or insightfulness of generalization. I therefore take the view that prosodic phenomena should be seen as an independent component of any model of language organization, which interrelates with other components in various ways: some features of the prosodic component interact with syntax, some with sociolinguistic categories, some with affective meaning, and so on; but there is no claim that one interrelationship is in some sense prior to the others. And while on the one hand I accept Bolinger's conclusions about the semantic conditioning of tonicity, I shall be arguing later in this chapter that tone-unit placement is in fact determined by syntax.[5]

There are however other difficulties with the generative approaches which ought to be raised before moving to the constructive part of this chapter. In particular, one has to comment on their curious semi-awareness of the problem of reliable data. They often remark on the methodological problems involved in their work, but—perhaps because of their traditional antagonism towards discovery procedures—they fail to do anything about it. Much of the difficulty arises out of a disagreement as to what are the basic (i.e. 'normal') data to take into account. Bresnan *et al.* seem to have used one of two techniques to establish their basic data: they have either used their own intuition to decide on normal intonation patterns, or they have asked their colleagues to read sentences aloud. Neither technique is a satisfactory basis for intonational study. I am not of course disputing the relevance of intuition as a datum for certain areas of linguistic analysis, but there seems no reason why one should assume that our intuition is an equally powerful means of judgment for all parts of language. Our conscious tacit knowledge of prosodic regularities is in fact negligible. It is well-known that response to a fixed set of prosodically-contrasting sentences varies widely from day to day. Some days we accept more sentences as possible than on other days; the range of semantic interpretations varies considerably (even when presented with the data in multiple-choice form); we rate as acceptable more the longer we are given to think about a sentence; and so on. Berman and Szamosi note one aspect of the complexity, but do so dismissively in a footnote: they feel that 'the oddness or normalness of a given stress contour depends partly on the speaker's ability to provide a satisfactory context', and add: 'It is interesting to note that those of our acquaintances who are most inventive in concocting contexts in which "semantically anomalous" sentences are acceptable found the widest diversity of possible stress patterns' (1972: 314). They are therefore—they say—hesitant about marking examples as ungrammatical. But they still do asterisk a large number of sentences, and their attack on Bresnan depends entirely on a naturalness condition of some kind, either by showing that other patterns than Bresnan's

5 The role of both semantic and syntactic factors in accounting for nuclear tone type and tonicity is discussed below, pp. 24ff.

are possible and normal, or by criticizing her outputs as being impossible or abnormal. The point is made also by Lakoff (1972: 286), who points to the normality of other stress patterns than those Bresnan gives, but who himself makes judgments about unacceptability, norms, contrastive stress etc., presumably on a personal intuitive basis. It would be very easy to go through most of the asterisked examples in this debate and provide contrasts which make them acceptable, without necessarily introducing a contrastive stress element, but Bolinger has already shown how elementary a matter this is.

In other words, the empirical basis of the whole argument is open to question ('insecure' is the word Chomsky uses for it (1969: 24)—and see his footnote 21 for his awareness of the problem of determining normal intonation, though he does not attempt a solution). As long as the analyst relies wholly on his own intuition for the verification of his prosodic hypotheses, his approach remains suspect: one can convince oneself in minutes that a pattern is possible, that problem patterns are idiolectal and dialectal (cf. the unsupported speculations in Berman and Szamosi 1972: 314), and so on. Before one can interpret claims that 'most people' do such-and-such in intonation, one needs some rather basic background information—like how many informants were asked, whether they were phonetically naive, whether they were well-educated, how the task was presented to them. At least Berman and Szamosi try, but their results are unimpressive. They give the following sentences as 'normal, non-contrastive, non-emphatic' patterns (312): (a) *We liked the proposal that George 'mentioned*; (b) *Whose church did they 'vandalize*; (c) *There are new worlds to 'win*; (d) *There are new areas to 'explore.* They say: 'Most people [sic] find that shifting the primary stress . . . to the head noun (or questioned noun) . . . results in sentences that are distinctly odd. (Of course, they can all be given contrastive interpretations, in which case there is nothing strange about them.)' (312–13). Bolinger took up the point that, given appropriate context, the above could be given just as contrastive an interpretation as the alternatives. I simply want to add that asking informants to judge for 'oddness' in these sentences does not obtain the agreement Berman and Szamosi claim. Even if one uses their technique, and asks informants to say the sentences out loud, there is considerable variability in the response. For example, when 30 educated and phonetically naive British English speakers were asked to say the above sentences aloud, the following tonic placements were obtained: (a) tonic on *liked* (4 times), *proposal* (4), *George* (8), *mentioned* (9); compound tonic on *liked* and *mentioned* (2), *proposal* and *mentioned* (2), *George* and *mentioned* (1); (b) tonic on *whose* (1), *church* (17), *they* (1), *vandalize* (11); (c) tonic on *worlds* (10), *win* (18); compound tonic on *worlds* and *win* (2); (d) tonic on *areas* (14), *explore* (11); compound tonic on *areas* and *explore* (5).

All of this indicates the unreliability of the data used in the above papers. To the extent that the authors realized the inadequacy of their own intuitions and asked other informants, their data are useful insofar as they make their methodology explicit. At times, however, their methodology seems positively in error. It would seem that one technique that was used was to present colleagues with a written version of a sentence and ask them to read it aloud (e.g. Berman and Szamosi 1972: 314, n. 11). The prosodic response was then taken as the basis of a judgment of normality. But this is in principle a suspect procedure. Berman and Szamosi give us no information about how they went about judging for normality, what statistical techniques they used (if any), and so on. Were their informants equally and consistently confident in their output (cf. Davy and Quirk 1969)? At the very least, one would want to present these informants with a set of alternatives which they would be asked to react to (e.g. by rank ordering)—otherwise one will reach premature conclusions (for example, assuming that the first pattern to be produced is the 'normal' one, whereas the sentence may have more than one version to which the term 'normal' may appropriately be applied, a possibility Berman and Szamosi themselves recognize (313) (though one which seems to be denied by Stockwell 1972: 87–8)). There was apparently some variability in referring to a certain set of sentences (315); Berman and Szamosi state: 'sentences like 40 are almost never ambiguous, because a unique stress contour is associated with each of the possible readings.' A footnote (13) adds: 'We refer, of course, to the most natural readings of the sentences, factoring out contrastive or other such marked interpetations.' But who decided the naturalness question here? Berman and Szamosi? Using their intuitions solely? Or does 'factoring out' mean what it says? My impression is that they, as others, are using informants in a thoroughly unscientific way, and the force of their case is correspondingly much reduced. (In any case it should be pointed out that notions of naturalness, contrastivity and markedness are extremely obscure. See further, Schmerling 1974.)

But there is a second problem with the reading aloud test: even with proper methodological controls, it works only with short simple sentences—and these are sentences which on the whole present few problems. As soon as a sentence gets at all complex, or as soon as the context is given in full, punctuation enters in. Now what does one do about this? If one leaves the punctuation in, in presenting a text to an informant, one is begging the question by giving the informants an explicit indication of where the tone-unit boundary falls. If one leaves it out, one is presenting the informants with an unfamiliar (and probably ambiguous) representation, to which they will be unable to give a 'natural' reaction. And there may be other difficulties, to do with the written medium or the spoken form, e.g. names beginning with a capital letter might tend to attract the accent. (This is not simply hypothetical: my same 30 informants were given the following sentences, separated from each other by other tasks: (a) *I've just bought some excellent badges*, (b) *I've just bought some Liverpool badges*. For (a), all 30 put the tonic on *badges*; for (b), 18 put the tonic on *badges*, and 12 on *Liverpool*.)

I can think of no way in which one can extract information about prosodic acceptability from informants without to some extent prejudging the results or introducing uncontrollable variables; and this is why I insist on the regulative function of the corpus. As far as I can tell, none of the authors being discussed—

except of course, Bolinger—have systematically analysed a corpus of spontaneously-produced, recorded material. If they had, many of Bolinger's criticisms would have been anticipated. Perhaps this is the traditional suspicion of
corpus-based work emerging again. But I would point out that one reason why
Chomsky's strictures of corpus work on syntax were so well-received was
because people had already spent years analysing the syntactic patterns of
corpora, and knew what the data were like. Chomsky's remarks made a great
deal of sense. But we are now talking of intonation, not syntax, and there we
lack a corresponding tradition of detailed descriptive work which we can use
as a basis for formulating more powerful hypotheses. Bresnan and others, it
seems, were jumping the gun. They were trying to develop a generative account
of prosodic patterns without having carried out the necessary descriptive
spadework. And this spadework means, in effect, the transcription of quantities
of spontaneously-produced material. No-one would claim that the description
of this material could be anything other than observationally adequate for the
corpus in question, but it can provide the necessary controls on the process of
extending the analysis into the realm of competence.[6]

The above debate is largely of historical interest now, in that alternative
theories of generative grammar have developed within which it would be
easier to incorporate prosodic phenomena (though the cautionary points about
methodology obviously still apply). For example, there was the basic difficulty
with the standard model of knowing what to do with intonational primitives
once they were permitted within the base component (cf. Stockwell 1960).
Semantically-oriented models of language structure, whether generative or
interpretive, will presumably find it much easier to take intonation into account,
because they allow a more direct relationship between intonational form and
semantics than could be present in terms of the standard model. Given a set of
semantic categories, one might postulate a prosodic component which works
along with the syntactic and lexical as a means of realization, as follows:

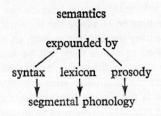

But I have not seen a detailed attempt to incorporate intonation into an approach
of this kind. Nor has the interpretive hypothesis been fully explored from this

6 This paragraph would have been unnecessary if generative authors had familiarized
themselves with the wealth of descriptive detail collected in the European pedagogical
tradition. It is really rather amusing to see examples of constructions attributed with
thanks to recent lectures of Ross or Lakoff, when they are cited in the work of Henry
Sweet and Joshua Steele.

point of view. In Chomsky (1969), tonicity provided the main argument for the view that semantic interpretation has to be partially determined by surface structure; but this essay was of course only exploratory: it illustrated the relevance of intonation in relation to the concepts of focus and presupposition[7] from only a small set of sentences, and it did not go into crucial questions of formalization. It was (and still is) quite unclear (a) how one would get from the rules of phonological interpretation, which would assign an intonation contour to surface structures, to the semantic rules, which would interpret a phrase containing an intonational centre as a focus of utterance, and how the semantic rules actually operate; (b) how certain surface-structure phrases would be marked to receive 'contrastive stress' ('by grammatical processes of a poorly-understood sort', 70), and in what ways these would be allowed to affect the operation of the phonological rules; and (c) how to account for gradience in naturalness of response in cases of contrastive stress, whereby 'naturalness declines far more sharply as larger and larger phrases containing the intonation center are considered as a possible focus' (76). In the absence of any suggestions as to how these problems should be tackled, the merits of an alternative approach, without taking sides on the generative v. interpretive issue, could usefully be explored. The main features of this approach are the splitting of the phonological component into two, the *segmental* and the *non-segmental*, and of the latter into a set of functionally distinct sub-components.

The present approach

Intonation cannot be slotted into one's model as a single category; it is not a unitary, homogeneous phenomenon. It is often talked about as if it were—when one hears references to 'the intonation of a sentence' or to 'the learning of intonation', for example. I have argued elsewhere that intonation is not a single system of contours or levels, but the product of the interaction of features from different prosodic systems—*tone, pitch-range, loudness, rhythmicality* and *tempo* in particular. For example, a particular tone (e.g. *falling*) can be seen to vary in terms of its relative height (e.g. *high* v. *low*) and width (e.g. *wide* v. *narrow*); a stretch of utterance can be articulated as 'parenthetic' if it is given *low* pitch range with optional *piano* loudness and *allegro* tempo. The various features are given a partly hierarchic organization, such that the basic unit of prosodic organization, the *tone-unit*, is seen to consist minimally of a *tonic syllable*, expounded by one of a set of *nuclear tones* (falling, rising, etc.), and optionally preceded and followed by other syllables involving differing degrees of pitch- and loudness-prominence. (The full system is given in Crystal 1969a: see especially Chapters 4 and 5. Further details will be found on pp. 60–61 and 92–5 below.) In the rest of this chapter, I want to look at the main structural characteristics of this model—and in particular at the concept of the tone-unit—from the point of view of how they might be integrated within a broader

7 'The focus is a phrase containing the intonation center; the presupposition, an expression derived by replacing the focus by a variable' (26).

model of language structure. What is immediately clear from this approach, regardless of its merits, is that there is far more to the study of 'intonation' than tonic placement, or *tonicity*. But the generative debate for some reason has arbitrarily restricted the subject-matter of intonation to tonicity. This is a restriction which goes back to Chomsky and Halle, and it needs to be removed. In fact it does not stop the writers from referring to other prosodic matters when they find it necessary to do so, but these references are always introduced in an *ad hoc* way, or not systematically distinguished from tonicity. In particular, there is a failure to give appropriate recognition to the independent roles of tone-unit boundary features and nuclear tone type, and to the systematic basis of other prosodic contrasts (such as pause, rhythm). The only exception, as far as I can see, is Stockwell (1972: 103ff.), who refers to two unpublished dissertations on the topic of phrase boundaries and intonation within the generative framework, and, in commenting on Pope's (1971) view that intonation assignment depends on prior stress assignment, argues for tonicity and tone to be seen as autonomous systems (96–7): 'It is quite likely that the contour, and its center, are altogether independent phenomena.'

The present view is based on an analysis of the prosodic patterns used in a corpus of some eight hours of informal, spontaneous conversation, constituting several varieties of educated southern British English. This analysis is intended to justify the particular theoretical approach used, which, for the sake of clarity, will be given some exposition first. Figure 1 is a first attempt at a model in which the main constructs required to handle my data are interrelated. The first four points which follow are preliminary assumptions, which I wish to take for granted for the purposes of this chapter.

(1) The model may be interpreted as a model of either production or reception; but for the purposes of illustration, I will outline its operation in terms of a process of production.

(2) *Meaning* and *phonetic substance* are taken as given: the question is to determine what components are necessary in order to interrelate them.

(3) A distinction between syntax and lexicon is here accepted, and represented using the labels *structures* (*sc.* syntactic and morphological structures and categories, as given in some grammatical handbook) and *lexical items* (as listed in some dictionary). It is assumed that the internal stress pattern of lexical items is given as part of this description, and no further reference will be made to stress in this paper. (This view of stress as a word-level concept is also Bolinger's, as already mentioned.)

(4) A distinction between *affective* (or attitudinal) and *cognitive* meaning is accepted as necessary for any analysis of intonational function. It is not assumed that these are the only two types of meaning which need to be recognized; nor is it assumed that a clear *a priori* distinction can be made between them. (The dotted line between *affective* and *structures* indicates the possibility of word-order variation, *inter alia*, expressing particular attitudes: see Charleston 1960.)

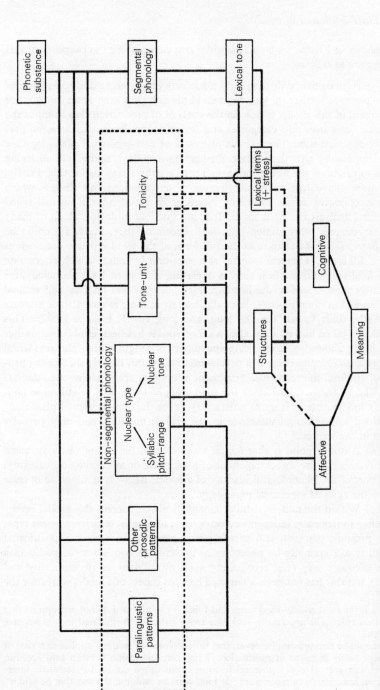

Fig. 1 Functional model: non-segmental phonology and other components

The points in Figure 1 which I consider controversial for the purposes of this chapter are as follows.

(5) A fundamental distinction is made between *segmental* and *non-segmental* phonology (see further, p. 52). Segmental phonology is seen as an interpretive component of this model which (in the analysis of production) has as input the syntactic structures and categories and lexical items, integrated in some previously-specified way. The various processes of non-segmental phonology are seen as operating *after* the segmental rules[8] have applied, as the lines emerging in the top right of the figure indicate. There are three reasons for this. Firstly, it is more convenient to specify the set of assimilations and elisions which become operative as an utterance increases in speed *after* a normal-speed segmental analysis has been made. It is not possible to decide which of many possible degrees of reduction (e.g. *have* becoming [həv, əv, v, f]) could be established as a base-form, and the full form of the word remains the obvious choice. Likewise, junctural features at a tone-unit boundary which operate on word-final segments are best seen as operating after word-level phonology, for obviously most words in the language may occur in non-final as well as final position within the tone-unit. Secondly, vowels in tonic monosyllables increase in length: short vowels become long, and long vowels become longer. This fact is best taken into account after a set of vowels has been established, rather than being allowed to complicate statements of length within the segmental component. Thirdly, there is a psycholinguistic point, namely that in the process of reading, the segmental graphemic properties are in a one-one relationship with phonemes, and since the model ought to be able to subsume both speech and writing, it is more satisfactory to see the non-segmental phonology as 'added to' segmental utterance in the spoken medium, and only partially added in the written.[9]

(6) A minor point is that *lexical tone*—that is, the use of pitch (or some other feature) as the direct exponent of a syntactic or morphological category, or as part of the phonological identity of a lexical item—is assumed to operate before the rules of segmental phonology.

(7) Within the non-segmental phonological component, this model recognizes five functionally independent categories: tone-unit, tonicity, nuclear type, other prosodic patterns, and paralinguistic patterns. In a more sophisticated model, it will certainly be necessary to present the two latter categories in a more adequate way (e.g. recognizing such distinctions as rhythmicality and pause), but this has not been attempted here, as unless this model works for the

8 This is the most widely-used term, and I find it useful; but I do not presuppose that any such rules will necessarily look like those currently formulated in a generative context.
9 It should be pointed out, however, that the metaphor of 'adding' applies to a view of language solely in terms of production. When comprehension is taken into account, the primary role of non-segmental features as an initial datum for semantic interpretation has often been recognized ('It's not what he said, but the way that he said it', etc.).

main non-segmental features of utterance, there is no point in trying to extend it to other areas.

(8) The main empirical claims made by this model are reflected in the solid lines connecting the various components. They are four. Firstly, it is claimed that the placement of tone-unit boundaries is determined by syntactic structure. Secondly, it is claimed that tonicity is primarily determined by lexical or semantic factors, sometimes by specific structures, and sometimes by affective information (as the broken lines indicate). Indirectly, of course, tonicity is dependent on syntax, in that tonicity requires the prior establishment of a tone-unit to define its domain, and tone-units are determined syntactically. The arrow in the figure indicates this indirectness. Thirdly, it is claimed that nuclear types are determined both by structural and affective meaning. Fourthly, it is claimed that other prosodic and paralinguistic patterns are determined by affective meaning, and are unaffected by syntax or lexis. This is very much a simplification, but it will suffice as a first approximation.

(9) Two other points should be noted. (a) As suggested in the earlier discussion, tone-unit boundaries are considered to have an independent organizational role from that of the tonic syllable expounded by a nuclear type. The motivation for this distinction is to take account of the facts of language acquisition mentioned above, when the first sign of language-particular patterning is the organization of what Weir calls 'sentence-like chunks' (1962) out of a largely undifferentiated babbling hitherto; these chunks are primitive tone-units, which operate some time before the appearance of definable nuclear tones or tonicity contrasts (the latter, of course, not appearing until the emergence of syllable sequences, much later). Some evidence for the distinction would come from the study of tongue-slips and related matters, where it is argued that the tone-unit is the fundamental unit of neural encoding, with slips rarely crossing tone-unit boundaries or affecting tonic placement (see Boomer and Laver 1968: 8–9; Laver 1970: 69ff.). (b) Other prosodic and paralinguistic patterns outrank tone-unit and other intonational organization, as the lines at the top right of the figure indicate, in that in output, variation in speed, rhythm, loudness etc. often reduce, subordinate or eliminate many of the intonational contrasts. The most important variable here is speed, whereby increased speed of utterance reduces the number of tone-units in an utterance, and vice versa. (This recalls Bierwisch's notion of 'optional phrasing' (1968).) Conversely, in input, one might expect initial processing of speed, loudness etc. to take place as a preliminary to more detailed processes (as in one's initial reaction to voice stereotypes—cf. Chapter 4).

Tone-units

I must now go on to consider the empirical content of the claims made in 8 above, using the corpus of data referred to earlier. What syntactic factors determine tone-unit boundaries? At the moment, it is an open question whether the tone-unit is best described with reference to the unit sentence or to some other unit, e.g. clause (as Halliday (1967) maintains, for instance) or element of clause structure (as Crystal (1969a: Ch. 6) argues). Bearing in mind the need to integrate one's treatment with generally-accepted models of grammar, the obvious starting-place would seem to be the sentence. Figure 2 indicates the operations required to assign tone-unit structures to sentences. (The grammatical apparatus used here, and in the following pages, is that of Quirk *et al.* 1972.) Given an input of a sentence, then (following the left-hand side of the figure downwards) if this sentence consists of one clause; and if this clause consists maximally of the elements Subject + Verb + Complement and/or Object, with one optional Adverb, in this order; and if each of the elements S, C, O or A is expounded by a simple nominal group: then the sentence will have a single tone-unit. This is considered to be the basic pattern. Examples are: /The big boy kicked the ball yesterday/, /We gave him a lift in the car/, /Go away/, /I asked him/, /He spoke/.

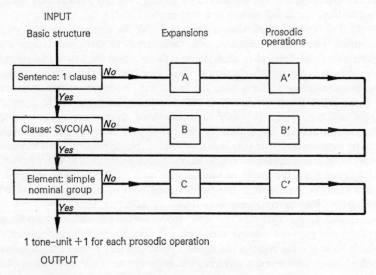

Fig. 2 Operations for assigning tone-unit structure to sentences

The above needs two clarifications, concerning the notions of clause structure and simple nominal group. As regards the former, it should be clear that different combinations of elements of structure will occur, depending primarily on the type of verb, e.g. SV, SVC, SVO, SVOO. I assume the classification of Quirk *et al.* (1972: §2.10). Minor (elliptical) sentences, e.g. S, O, are also subsumed under the above statement. Concerning the second point, Quirk *et al.* distinguish 'simple' nominal groups (§13.76), in which a noun is modified only by closed-system items (*the, that* . . .) or realized solely by a pronoun or proper name, from 'complex' nominal groups, which involve heavier modification. Within complex groups, they distinguish (i) modification consisting of one adjectival premodifier and/or one prepositional phrase postmodifier, from (ii) all other cases of 'multiple' modification. They discuss these distinctions from the point of view of the stylistic differentiation of texts. From the intonational point of view, however, it makes better sense to class together simple and type (i) complex groups, as they are identical as far as intonational distribution is concerned. 'Multiple' for me therefore includes all nominal groups containing minimally either two premodifying elements (determiners excluded) or two postmodifying elements (cf. C3 below).

Returning to the top left-hand corner of Figure 2, we find that various possible syntactic *expansions* occur at each of the grammatical levels recognized in the model. Each expansion carries with it a *prosodic operation* which involves the placing of a tone-unit boundary (or boundaries) at a point in the construction which demarcates the point of expansion of the basic structure, and which does not already have a boundary present (due to some previous prosodic operation). Thus at clause level, the sentence may contain an indefinite number of clauses: each clause is then subjected to a prosodic operation which gives it an intonational identity. The output from the clause level is then fed into the next level, and *each* clause in the sentence is analysed for its element structure: if it contains other elements than those recognized in the basic pattern above, or a marked order of elements, each of the expansions (under which term I subsume re-ordering) is given an intonational identity. The output, as a sequence of elements of clause structure, is then fed into the next level, and each nominal group (or phrase containing a nominal group) is analysed for its complexity, in the above sense, any expansions being intonationally identified. No further levels of grammatical structure affect tone-unit boundary placement. The output of tone-units is therefore ready for analysis in terms of placement of the tonic syllable (see pp. 22ff.).

Now follows the set of expansions which need to be recognized in order to account for the corpus. This is at present little more than an inventory. Doubtless it will prove possible to interrelate these structures more elegantly, but in the first instance I was anxious to present the facts with a minimum of theoretical overlay. The symbol : separates a syntactic expansion from its prosodic operation. / =tone-unit boundary. A, A', B, B', C, C', refer to Figure 2.

Expansions A: Prosodic operations A'

(1) *Structural parallelism: put* / *after each component*, e.g. /he came at three/ left at four/ was home by five/ and in bed by six/.

(2) *Coordinate clauses:put* / *after each component*, e.g. /John picked up the phone/ and a voice asked him the time/; /either you've got the answer/ or I have/; /he asked me what I'd said/ and whether I was interested in more/. There are a number of categories of exception to this rule, which have not been fully explored. The most important case is Ellipsis. No boundary is used if the Subject of a coordinated clause is elided, and a sequence of coordinated verbs

produced, e.g. /Susan will sing and dance/. On the other hand, the ellipsis of Object or Complement or part of the Verb from the first clause in a coordination requires the prosodic operation: *put | at the point of ellipsis, and optionally at the parallel point in the coordinated clause*, e.g. /Gerald likes/ but Peter hates/ Mary/ (cf. Quirk *et al.* §8.91); /it wasn't Jim/ but John who asked her/ (cf. Quirk *et al.* §14.18).

(3) *Subordinate clauses*

(i) *Adverbial initial: put | after clause*, e.g. /when he comes/ tell him I'm out/.

(ii) *Adverbial medial: put | on either side*, e.g. /the man in the corner/ if you must know/ is my cousin/.

(iii) *Adverbial final: put | before clause.* The conditions operating here are not entirely clear. / is obligatory if the adverbial status of the construction needs to be made clear, e.g. /tell me/ to save time/ (= in order to save time), as opposed to /tell me to save time/, which is ambiguous between adverbial and object. It is also obligatory when the preceding sentence structure is long or complex, as in /you're all going out to the museum on Saturday/ if the weather stays fine/. (The question of whether phonological length of the preceding structure as such is a determining factor needs to be investigated.)

(iv) *Nominal as subject: put | after subject* (cf. Quirk *et al.* §11.16), e.g. /what I said/ was of the utmost importance/; /how the book will sell/ is impossible to say/.

(v) *Medial non-restrictive: put | on either side*, e.g. /my brother/ who's abroad/ sent me a letter/; /the man/ dressed in a raincoat/ came towards me/. The boundary between non-restrictive clauses and phrases is by no means clear-cut (cf. Quirk *et al.* §3.31 and C4 below).

(vi) *Final non-restrictive: put | before.* This includes those with sentential antecedent (cf. Quirk *et al.* §13.15), e.g. /He likes linguistics/ which surprises me/.

(vii) *Appositive: put | after* (cf. Quirk *et al.* §13.16) e.g. /the fact is/ that he doesn't love her/.

(4) *Medial parenthetic clause: put | on either side*, e.g. /each one of the children/ I insist/ will have to go/; /Michael Smith/ he's the one in the black suit/ has just got married again/. There is no clear boundary between clause and phrase here, once again, as Quirk *et al.* point out; consequently one might include here (rather than under C below) examples of the following type: /Michael Smith/ the man in the black suit/ has just got married again/. Exclamatory asides, because of their parenthetic properties, ought also to be taken at this point, and not with apposition under C, e.g. /John/ the butcher/ he's ruined all my plants/—which might be contrasted with /John the butcher/ . . ., where John deals in meat.

(5) *Direct speech: put | after the reporting verb*, e.g. /then they said/ who's coming/ (=. . . said, 'Who's coming?'); /tell me/ where's your brother/; /naturally he said/ I'm very interested/ (= 'Naturally,' he said, 'I'm very interested.')

(6) *Comment clauses* (cf. Quirk *et al.* §11.65)

    (i) *Initial: put | after,* e.g. /you know/ I think it's going to rain/—cf. /you know I think . . ./

      (ii) *Medial, emphatic: put | on either side,* e.g. /and Mrs Jones/ you know/ came too/ ('you know' = 'you do know her, don't you').

    (iii) *Final, emphatic: put | before,* e.g. /and everything came out quite well/ you know/.

(7) *Tag utterances: put | before,* e.g. questions, /you're staying/ aren't you/; statements, /that was a lark/ that was/; /he likes a drink/ Jim does/. The statement clauses with elided verb might also be included at this point, e.g. /he's coming/ John/; cf. Quirk *et al.* §14.50.

Expansions B: Prosodic operations B'

(1) *Initial vocative: put | after,* e.g. /John/ are you coming out with us/.

(2) *Adverbials* (conjuncts/disjuncts, in the sense of Quirk *et al.* Ch. 8)

    (i) *Initial: put | after,* e.g. /therefore/ I think he's right/; /normally/ he doesn't take medicine/ (cf. /he doesn't take medicine normally/ = 'in the usual manner'); /every six weeks/ he visits us/. I also include interjections, etc. at this point, e.g. /well/ I think he will/.

    (ii) *Medial: put | on either side,* e.g. /he did say/ on the other hand/ that he'd like to/; there were /with respect/ twelve people there/.

    (iii) *Final: put | before,* e.g. /I didn't ask him/ anyway/; /he didn't read the book/ stupidly/ (i.e. 'unfortunately'). Only a subset of conjuncts and disjuncts operate in this way (cf. Quirk *et al.* §8.91); I have not investigated how this subset might be defined.

(3) *Adverbial sequence: put | after each element,* e.g. /I spoke to him quietly/ without fuss/.

Expansions C: Prosodic operations C

(1) *Structural parallelism: | put after each component,* e.g. /I want to see the girls from class 1/ the boys from class 2/ and all prefects/; /he's gone to buy gin/ whisky/ eggs/ and tea/.

(2) *Multiple heads*

    (i) *Separate premodification: put | after first head,* e.g. /in that shop you'll find some very nice chairs/ and tables/ (i.e. the tables are not necessarily very nice; cf. / . . . very nice chairs and tables/).

    (ii) *Separate postmodification: put | after first head,* e.g. /the man/ and the woman dressed in black/ came to see us/ (i.e. only the woman is dressed in black; cf. /the man and the woman dressed in black/ . . ., where both are).

(iii) *Non-restrictive apposition* (cf. Quirk *et al.* §9.133): *put / on either side of the apposed phrase*, e.g. /Mr. Jones/ the architect/ is over there/—cf. /Mr. Jones the architect/ . . ., which is restrictive, and implies an opposition with 'Mr. Jones the butcher' or 'Mr. Smith the architect'. This also includes the use of apposition markers (cf. Quirk *et al.* §9.138), e.g. /the plane/ or rather the elephant/ will be there by two/.

(iv) *Noun phrase tags: put / before*, e.g. /they're all the same/ these unions/.

(3) *Multiple modification*

(i) *Premodification, general adjectives: put / after each component except the last*, e.g. /I was talking to that very tall/ pretty/ rather awkward girl/. This also includes coordinated premodification, e.g. /an equally serious/ but more interesting situation/ is. . . . In Subject position, / is put after the completed Subject element, e.g. /the very tall/ pretty/ but rather awkward girl/ was talking . . ./. The term 'general' excludes certain adjectival categories which display order-restrictions (e.g. colour, nationality) and which would not be split intonationally, e.g. /the big red house/: see Quirk *et al.* §13.65. However, if C1 is applied, and the adjectives are introduced as if in a list, even order-restricted adjectives are affected, e.g. /it was a big/ red/ Gothic kind of building/.

(ii) *Postmodification, in subject: put / after subject* (cf. Quirk *et al.* §13.39), e.g. /the man in the raincoat standing near the bus-stop/ is my brother/. An additional / is introduced where ambiguity has to be avoided, cf. /the man with the dog/ sitting near the bus-stop/ . . . and /the man with/ the dog sitting near the bus-stop/ . . .

(iii) *Postmodification, in passive agent: put / before agent*, e.g. /the butler had been fiercely attacked/ by a man wearing a raincoat and holding a gun/.

(iv) *Postmodification, in non-final object: put / after object*, e.g. /I gave the book you'd been waiting for/ to the man from upstairs/. This seems obligatory only when the postmodification is clausal, but there is a strong tendency for / to be used even with phrases, e.g. /I gave everyone in the room/ a big wave/.

(4) *Medial non-restrictive phrases: put /on either side*, e.g. /the man/ in a raincoat/ came towards me/.

An illustration of the application of the above rules to the corpus is as follows. Here is a sentence as it was first transcribed (though I omit certain features of transcription not relevant to this chapter). Short and long pauses are represented as . and – respectively; words containing the tonic syllable are in small capitals, with an indication of the pitch movement over the stressed syllable (′ rising, ` falling).

the second deplorable thing ABOUT it/ – is the FACT/ . that . THIS CHAP/ . a NEUROTIC/ – his mother calls him a NEUROTIC/ from the age of TWO/ . who can't stick in the army for twenty-four HOURS/ is the kind of PERSON/ who is made a public idol of the DAY/ –

Given only a grammatical specification of this sentence in terms of Quirk *et al.*, the following prosodic operations would apply:

(a) *clause level:* / after *fact* (under A3 vii), the first instance of *neurotic* and *two* (under A4), *hours* under A3v), *person* (under A3vi), and *day* (sentence-final). The sentence now looks like this:

> The second deplorable thing about it is the fact/ that this chap a neurotic/ his mother calls him a neurotic from the age of two/ who can't stick in the army for twenty-four hours/ is the kind of person/ who is made a public idol of the day/

(b) *element level:* no operations applicable.

(c) *group level:* / after *it* (under C3i), *chap* (under C2iii), *neurotic* (under C3iv). The sentence is now in its proper tone-unit form, and goes forward for tonicity insertion, obligatory pause insertion (e.g. pauses required around the appositional group, *a neurotic*), etc.

Out of the 12,000 tone-units examined, about 100 were incapable of prediction from the above rules.[10] How are these to be dealt with? An example of such a sentence was /we gave him/ a lift/ on a Tuesday/, where the two internal boundaries are not predictable from the above rules. There are only four possible explanations. Firstly, the usage is sociolinguistically explicable (or 'stylistically' explicable, in the sense of Crystal and Davy 1969): that is, it is predictable for the entire output of a particular group, e.g. sports commentator or political speech-maker. This hypothesis would be easy to check statistically. Secondly, the usage is individually explicable: a predictable idiosyncrasy, which may be analysed as part of voice-quality or idiolect. There would presumably be no difficulty in verifying this hypothesis either. Thirdly, the usage is (socio- or psycho-) linguistically unpredictable because of performance interference, e.g. a physiological reflex (such as a cough, or a pause for breath) interrupts speech flow, or the speaker arbitrarily chooses to restart a construction. In all such cases, there will be some other indication than the non-segmental anomaly that an aberrant utterance is in progress. Lastly, the usage is attitudinally predictable: tone-unit boundaries are put in or omitted because of the attitude of the speaker. This is the problem area, because of the difficulty of specifying precisely the range of possible attitudes. But in principle it should be clear that, given an alphabet of affective category-levels applicable to the whole of a sentence (and not just the non-segmental component), it would be possible, given enough data, to establish the attitudinal conditions which affect

10 To avoid the charge that the transcription was biased by an awareness of the grammatical constraints outlined in this chapter, I should make it clear that the prosodic transcription of the data used here was carried out between 1963 and 1970, the transcription being checked by at least two analysts, the sole criterion that they were given to work with being auditory agreement as to the prosodic variables involved (see Crystal 1969a: Ch. 1). The above analysis was prepared for a conference in 1973. It is of course possible that we were all of us being unconsciously influenced in our transcription by some innate knowledge of these rules!

the placement of tone-unit boundaries. For example, one might say: if the utterance is interpreted as X (excited, tired, irritated . . .), then Y prosodic operations apply. Impressionistically, this is not difficult to do. The above sentence is explicable in this way, for instance: here a husband's story had been interrupted by his wife, who had queried whether the hitch-hiker had been picked up on a Tuesday; the husband, plainly irritated, replied with the above. One might then hypothesize that in the attitudinal context IRRITATION, optional tone-unit boundaries are introduced starting at clause level and continuing downwards, depending on the degree of irritability present, up to and including the morphemic level, e.g. /we gave him/ a lift/ on a Tuesday/; /we/ gave him/ a lift/ on/ a Tuesday/; /we/ gave/ him/ a/ lift/ on/ a/ Tuesday – /in/dis/putably/, he might have added! The matter obviously requires further study. Given the above norms, under what circumstances will data present (a) more and (b) fewer tone-units? Other prosodic variables will have to be considered (especially *tempo* and *pause*), as will the question of the type of grammatical unit with which tone-units can best be correlated. There is some evidence in the data, for instance, to suggest that clauses and sentences are the units of organization for relatively informal, fluent discourse, but elements of clause structure for more formal or less fluent situations. It is hoped that, using the cautionary perspective and normative framework of the present approach, such questions— along with the descriptive and methodological issues raised earlier—will begin to be systematically investigated.

Tonicity

It should be clear from what has been said so far that a great deal of prosodic categorization needs to have taken place before one can raise questions of tonic placement. The present section assumes that questions of tone-unit boundaries have been resolved, and that our data consist of utterances analysed into a sequence of tone-units. Figure 3 assumes an input of a tone-unit, indicated by / . . . /, containing a grammatical structure (as specified above) which can now be seen as a string of words. Minimally, a tone-unit consists of a single word, e.g./JOHN/, though one should note the possibility under certain conditions of tone-units consisting of bound morphemes, as in the case of *indisputably* above. Under such a circumstance, there are no problems of tonicity, as this word will contain the tonic syllable (which is the primary stress-prominent syllable of the word). The question now is to determine the conditions on tonic distribution when more than one word is involved, and in order to do this, a classification into *lexical* and *grammatical* types is required. This distinction is longstanding in the literature, and I do not propose to defend its theoretical status here (for a critical discussion of the distinction, and detailed references to its use, in various terminologies, see Crystal 1966b). It seems adequate to specify the category of grammatical item by listing. I propose to use the terms *lexical item* and *grammatical item*. Lexical item is chosen, rather than (say) 'open-class word,' in order to avoid the misleading implication of the term 'word': lexical items include many kinds of multi-word units, with an invariable or unpredictable internal structure, and which have to have their prosody dealt with in the same way as simple words. Included under this heading, therefore, are: idioms (e.g. at ANY rate, ANY old thing), compound names (e.g. the WINSLOW boy), compounds (e.g. TOY factory), and phrasal verbs (e.g. look UP to). Prominence within lexical items, whether single or multi-word, is not dealt with in this chapter. The following is the inventory of types of grammatical item recognized: pronouns (*I* etc., *myself* etc., *someone* etc., *my* etc.), conjunctions, prepositions (including complex prepositions; cf. Quirk *et al.* §6.5), auxiliaries, the items *not*, *it* (extrapositive) and *there* (existential), anaphoric items (*this* etc.,[11] *one(s)*, *so*, *some*, *any*, etc.), and determiners (*the*, *my*, *all*, *each*, etc.).

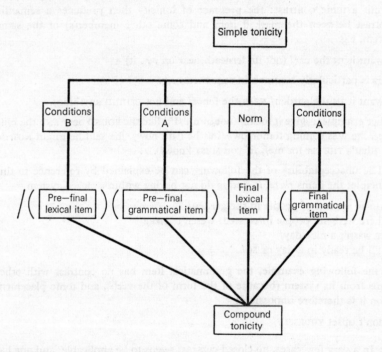

Fig. 3 Factors affecting tonic placement

Figure 3 asserts that a tone-unit will consist of minimally one lexical item, and that in any string of lexical and grammatical items, the norm of tonic placement will be on the final lexical item. (This is a fairly traditional and uncontroversial claim. The only exception to this generalization about single-item units seems to be tag utterances (cf. A7 above), which may consist wholly of grammatical items.) From the statistical point of view, 80 per cent of all multi-word tone-units in the corpus displayed this pattern. The problem is

11 Ostensive, summarizing etc. uses of *this* etc. must be taken separately as nominal, and treated thus intonationally (cf. below), e.g. /look at *that*/, /I want to say *this*/.

how to handle the remainder. There are three other possibilities: either the tonic will occur
(a) on a grammatical item following the final lexical item;
(b) on a grammatical item preceding the final lexical item; or
(c) on a pre-final lexical item.
It would seem that the conditions operating upon positions (a) and (b) are the same, and these are labelled **A** in the figure.

A1 The main principle here is that only those grammatical items which operate clearly as members of a closed system (see Quirk *et al.* §2.12, and below) permit a tonic contrast: the presence of tonicity then produces a semantic contrast between the marked item and some other member(s) of the same system, e.g.

/I want it IN the car/ (not underneath/near/on . . . it)

This is particularly common in sequences, e.g.

/I want it IN the garden/ NEAR the fence/ and not BEHIND anything/.

Other examples: /give it to ME/ (not him), /I'd like the ROUND one/ AND the blue one/, /he WAS coming tomorrow/ (but he isn't now), /he said he might NOT do it/, /that's THE car for me/, /if you MUST know/ . . .

The unacceptability of the following can be explained by reference to this principle: the items *there*, *it*, and *so* do not belong within a closed system.

*/THERE are lots of people in the garden/
*/there were SIX people interested/ weren't THERE/
*/IT wasn't a nice day/
*/it'll be ready in a day or SO/

In the following example, the grammatical item has no contrast with other items from its system (because of the form of the verb), and tonic placement upon it is therefore impossible:

*/don't upset YOURSELF/

A2 In a very few cases, no closed contrast seems to be applicable, and one has to assume that it is the attitude of the speaker which has conditioned the tonicity (cf. p. 20), e.g.

/what are you doing it FOR/ (context, e.g. IMPATIENCE).

Here, I do not think it would be plausible to argue that a contrast was intended with any other particular preposition(s). Likewise, in cases where the preceding context makes it clear that no systemic contrast is operative, speaker's attitude must apply, e.g.

X /JOHN'S coming to the party/
Y /why did you ask HIM/ (context: SURPRISE).

B It is a more complicated matter to state the conditions which permit the placement of the tonic on a pre-final lexical item. It would be relatively simple if the constraints were wholly syntactic in character, as much of the literature suggests (cf. above), but in fact (as Bolinger argues) very few are. I have been able to detect five cases only where the occurrence of pre-final tonic can be related unequivocally to a specific feature of sentence structure; and it is for this reason that the line between *structures* and *tonicity* is left broken in Figure 1.

(1) *Final adverbial disjunct/conjunct:* here, the tonic is placed on the next previous lexical item, and the adverbial is prosodically expounded as a nuclear tail (or as prosodically subordinate, or as the second part of a complex tone),[12] e.g.

/he didn't DO it of course/
/that's a hard decision to have to MAKE though/
(Alternatively, /he didn't DO it [of COURSE]/
/he didn't DO it of COURSE/.)

(2) *Final direct speech marker:* here, the tonic is placed on the next previous lexical item, and the marker is a nuclear tail, e.g.

/I don't want to go OUT he said/

(3) *Final vocative:* the tonic is placed on the next previous lexical item, and the vocative is nuclear tail, e.g.

/it's the BAKER Mr Jones/ (contrast apposition above)

(4) *Lexical sets in coordinate structure:* the tonic is placed on the items belonging to the same set, e.g.

/this book cost FIVE dollars/ and this one THREE dollars/
/ONE egg/ or TWO/

(5) *Question-word government:* the tonic is placed on the governed item,

/what TIME does your watch say/
/how many BOOKS has she written/
/whose CAT is in the doorway/
/isn't it wonderful how NICE she looks/

Note: this might be subsumed under 6 below, as 'new' information.

The vast majority of cases of pre-final lexical tonic can be accounted for only by referring to some kind of semantic or lexical conditioning, however. This conditioning is sometimes referred to as 'lexical presupposition', and there are doubtless many sub-categories to be distinguished. For the moment, I have dealt with this area under the single heading.

12 For an explanation of these terms, see Crystal 1969a: nuclear tail, 223ff.; prosodic subordination, 244ff. and below (p. 26); compound tones 218ff. and below (p. 27).

(6) *Comment on previous lexical item:* This relationship can of course be defined positively or negatively: positively, one would say that the tonic is placed on the NEW lexical item (or information); negatively, that it is not placed on the GIVEN lexical item (or information), even if this is final in the tone-unit, e.g.

X /that was some ACCIDENT/ WASN'T it/
Y /a TERRIBLE accident/

/she's UNHAPPY/ VERY unhappy

This category would have to include cases where the final lexical item in the tone-unit is assumed by the speaker to be familiar or obvious: the tonic is then brought forward onto the item which the speaker considers to be new, e.g.

X /what have you got THERE/
Y /it's a VERPLOORG grammar/

This subsumes the kind of example cited by Bolinger (1972: 638), where the unnecessary information is de-accented, though none of the utterances were contrastive, e.g.

/he has a YELLOW streak/
/they STRANGLED him to death/
(What happened?) /I just broke the CAR window/
/come over to OUR place/

It might also subsume attitudinally extreme lexical items, which always display a strong tendency to attract the tonic, e.g.

/it's a TREMENDOUS result/
/that's a FANTASTIC thing to say/

(7) It is perhaps worth distinguishing from within this general category the formally distinct lexical conditioning that occurs in cases of linguistic inventiveness, where one finds nonce items or semi-institutionalized compounds (cf. Quirk *et al.* §13.45). In such cases, the new item attracts the tonic, e.g.

/it's a look-at-me-I'm-ORIGINAL sort of book/
/that shelf is a do-it-YOURSELF job/
/that's the IN-THING these days/

It is unlikely that any greater precision will be introduced into the analysis of the semantic conditioning of pre-final tonic placement until more adequate studies of semantic relationship are written. But one other concept must be introduced at this stage, namely that the intonation system allows for a double focusing of information by the use of a compound or subordinate tone. This is referred to as *compound tonicity* in Figure 3. Compound tones are of the form `` `+´ ``, `` ´+` ``. The criteria for their identification are given in Crystal 1969a (218–19). They are 'combinations of two kinetic elements of different major phonetic types acting as a single tonal unit. . . . The syllables between the two kinetic elements must display an evenness of pitch pattern, continuing the pitch movement in a "trough" or sustained arc from one to the other. . . . The phonetically dominant element is usually the first. . . .' A subordinate tone is symbolized as '[`] or '['[']: criteria for their identification are given in Crystal 1969a (245): 'The primary characteristic of the subordinate tone-unit is that its pitch-contour, while having a complete and independent shape within itself, falls broadly within the total contour presented in the superordinate tone-unit. . . . The nuclear type postulated as subordinate must repeat the direction of the nucleus in the superordinate unit, both nuclei being one of the two primary categories, fall or rise. . . .' For example,

/he SAID he was COMING/

/he'll DO it you KNOW/

/there's a MAN [in the GARDEN]/.

Semantically, the effects involved here must be seen in terms of the distribution of information (we are not at this point dealing with the choice of tones, e.g. fall-plus-rise v. rise-plus-fall, which is relevant to the next section). They can be seen by contrasting these examples with other possible realizations of the sentence, in particular as a single major tone-unit, and as two separate tone-units:

(a) /there's a MAN [in the GARDEN]/ or / . . . in the GARDEN/

(b) /there's a MAN in the garden/

(c) /there's a MAN/ in the GARDEN/

In (a), *man* carries primary information, but *garden* has some information value also; in (b) *garden* is assumed to be given; and in (c) both *man* and *garden* are equally new.

It is possible to double focus on any combination of lexical and grammatical items:

lexical +lexical, as just illustrated

lexical +grammatical, e.g. /well ASK HIM/;

grammatical +grammatical, e.g. /why doesn't HE give it to HIM/;

grammatical +lexical, e.g. /it's UNDER the WINDOW/.

Doubtless it will be possible in due course to make a subclassification of the types of semantic relationship involved in double focus. One such relationship, for example, is that between general and specific instantiation, illustrated by statement tags, e.g.

\   /
/he's a FOOL is JOHN/

        \   /
/it's a great THING DRINK/

One other point should be made. Compound tonicity applies within tone-units. It is however possible for certain tone-unit sequences to be conflated, one tone-unit being used instead of the predicted sequence above, but only if a compound tonicity structure is used. There is then a corresponding reduction in the information-load of one of the tone-units. This happens regularly only with grammatical structures whose use is clearly subordinate, in particular tag utterances (cf. A7, C2iv) and medial and final adverbials (A3ii, iii, B2ii, iii). Occasionally, this happens with final non-restrictive and appositive clauses (cf. A3vi, vii).

     \   /   \   /
/he's COMING ISN'T he/ v. /he's COMING/ ISN'T he/

The main phonetic criterion distinguishing these two cases is that the initial pitch level of the rise on ISN'T is lower in the first case than in the second; also the second allows a pause between the two units.

Tone

The analysis of the pitch movements which expound the tonic syllable (or nucleus) of a tone-unit has been much neglected in recent theoretical discussions of intonation, though this issue was very much to the fore in early pedagogical studies, and a number of phonetic classifications have been made. The approach presented in Crystal (1969a) argues that the range of nuclei in a language is best seen in terms of the interaction between two systemically distinct features, *syllable pitch range* and *tone*. The former refers to the relative pitch height of a syllable, syllable-onset or -termination, in relation to preceding or subsequent syllables; the latter to the pitch-direction followed throughout a tonic syllable. For example, the traditional concept of 'high rising tone' is seen as the product of two separate systemic selections: high (v. mid, low etc.) and rising (v. falling, level, falling-rising etc.). It is clear that there is in principle a very large number of phonetic possibilities that a language might use—high falling, high falling-rising, high falling-level, high level-falling, etc. The question is to determine the number of basic phonological categories required, to provide a model for their interrelationship, and to give adequate recognition to the range of functions they possess.

Methodologically, this is probably the most difficult area of all for the intonation analyst, some of the reasons for this being discussed in Crystal 1969a (Ch. 7). But this book did not pay sufficient attention to the underlying malaise in this area of intonation study, which is a failure to think theoretically about the subject: crucial theoretical terms tend to be used loosely, and their implications are missed. Three terms in particular are widely used, but their status remains largely uninvestigated: *context, system* and *connected speech*. They are fundamental to any general explanation of intonation, but they must be used carefully and precisely in order for this to be achieved. As a general indication of my attitude, I would say that the concept of context has been much overrated, that of system much underestimated, and the complexity involved in constructing a model of intonation for connected speech largely ignored.

Statements referring to the importance of context in intonation analysis are found throughout the literature. They reflect a movement away from the view that a nuclear tone (e.g. low rise) expounds a single, 'basic' meaning, always present regardless of context (though contextual variations may add certain overtones), to a view that there is no common meaning underlying all instances of its use, the interpretation of each instance being totally dependent upon the context in which the tone occurs. Certainly it is difficult to defend the first position, in any strong sense. A collection of instances of any tone bring to light a large number of possible attitudinal implications, and identity between the different instances seems possible only by a process of simplification (in which some attitudes are selected as being more fundamental than others, which are considered marginal) or by a process of generalization, whereby all the implications are subsumed under some extremely broad attitudinal label (e.g. 'emphasis', 'self-involvement'). Neither of these processes is desirable: the first approach may have pedagogic value, but it begs crucial theoretical questions as to what is central and what is marginal; and the generality of the labels in the second approach is such that they are vacuously applicable to almost every nuclear type one might find. In any case, one might add, why *should* one be looking for a single meaning that can be traced through all instances of a given category? No-one would expect this for other kinds of formal category. The point has been much discussed, in linguistics, philosophy and elsewhere, and I will not go into it further here.

The second position seems on the face of it to have a lot in its favour. In particular, there is the difficulty of finding a single sentence with a *totally* unacceptable nuclear tone: it is always possible to think up some context which makes the sentence appear quite normal, even though the context discovery-procedure may itself be an involved process, as Haas has pointed out (1973). Analysts asterisk intonationally-transcribed utterances at their peril, as Bolinger regularly shows; and much of the discussion in recent years has taken the form of criticism of proposed semantic generalizations on grounds of contextual inadequacy. But this position is not as clear-cut as it seems. For instance, it ignores the important question, discussed by Haas (*ibid.*), that contextualization is itself a complex process, involving various procedures and degrees of intuitive confidence: the degree of difficulty encountered in thinking up a context is itself a significant factor in deciding the overall acceptability of that utterance. But more important than this, the position remains unintelligible without clarification of the term 'context'. It is a term which has been used in a variety of senses—or so it would seem, for it is rarely explicitly defined. It has been used to include some or all of the following: the co-occurring formal structure of an utterance (whose intonation is being analysed), the formal structure of utterances preceding or following the focal utterance, the intonation patterns preceding the focal utterance, the observable situation in which the utterance takes place, factors in the observable situation preceding the focal utterance, the presuppositions in the mind of the speaker, or hearer, and other things besides. Given such a broad interpretation, it would not be surprising for the meaning of an intonation pattern to be wholly dependent upon context; but of course this says nothing, until the specific conditioning claimed to be operating within each kind of context is explained, and some kind of criteria set up. 'Finding a context' for intonation patterns by adding a previous utterance or giving a brief cue-specification in brackets provides pedagogic plausibility, but no explanation.

When one looks closely at the various possible senses of context, however, one finds that certain of them are quite inoperable or irrelevant for the specification of intonational meaning. One may, to begin with, dispense with general appeals to mental presuppositions and unobservable aspects of 'the situation' in which the utterance occurs. It should be obvious that, unless we are provided with some objective linguistic, visual or other evidence to indicate that a presupposed state of affairs or a change in the co-occurring situation is conditioning the structure of interpretation of an utterance, we have no alternative but to assume that nothing contrastive is presupposed, that no change is taking place, that mutual attitudes are constant, and that the process of interpretation based upon an appeal to observable characteristics of the situation (see below) should continue unaltered. For example, if in a conversation the mood of one of the participants changed (e.g. boredom setting in), but at the time there was no formal sign that this had happened within the pattern of the utterance, and retrospective analysis of a tape failed to produce any consistent interpretation of boredom at this point, then this information must be disregarded. (The fact that it is often not disregarded is due to the speaker-orientated approach to intonation, whereby the analyst uses his own intuition to interpret his own usage, and thereby frequently fails to realize which aspects of his semantic introspection were expounded in his utterance, which were not, which were a reflex of aspects of his personality, and so on. The danger is always to read too much meaning into a pattern.) The same reasoning applies when questions of ambiguity are raised: an utterance is not intonationally ambiguous until such time as the participants recognize it and accept it as relevant for the conversation. If A sees a possible ambiguity in B's utterance, but discounts it (as unintentional, or for some other reason), then it would be misleading to extract the feature concerned and refer to it as 'potentially ambiguous', or in some such way. *A fortiori*, if none of the participants detect any ambiguity at all, and retrospective analysis fails to produce any consistent interpretation of an utterance as ambiguous, appeals to potential ambiguity must be disregarded. (References to such notions are usually due to looking at sentences in isolation, instead of in connected speech. Of course many sentences are intonationally ambiguous in isolation: to take these, and then to say that 'context resolves the ambiguity' is questionable, to say the least, for if connected speech had been studied in the first place, the question of ambiguity would never have arisen. Similar views have been expressed over the supposed ambiguity of sentences like 'Flying planes can be dangerous', e.g. Noss 1972.) Most of the time, we produce or interpret an utterance's intonation using the assumption that it will be un-ambiguous, and that there is no change taking place in the co-occurring situation that could affect the process of interpretation. Only when there is clear evidence to the contrary, do we need to talk about the notion of context.

Eliminating such matters from our discussion reduces the notion of context to more manageable proportions. Specifically, five variables need to be distinguished:

(1) The co-occurring syntactic and lexical pattern of utterance. There are a number of formal notions (e.g. sentence final v. non-final) which are pre-requisite for any semantic analysis of nuclear tones. This aspect of contextual influence will be discussed further below.

(2) Preceding and subsequent syntactic and lexical patterns. I have not explored discourse organization as a whole in relation to the selection of nuclear tones, but in principle it should be clear that there could be a considerable influence here, e.g. a sequence of parallel sentence structures (as in a series of rhetorical questions) would strongly motivate a corresponding sequence of parallel choices of nucleus.

(3) Preceding and subsequent intonational patterns. See further below.

(4) Relevant co-occurring and preceding semiotic behaviour, especially facial expression, but including all forms of kinesic and proxemic behaviour. The importance of context in this sense is well-known, though under-estimated (see further, Crystal 1969a: Ch. 7).

(5) Co-occurring and preceding observable alterations in situation. This is the traditional core of the notion of context in intonation studies. The choice of intonation is referred to such situationally-conditioned attitudes as politeness, surprise, anger and so on; and it is this aspect of context which has been over-rated. The range of 'attitudes' to be considered under this heading is very wide, and it is the multiplicity of semantic labels and the problems of quantifying affect which have led to pessimism in the semantics of intonation and the ex-treme reliance on the notion of context. Doubtless it will be possible to make much progress in these areas, once we have available more adequate analyses of affective states and their linguistic categorization, so that the idea of situ-ational context might become more explicit. But in the meantime it is important to realize that this aspect of context is by no means the cornerstone of inton-ational semantics: it is in fact very much dependent upon the other senses of context (1–4) above. The following dialogue provides an example:

A /you've got something in your HÂIR/ (said in a jocular tone, thinking that it is no more than a fallen leaf)

B /HAVE I/

The low falling tone here, where one might have expected a livelier reply (such as a high rise) to suit A's jocular mood, provides a contrast that indicates B's displeasure—let us call it 'offended'. But it would now be most misleading to say, as is often said, 'One of the meanings of the low falling tone is "offended" '. It would be absurd to see the low falling tone as 'containing' a range of meanings, one of which is 'selected' at this point in context, for obviously the range of meanings the low fall (or any other tone) could contain are as many as there are contextual conditions, and hence no analytic progress would have been made. Rather, this example shows the importance of the other contextual factors in accounting for a particular effect. Sense 1 is relevant, for with a less abrupt syntax and lexis, there would be less likelihood of an offensive interpretation. Sense 2 is relevant, as if B had been replying in this manner in previous discourse, A would have grounds for discounting the offensive interpretation. Sense 3's relevance has already been referred to, namely the contrast between A's and B's intonation. And sense 4 is relevant, as the offensive interpretation could disappear entirely if an appropriate facial expression or gesture were involved. Indeed, when one considers 1–4, it is difficult to see what need there is to refer to sense 5 of context at all.

I would in fact want to argue that sense 5 is largely irrelevant to the semantic analysis of intonation. It is only occasionally that one may make a confident prediction of an intonational pattern from an observed situational event, and vice versa. There is no guarantee that an angry situation (let us say) will produce an attitude of anger in any individual, and none that an angry attitude will produce an 'angry' intonation pattern. The controlling variables are personality (e.g. some people are more controlled than others) and sociolinguistic (e.g. some social situations are more conducive to angry scenes than others). Even on the basis of a clearly observable situation, then, it would be misleading to assume that the interpretation of the situation should be allowed to influence one's semantic analysis of the intonation. Indeed we are aware of this, for we say such things as 'John kept very calm—there wasn't even a tremor in his voice', which indicate the possibilities of intonational disassociation from the accompanying situation (or 'displacement', in the terms of Hockett and Altmann (1968); see further, Chapter 3.

The observable situation probably has an important role to play in the initial stages of any discourse, where it establishes norms (e.g. of formality, intimacy, excitement) for the dialogue. It then proves unnecessary to refer again to situation unless major variations in it arise. There have been in fact only a handful of occasions in my own conversational data where an observable change in the accompanying situation directly influenced the intonation. One occasion was when a third speaker entered the room; as he was a stranger to one of the participants, the speech became more formal and the intonation altered. Another was when the door-bell rang, and a puzzled tone came into A's voice. These occasions were isolated. For the most part, one can listen to a tape without referring at all to the ongoing situation. (The impression of the opposite is probably due to the emphasis on the more action-packed kind of situation found to be important in foreign-language teaching, which motivates so much of available intonational materials.) The language is self-contained, and the interpretation of the intonation depends essentially on the semiotic (linguistic and non-linguistic) contexts. (The analysis of non-vocal semiotic features is not dealt with further in this book.) The problem for the intonation analyst, therefore, is to develop an adequate model of the contrastive possibilities operating as one moves from nuclear tone to nuclear tone in the stream of connected speech. And in order to do this, he has to clarify what is involved in the other vague theoretical notions mentioned above—the notion of an intonation *system* in relation to *connected speech*.

The concept of 'system' is generally discussed with reference to three criteria: a system contains a finite number of members; it is reciprocally exclusive (two or more members may not be selected at a particular point in a syntagm); and it is reciprocally defining, i.e. the most precise and economical statement of the meaning of an item is in terms of the other members of the system of which it forms a part. The set of nuclear tones in English is normally referred to as a system, but little attempt seems to have been made to show that these conditions have been met. The notion of reciprocity of definition is particularly important. What this implies is that attempts to define the meaning of a nuclear tone cannot be successful until we know two things: (a) what tone the previous discourse (or, in a discourse-initial position, the previous observable situation, semiotic frame, etc.) leads us to expect; and (b) what tone we actually get. Regarding the first point, one might construct a taxis of tonal possibilities, such that, given a sequence of tone-units and tonic syllables, the selection of any tone is made dependent upon the selection of the previous tone or tones. Given the selection of the first tone in a string, then one may see a progressive influence of the type

A–B

B–C

C–D . . .

such that a primary factor influencing the selection of any tone is going to be functional compatibility with the previous one(s). For example, one might expect, given the occurrence of a rising-falling tone, to find clusters of such tones at a particular point in discourse; this is in fact what one finds. (This is reported in Crystal 1969a: 241 ff., where the notion of 'tonal reduplication' is introduced, but the value of the statistical analysis reported in this earlier work is extremely limited, little account having been taken of the grammatical contexts of the various tones.) A more important illustration of functional compatibility emerges from the statistical fact that, for any sample of data, between 50 and 60 per cent of the nuclei will be falling tone, the vast majority being low falling in type—in other words the 'neutral' intonation for statements, as generally reported. As Quirk *et al.* say (1972: 1044), 'a tone unit has a falling nucleus unless there is some specific reason why it should not.' Of the remaining 40 per cent of nuclei, half of these are low or mid rising or level tones whose use is wholly conditioned by the accompanying syntax (see below) for the signalling of dependent non-final structures. In other words, between 70 and 80 per cent of nuclei are semantically 'neutral'. The problem comes in accounting for the remaining tones, and the non-neutral use of the low falling and rising tones. But as a general principle, I would wish to argue that the vast majority of tones in connected speech carry no meaning—that is, they communicate no new information, because their occurrence is syntactically predictable. The problem of specifying nuclear meaning comes when a tone is used unpredictably in a specific syntactic context, or when (as stated in point (b) above) the discourse leads us to expect a particular tone, and we are given another. Both these cases involve us in looking at the nature of tonal relationships within the nuclear system.

For the rest of this chapter, I shall restrict the discussion to the following nuclei:

'low fall', viz.	�‾	, symbolized as ↓
'high fall', viz.	‾‾	, symbolized as ↑ `
'low rise', viz.	⟋	, symbolized as ↓
'high rise', viz.	‾	, symbolized as ↑ ´
'level', viz.	‗	, symbolized as -
'rise fall', viz.	⌒	, symbolized as
'fall rise', viz.	⌄	, symbolized as ˅

The other phonetically distinct nuclei in English are not dealt with here (e.g. 'fall-level', 'rise-fall-rise'): statistically they are a very minor group, and semantically it will probably be possible to see their analysis as a straightforward extension of that suggested for the 'major' tones. Certainly, if the approach is not plausible for the above seven categories, it will not work for the others.

In this approach, then, we are given a tone-unit and tonic syllable, along with all co-occurring syntactic and lexical information. The first task is to determine the extent to which grammatical factors have to be taken into account in arriving at a semantic specification of the tones. Here one has to be very rigorous over what is to count as a grammatical function of intonation. If the criteria are not exact and explicit, the grammar quickly becomes overloaded with spurious categories and artificial distinctions (for example, degrees of 'exclamatory force' and 'personal commitment'). This is the difficulty which I find with Halliday's approach to intonation, for instance (see Crystal 1969b). To avoid this difficulty, the present approach uses a much more restricting criterion: one allows as grammatical only those uses of intonation which can be shown to expound categories *already required* by a grammar. Given a grammar of English which uses such notions as dependent clause, negation, restrictive and non-restrictive, and sentence completion, for instance, then if one can show intonation expounding these concepts, this can be said to be a genuinely grammatical function of intonation for this grammar. Note, too, that in all such cases we are dealing with a grammatical system in the strict sense, viz. a finite, mutually defining and mutually exclusive membership—e.g. restrictive v. non-restrictive positive v. negative. In this way, one would need to establish six conditions on the use of nuclear tone, in order to account for the following grammatical distinctions (all of which are taken from recently-published grammars of English):

– or ´   non-final tonic in sentence: *syntactic dependence*, e.g.

/what he SAID/ was are you COMING/

/he won't go HOME/ until she comes BACK/

´   final tonic in sentence: *continuity*, e.g.

incomplete listing: /would you like TEA/ or COFFEE/ (cf. . . . . TEA/ or COFFEE/)

: *expectation of response*, e.g.

tag question: he's COMING/ ISN'T he/ (cf. . . . . ISN'T he/)

question (v. exclamation): weren't they PUNCTUAL/ (cf. . . . . PUNCTUAL/, */how WELL she sings/ DOESN'T she/)

↑´   *contrastive question*, specifically echo utterance marker (cf. Quirk et al. 1972), e.g.

/John's going to the OFFICE/

/to the ↑ WHERE/

and also in certain types of rhetorical question, and indicating the penult in a list, e.g.

/we want EGGS/ BUTTER/ ↑ BREAD/ and TEA/

↑ `   *contrastive focus*, e.g.

/he's HAPPY/ in fact he's ↑ VERY happy/

˘   *contingency*, especially negative implication, where the polar contrast is clear, e.g.

/I didn't give her ANYTHING/ (cf. .... ANYTHING/)

/I SHOULD go/ (but I won't) (cf. .... SHOULD ...)

/we do admit STUDENTS/ (but not ANY STUDENTS/)

/it's GOOD/ (but not THAT GOOD/)

/John won't sit still until the TAXI comes/ (cf. .... STILL/ ... TAXI ...../)

↓ `   final tonic in sentence: *unmarked*
non-final tonic in sentence, see below under attitude.

It may be possible, with further study, to add to this list; but meanwhile it would seem prudent to restrict one's claims about grammatical function—which are extremely strong claims to make—to those cases about which there is clear and extensive evidence.

By distinguishing the three phonetic variables which underlie the above nuclei (viz. general pitch direction (falling-type v. rising-type), pitch-range (high v. low start) and complexity (viz. ^, ˘), the following systemic relationship might be hypothesized between tonal type and grammatical function:

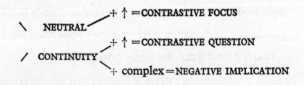

Note: (a) There seems to be no grammatically-conditioned equivalent to fall-rise under the heading of falling-type tones. Rise-fall cannot be predictably related to any grammatical contrastivity, and its description thus comes under the heading of attitude, below.

(b) Labelling ` as *finality*, as is sometimes done, is to be misled by the labels used, the term *continuity* suggesting its opposite. The only clear sense for which the term *final* might be applicable, in a grammatical context, is 'final in a string', such as a sentence, and this would handle only a small proportion of the low falling tones in the data.

Specifying further semantic differentiation for the tones in the above contexts is a purely attitudinal matter, and here the problem of labelling arises. As pointed out in earlier work (Crystal 1969a: Ch. 7), descriptive labels in intonation are generally unclear. It is often uncertain, for example, whether a label like *interrogative* is being used to refer to an attitude, a syntactic pattern or category, or a speech-act. Likewise, labels tend to be used in a fairly arbitrary way, such that one is uncertain of the structural meaning-relations which may be operating between them—a pair of labels, such as *sarcastic* and *ironic*, may be being used synonymously, hyponymously, incompatibly, and so on (see Lyons 1968 for these relations). In the absence of explicit criteria and an agreed semantic theory, it is not surprising that descriptions of nuclear meanings do not take us very far, and are often contradictory. But while a great deal of empirical psycholinguistic work remains to be done on how these labels are used, it should still be possible to develop some theoretical ideas about the way in which our semantic interpretations are organized and how they are arrived at, and thus reduce somewhat the amount of arbitrariness in our descriptions. One suggestion towards this end is developed below: it is based on the view that any explanation of intonational meaning cannot be arrived at by seeing the issues solely in either attitudinal or grammatical terms. It is precisely the interplay between the interpretation of an intonation pattern in grammatical terms and its interpretation in semantic (attitudinal) terms which is of interest, as there are grounds for believing that the two sets of 'meanings' are to some extent mutually defining. A low rising tone, for example, may in syntactic terms be given an interpretation as 'marker of syntactic continuity'; but in attitudinal terms, one might talk of 'inconclusiveness' and a range of related labels. Likewise, the fall-rise might in a grammatical context be defined with reference to a category of contingent negation; attitudinally, with reference to such labels as 'uncertainty', 'doubt', etc. (see below). There would seem to be a certain analogousness between the two dimensions of interpretation, which any analysis should take into account. The present approach insists upon a dual account of the meaning of any nucleus, distinguishing, but interrelating, its grammatical and its attitudinal roles. In this way, it is hoped, one might arrive at a solution to the problem of nuclear meaning posed at the beginning of this section, by postulating a stable 'core' of meaning (partly grammatically, partly attitudinally defined) and a 'periphery' of attitudinal nuances which rely for their interpretation on the co-occurring lexis, semiotic features etc. (see Crystal 1969a: 284f. for examples).

A first attempt at specifying the attitudinal core of the above tones is as follows:

–   final tonic in sentence: *absence of emotional involvement*, which may be interpreted as sarcasm, irony, boredom etc., e.g.

/it was a FASCINATING lecture/

non-final tonic in sentence: implication of routineness—perhaps arising out of the dominant sense of the level tone in final position.

↓′   final tonic in sentence: *personal inconclusiveness* (cf. the continuity sense above)—specific labels used here are non-committal, unaggressive, etc., which are a short remove from polite, respectful etc.
: *social openness*, perhaps arising from the interest, etc. implied in the expectation of response sense given above (p. 35)—specific labels used here are casual, friendly, persuasive etc., and (with appropriate kinesic accompaniment) warning, grim etc.

non-final tonic in sentence: *attitudinally neutral*

↓‵   final tonic in sentence: *attitudinally neutral*
non-final tonic in sentence: *personal definitiveness*—specific labels used here are abrupt, insistent etc.
: *unsociability*—specific labels being cool, irritated, rude etc.

↑‵   in any position: *definite emotional commitment*—specific labels being emphasis, surprise, warmth, selection depending very much on kinesic accompaniment.

↑′   in any position: *definite emotional inquiry*—specific labels being query, puzzlement, surprise etc.

˅   in any position: uncertain outcome—doubt, hesitation etc., leading to suspicion, threatening etc.

˄   in any position: *definite outcome*—impressed, satisfied, smug etc., or the reverse, depending on kinesic accompaniment.

In the same manner as above, the systemic relationship between these tones may be outlined as shown on page 39.

Figure 4 presents a schematic account of the main English nuclei, in the light of the discussion so far. The various tones are given a preliminary classification into two main types, the general direction being falling and rising respectively. Various grounds for such a distinction were discussed in Quirk and Crystal (1966), but there was no discussion of the general theoretical implications. Level nuclear tone is placed at the top, as apart from being mid-way between fall and rise phonetically, it takes on the functions of either fall or rise, depending on its distribution. Within each phonetic type, the tones are ordered on the basis of their twofold potential function, grammatical and attitudinal. The scale of *specificity of grammatical function* refers to the degree of restrictiveness

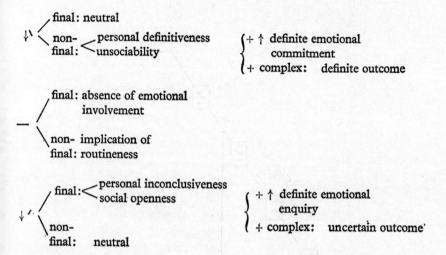

of the syntactic conditions which predict the occurrence of a tone: some of these conditions are fairly general (e.g. 'occurring finally in statements'), whereas others are quite specific (e.g. 'occurring on words beginning with the morpheme *any-*'). The further down the scale a tone appears, the more specific the definition of the grammatical conditions required to predict it. *Degree of affective involvement* refers to the amount of attitudinal implication carried by a tone, 'amount' here referring to the consistent use of a range of descriptive labels (angry, pleasant, very X, etc.). The further down this scale a tone is placed, the more labels are needed for its complete semantic specification. The line A–A indicates the extent of the area of grammatical function: in other words, this model claims that all other nuclei in English can be described without reference to grammatical constraints, and are assumed to be attitudinal intensifications of the attitude-types already described. (Attitudinal intensification applies only within a phonetic type, however, e.g. ⌃⁄ intensifies ˅, ˅˄ intensifies ⌃, and so on.) Grammatically, all that can be said about complex tones is that they are distributionally restricted to the ranges of the simple tones of the same phonetic type: for example, ⌃ may be used in all places where ↓ˋ or ↑ˋ go, and simply adds attitudinal information to the utterance. If ⌃ were to replace, say, ↓ ′, however, then there would be a corresponding change in grammatical function, but this would result, not from the pitch-complexity of the tone, but from its status as being basically falling in type.

There is no evidence of any grammatical constraint operating upon syllabic pitch-range, apart from the basic high v. low distinction used above. Rather, the three independent scalar values involved (pitch height of tonal beginning, pitch height of its termination, and overall width) should be seen as producing

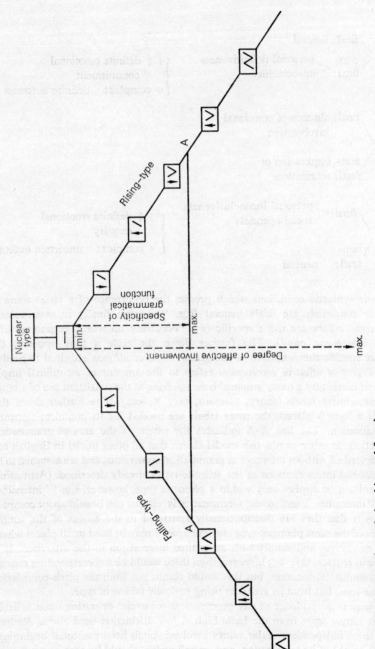

Fig. 4 Nuclear type interrelationships and function

formal contrasts capable of being interpreted semantically as sets of gradable antonyms. For example, width can be seen as a contrast between maximally *wide* and minimally *narrow*, with a semantic specification as follows:

wide: increased positive implication, definitiveness of commitment, and emotional involvement;
narrow: increased negative implication, non-commitment, emotional non-involvement.

But these comments at present are no more than suggestive.

So far we have been talking about the semantic interpretations as produced by an ideal intonation-user, who takes a syntactic context and uses the predicted tones above to produce the stated result. But there are some 5 per cent of cases in my data where the user did not produce the predicted tone in the syntactic context. How are these to be handled? To consider them as performance errors would be both naive and erroneous, as the very deliberate use of p. 31 suggests. Clearly, the model has to be extended to account for such cases, and I would propose the following. By 'expected tone' (E) I mean the tone which the grammatical context normally requires, as outlined above (p. 35); by 'obtained tone' (O), I mean the tone which actually occurs in the data. Where there is identity between E and O (which happens 95 per cent of the time), no further semantic specification is required to that given above. But where there is not, a further dimension must be added to Figure 4. The three phonetic variables of pitch direction, complexity and range are interrelated, as in Figure 5, and a possible formalization given in the accompanying Table. An arbitrary value of 1 is assigned to each feature, and the tones are matched in terms of increasing differentiation, using the model as a basis. The higher the number, the point of greater formal divergence; and it is then hypothesized that this will also be the greater semantic divergence also. In this way, some interesting hypotheses are generated, e.g.

$$E = \check{\ }, O = \downarrow\grave{\ } \equiv E = \downarrow\grave{\ }, O = \check{\ } \text{ etc.}$$

(i.e. replacing a more marked tone by a less marked one is equivalent to replacing a less marked tone by a more marked one)

$$E = \downarrow\prime, O = - \equiv E = \uparrow\prime, O = \downarrow\prime \text{ etc.}$$

The testability of these hypotheses now needs to be investigated. Equivalence might be measured in terms of quantity of labels, interrelated in semantic structure, or by obtaining reactions to sets of labels, using Osgoodian differential techniques. It is to be hoped that analysts will now turn their attention to such matters, if the present hypothesis is felt sufficiently plausible to warrant the effort.

Comparative implications

The above analysis, I would claim, provides evidence in support of the model of non-segmental phonology outlined in Figure 1. But so far, the only data

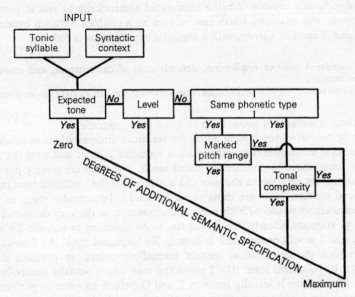

Fig. 5 Additional semantic specification for nuclear types

		O			
	↕\	—	↕/	↑/	V
↕\	E=0	1	2	3	4
—	1	E=0	1	2	3
E ↕/	2	1	E=0	1	2
↑/	3	2	1	E=0	1
V	4	3	2	1	E=0

Table 1 Hypothetical values for nuclear differentiation

which has been presented is from Southern British English (Received Pronunciation).[13] A necessary next step is to carry out an identical analysis of data

13 The cautionary point should be made that the dialect differences between this and American English should be borne in mind for readers more used to the latter. Specifically, differences in nuclei should be watched, especially (i) the use of the high fall-rise for British low fall, with no necessary interpretation of contingency (see below); (ii)

from other dialects and languages, to determine the extent to which the above categories and processes are universally applicable. No conclusion on this point is attempted here—nor is it possible to reach any such conclusion in view of the general absence of analysed corpora for other languages. But an illustration of the applicability of the above procedure to other languages, using the English examples as a point of comparison, does bring to light some interesting correspondences and differences.

Three Brazilian Portuguese speakers (from São Paulo) went systematically through my classification for English, translating the sentences into Portuguese, and testing the possibility of alternative intonational processes upon themselves and other native-speakers.[14] Naturally, this brings to light only a proportion of the intonational patterns in Portuguese which have to be accounted for, and the naturalness of the informants' responses needs further confirmation, but the results are still interesting. Almost all the sentences were capable of translation without radical alteration in their structure, and an identical intonation pattern was used in the majority of cases. The main differences were as follows:

Tone-unit boundaries

(i) Strong tendency to incorporate initial adverbials into the tone-unit (cf. A3 above and B2), e.g.

/Normalmente ele não toma REMEDIOS/ ('Normally she doesn't take medicine')

(ii) Strong tendency to incorporate initial Noun clauses into the tone-unit (cf. A3iv), e.g.

/Como o livro vai vender e impossivel DIZER/ ('How the book will sell is impossible to say')

(iii) No boundary after appositive subordinate clause (cf. A3vii), e.g.

/O fato e que ele não GOSTA dela/ ('The fact is that he doesn't love her')

(iv) Final comment clauses have separate tone-units (cf. A6), e.g.

/Nos vamos AMANHÃ/ SABE/ ('We're going tomorrow, you know')

the use of high narrow rise for British low fall, with no necessary interpretation of query; (iii) a more extensive use of level tone than in British, in place of the low fall and rise; and (iv) more narrowing on rising tones, with no necessary reduction in intensity of emotion. See further Engler and Hilyer (1971). On Australian English, see Adams (1969), Burgess (1973), Flint (1970).

14 I am indebted to Antonieta Celani, Leila Barbara, Stella Pilar and other colleagues from the Cultura Inglêsa and Catholic University of São Paulo, for their help in verifying the statements about Portuguese used in this chapter.

Note: This accounts for the familiar error made by Portuguese speakers in

learning English, e.g. /We're going TOMORROW/ you KNOW/.

(v) Final adverbial conjuncts, etc. regularly have separate tone-units (cf. B2), e.g.

/Ele CHEGOU/ FINALMENTE/ ('He arrived finally')

Note: As previously, a common learning error, to give the final adverbial a separate tone-unit.

(vi) Vocatives always have a separate tone-unit, even in final position (cf. B1), e.g.

/voce vem CONOSCO/ JOÃO/ ('Are you coming with us, John')

Note: As previously, a common learning error, as in /good MORNING/ Mr JONES/.

Tonicity

The tendency is to keep the tonic syllable on the last item in the tone-unit, whether grammatical or lexical. This tendency seems to have general applicability: for example, it applies even when one has repeated items in coordinate structures (cf. B4), e.g.

Esti livro custa cinco DOLARES/ e esti aqui tres DOLARES/

(accounting for the learning error of /this book costs five DOLLARS/ and this one three DOLLARS/). It is also seen in the avoidance of a tonic on the grammatical item, even in a sequence (cf. A1), or in idioms (for example, in the reading of football results on the radio, the tonic is always on the numbers, which contrasts with English drawn games, where the tonic is brought forward onto the name of the team, as in

/Liverpool EIGHT/ READING 'eight/

but /Liverpool OITO/ Reading OITO/).

It was difficult to establish any precise principles for tonicity, though, because of the differences in grammatical patterning between the two languages, e.g. the considerable differences in thematic construction, as in:

(/The hat was BLUE/ = /Chapeu era AZUL/
/The HAT was blue/ = /Azul era CHAPEU/)

All that can be said is that this is probably the area of greatest divergence between English and Portuguese, and thus the area where one has to be extremely cautious before talking about intonational universals.

Tone

(i) In tag questions, pitch-range is more important than tonal direction: Portuguese speakers use either falling or rising tones for both 'asking' and 'telling' senses, distinguishing the senses by a high beginning-point for the tone (for 'asking') and a low beginning-point (for 'telling'), viz.

	English	Portuguese
Asking	↓′	↑′ or ↑ˋ or ↑⁻
Telling	↑ˋ	↓, or ↓ˏ or ↓⁻

(ii) Attitudinal clashes occur with level tone, which is widely used in place of English low fall and low rise in their neutral distribution, and fall-rise, which is found where English would expect both low falling and rising tones.

(iii) Phonetic difficulties occur especially with: low rise on long vowels in monosyllables; high rise with a nuclear tail of any length (the tendency is to introduce a separate tone-unit or sequence of units, each with a high rising tone).

Conclusion

The aim of this chapter has been to draw together a number of previously unrelated observations and principles, and attempt to provide a coherent model of intonational patterning which could be extended to handle other prosodic features and be integrated within linguistic theory as a whole. In the process, a number of further research tasks have become apparent, the more important of which are now listed.[15]

(1) The need to establish the attitudinal and stylistic conditioning on tone-unit boundaries. Given the above norms, under what circumstances will data

15 Recent work on the relationship between intonation and syntax in English includes: Allerton and Cruttenden (1974), André (1974), Cruttenden (1970), Fox (1973), Halliday (1970), D. Harris (1971), Hartvigson (1969), Langacker (1970), Shen (1969), Shevchenko (1972), Stageberg (1971), Watanabe (1972), Wode (1972a,b). See also Copceag and Roceric-Alexandrescu (1968), Delattre (1970), Grundstrom and Léon (1973), Hornby (1971), Léon (1970, 1972), Lieberman (1970), Rodón (1970), Rountree (1972), Sotkis (1972), Vanderslice (1970a), Vanderslice and Ladefoged (1972), Walch (1973), Yorio (1973).
    Recent work on the intonation of languages other than English includes: Bagmut (1970), Blount (1970), Cohen and 't Hart (1970), Collier (1971), Collier and 't Hart (1970), Debreczeni (1972), Elert (1970), Feldman (1973), Gonzalez (1970), Guentherodt (1969), Halim (1970), Hirvonen (1970), Imazu (1973), Isačenko and Schädlich (1970), Kvavik and Olsen (1972), Lepschy (1968), Morais-Barbosa (1966), Nash (1973), Nikolaeva (1969), Pilch (1970), Sethi (1971), Van Katwijk (1974), Vende (1969), Weinberg (1971), Wittman (1970).

present (a) more and (b) fewer tone-units? Other prosodic variables will have to be considered (especially *tempo* and *pause*) as will the question of the type of grammatical unit with which tone-units can best be correlated. There is some evidence in the data to suggest that clauses and sentences are the units of organization for relatively informal, fluent discourse, but elements of clause structure for more formal or less fluent situations.

(2) The extension of the discussion to handle inter-sentence relations is necessary. The notion of 'connected speech' is still the weak point of inquiry. One hopes, as this comes to be more thoroughly investigated, that appropriate attention will be paid to intonation, along with the other variables.

(3) Non-vocal semiotic activity has not been studied in this chapter, but its importance as the only way of salvaging a non-verbal concept of 'context' should be apparent from the above. Experimental situations in which the effect of controlled variation in kinesic activity upon intonation should be devised.

(4) Enough work in structural semantics has now been done to make an analysis of the meaning-relations operating between the various attitudinal labels feasible. In particular, more broadly-based studies of informant reaction need to be undertaken.

(5) The concept of equivalence needs to be further investigated, and if found wanting, some alternative way of handling the distinction between intonational norm and deviation devised.

(6) The entire approach needs to be applied to languages as unrelated to English as possible, in order to build up a body of data that can bear on the question of universals (see also Chapter 2). In this respect, the need for adequate corpus-based work ought not to be underestimated.

2
Current trends in paralinguistics

Defining the starting-point for a discussion of paralanguage's currency and trendiness is not a difficult task. There has already been one well-organized attempt to summarize the state of the art, in this subject, with the 1962 Indiana University Conference on Paralinguistics and Kinesics, which was later published under the heading *Approaches to semiotics* (Sebeok, Hayes and Bateson 1964). In retrospect, it is clear that this conference performed two major roles. First, it brought together the rather scattered material which had been published or mimeographed in the few years since the stimulating specification of the field by Trager, Smith and their associates, and attempted to establish explicitly the general principles which seemed to underlie the various approaches. Secondly, in trying to define the subject, and to relate it to the other branches of semiotics, a number of promising lines of inquiry were suggested, and sometimes very specific research topics outlined. In these ways, the conference participants provided considerable bibliographical information, and presented a fairly complete picture of the pre-1960 period in paralinguistic studies. It therefore should not be too much of a simplification to consider current trends in paralanguage as running from the date of that conference to the present. Indeed, much of the research which has taken place over the past ten years has in fact been influenced, directly or indirectly, by the work of this conference.

In my view, there are three main trends in paralinguistic study in the 1960s: (a) further development of the approach outlined mainly in Trager (1958), including its increasing application to other (non-linguistic) areas; (b) the development of other approaches not within the Trager-Smith framework; and (c), partly as a result of these first two trends, the development of considerable theoretical confusion. It is profitable to begin by suggesting some reasons for the latter.

Part of the reason for the confusion which surrounds paralinguistic study at the present time is certainly due to the way in which linguistics developed during the 1960s. The early definitions of paralanguage, and the descriptions of paralinguistic effects, as we shall see, were made exclusively within the theoretical and descriptive framework provided by Trager and others (see Trager 1949, Trager and Smith 1951, Smith 1952, Trager 1958); but to follow their account of paralanguage, one had really to understand their whole approach to linguistic analysis. For example, it was not possible to appreciate the basis of their distinction between some types of pitch movement and others (e.g. between overhigh/overlow pitch height, which were considered paralinguistic, and the four pitch levels, which were phonemic, and hence linguistic) without

understanding their 'emic' approach to prosodic features, and this in turn
would have to be seen in the context of what in their view constituted 'linguistics proper' (see below). But in the 1960s, the theoretical approach begun
by Trager and Smith became largely of historical interest within linguistics
(though certain aspects of their description continued to be used); and with this,
the status of paralinguistic study became unclear. A number of factors contributed to this situation.

An important factor is the absence of any reassessment of their views in the
light of other developments in the course of the past ten years. When a theory
(in this case, generative theory) is so much in the ascendant, any earlier linguistic
approach which does not take cognizance of the claims of that theory, and attempt
some comparison with its own claims, is necessarily going to distance itself
from the eye of the majority of linguists and become, in effect, of historical
interest. In the present case, it would have been beneficial for the development
of paralinguistic study if Trager, or someone, had discussed it in the light (or
darkness) of the competence/performance distinction, for its accountability in
terms of this dichotomy is by no means clear. Or again, paralinguistic effect
could usefully have been brought into the discussion of meaning-relations, in the
sense of Fillmore (1968a), or of syntactic presuppositions (cf. Fillmore 1968b,
Chomsky 1969), in view of the close relationship between paralanguage and
intonation, and the relevance of these effects in determining certain types of
structural contrast.[1] But as far as I am aware, such matters have not been raised,
and the general differences between the views of Trager as presented in *The
field of linguistics* or *An outline of English structure*, and generative grammar,
have simply become more marked with the passage of time.

Trager and Smith themselves seem to have recognized the passing of an
era, as the rather wistful foreword to the seventh and final printing of the
Outline (in 1966) indicates.[2] And neither they nor their colleagues have answered
in print the fairly steady flow of criticism which has been levelled at their
approach over the past twenty years (e.g. Bolinger 1949, 1951, Chomsky *et al.*

[1] The application of case grammar in the University of Edinburgh (Dept of Child Life
and Health) project on language acquisition allowed for paralinguistic features in the
interpretation of utterances: 'an utterance needs to be interpreted before it may be
categorized, and interpretation may depend on the syntax and semantics of the utterance, on its prosody, on its co-text (discourse relations), or on extralinguistic information'. Paralinguistic features are in fact specifically mentioned in the presyntactic
section of their analysis. (Information from a preliminary draft of an Appendix out-
lining their descriptive apparatus, May 1968.)
[2] 'The hoped-for writing of a completely revised *English structure* has not come to
pass, but a considerable amount of progress has been made and the results of this
research is beginning to appear now in various places. Consequently, the sixth printing
being exhausted, it has been decided to make this the final printing of the *Outline of
English structure*, to meet the continued demand for copies. But users are urged to
remember the original date of publication, to search out the comparatively few publications that have appeared since then which stem from the same analytical foundation,
and to use the book's conclusions not as the final word but as points of departure for
further analyses.'

1956, Stankiewicz 1964: 265–7, Crystal and Quirk 1964 or Lieberman 1965).[3] Perhaps part of the reason for the failure to defend the approach lay in its pioneering status, which seemed to generate a certain complacency over theoretical matters. Markel's comment at the Indiana Conference is indicative of this, and other examples of the same attitude can easily be collected: 'I think we will find, if we go over the list, that everything we want to call paralanguage is covered by Trager's system. We would also find those things that are not covered are not paralanguage; they are psycholinguistics or metalinguistics.' Trager himself takes a more reasonable view of the limitations of his approach (as the foreword quoted in footnote 2 suggests), referring to it only as a 'guide to observation' (1964: 22); but one would never guess this from the subsequent applications of his approximation by others in such fields as psychotherapy or anthropology, where the completeness of the description and the adequacy of the underlying theory is assumed. Trager's 1958 paper is however a first approximation towards a description, not a theory. It is not a 'system' in any theoretical sense (cf. Duncan 1969: 119, and above, p. 33), but rather an inventory and notation of effects made on fairly *ad hoc* principles.

There were other reasons for a restricted interest in paralinguistic studies amongst linguists in the 1960s, to the extent that it is given no mention at all in such standard textbooks as Gleason (1961), Robins (1964), Hall (1964), Lyons (1968) or Malmberg (1968). The link with semiotics, for instance, has in a way been a hindrance as well as a help, in that its description along with the relatively indiscrete and unstructured non-vocal modes of communication has tended to minimize attention to any features of a more clearly 'linguistic' character that it might display. And the almost exclusive emphasis on paralanguage's affective function was doubtless a further factor which made many linguists feel that this was not an area of importance to investigate. Most linguists were—and are—of the opinion that paralanguage is at best of marginal significance to linguistics, and equally well or more appropriately studied by other disciplines. The 'marginal' view is of course reinforced by the (rather unfortunate) terms used. Labels like 'para'language (cf. 'supra'segmental) reflect a theoretical viewpoint which sees effects of this kind as 'additional'.[4] It is by no means easy to wriggle out of this terminological straitjacket in order to argue a more central linguistic view of these phenomena, but it is important to try; and one of the major trends in paralinguistic study in the 1960s has been to present this alternative.[5]

Paralanguage was of course a marginal field for Trager too, but at least there its relationship with aspects of language which were considered more central was fairly explicit, and the techniques of classification and description were

3 Trager's (1964) reaction to Crystal (1963) simply reasserts his original position, and does little more than clarify the extent of the difference between the two positions.
4 Cf. such definitions of 'prosodic features' as Carrell and Tiffany's (1960: 260): 'the variables which add the "plus" values to communication. . . .'
5 The fallacy of assuming that those areas of language that one's available linguistic techniques cannot handle are therefore less important was stressed by Birdwhistell in a paper in 1959: See the quotation on p. 69.

modelled on familiar linguistic lines. The term 'paralanguage' filled a slot in Trager's overall descriptive framework, entering into the definition of the whole, and receiving its own definition and status from its relationships with other categories of the theory. And once the parent-theory came to be considered inadequate as a view of language, then necessarily paralanguage's status became unclear. The mid-1960s saw the retention and development of many of the *descriptive* insights of the approach, but with less and less reference being made to the theoretical principles which had earlier been established to account for them. The development of paralinguistic ideas within semiotics, and their application to such fields as psychotherapy, anthropology or language teaching, was almost entirely a descriptive development, which was of course welcomed by scholars from these fields, who had lacked any means of formalizing these features of behaviour hitherto. Similarly, the Trager/Smith description of phonology, and accompanying notation, continued to be used as a basis for teaching about English and about linguistics in many influential textbooks (e.g. Gleason 1961), and has been given a new lease of life by Chomsky and Halle (1968). But exposition and examination of the theoretical basis of the description has not taken place during this time. One thus finds the development of a situation in which a widely-used descriptive framework rests on a largely implicit theoretical foundation; and in the absence of analytic criteria being made explicit, one naturally finds arbitrary descriptive decisions, ambiguous cases being forced into one or other of the set of choices provided by the framework, and, following on this, inconsistency in the use of terms by various scholars.

'Paralanguage' itself, as a term, was particularly affected by the lack of any explicit theoretical foundation. In the mid-1960s, one finds an increasing number of references to the 'language and paralanguage' of a community, without further comment—as if the latter were in some way a reality which existed independently of one's specific approach to language.[6] Scholars of radically different theoretical persuasions who had cause to refer to paralanguage would refer to Trager (1958) and assume that the conceptual relationship between that paper and their own approaches was obvious. Significantly, the number of references to Hill's brief remarks (1958: 408-9) increases during this period—significant, as paralanguage for Hill subsumed kinesics, an extension of the term which most of the early workers in the field did not intend, and which is still very much a minority view. Thus, while the existence and relevance of paralinguistic effects has been recognized by many scholars in various disciplines, in the absence of any theoretical nucleus to provide a baseline for comparing and assessing modifications and extensions in the use of terms, a

6 Cf. Abercrombie (1968: 55): 'the term paralanguage . . . seems to me potentially misleading: it can give the impression that, because there exists a (more or less) homogeneous entity called *language*, there must be, existing beside it, a comparably homogeneous entity called *paralanguage*. I believe this is not so. . . . These non-verbal, though conversational, activities to which the word paralanguage refers are far too diverse, too little codified, too uninvestigated, and too insufficiently understood, to be given the air of unity which a noun confers on them.'

multiplicity of definitions and characterizations of paralanguage have developed, and produced a general state of confusion. In trying to classify some of these differences, I shall concentrate on those papers which explicitly refer to their subject-matter as falling under the heading of paralanguage. There are of course other studies which deal with similar effects, though not labelling them 'paralinguistic', and I shall refer to these in passing later.[7]

A preliminary point which has to be made is the quite remarkable range of subject-matter which is allowed under the heading of paralanguage. In the process of accumulating information for this chapter, I wrote to a number of scholars asking them what work, if any, they were doing within this field. The term 'paralanguage' was deliberately not defined in my letter. Excluding those who expressed uncertainty as to whether their work did fall under this heading or not, there was still considerable variability in interpretation. All of the following were suggested: animal vocalization (or some aspect of it), memory restrictions on language, recall ability for language, utterance length, literary analysis, environmental restrictions on language use (accounting for such matters as word or phoneme frequency differences in social groups), glossolalia, and emotional expression in general language disturbance—in effect, a fair proportion of sociolinguistics and psycholinguistics. These were, however, marginal interpretations of paralanguage, compared with the senses classified below, which I would consider to be the most widespread and influential uses of the term. The fact that there were seven distinct 'basic' senses, of course, simply indicates the distance this subject has to travel before its claims to be scientific can be taken seriously. I shall illustrate these senses in terms of the increasing restrictedness of the phenomena allowed in under the heading of paralanguage.

(1) *Including non-human as well as human vocalization.* Austin's (1972) 'sound-signal systems' are illustrated from various animal species as well as man, and referred to as paralanguage. Abercrombie (1968: 56) restricts the term to human behaviour, but implies a parallel with animal communication. Hockett (1960) refers to paralinguistic phenomena in his discussion of animal communication and the origin of speech, but it is unclear whether the term should be construed in a purely 'human' sense. Increased study of human paralanguage over the past few years has, however, shown more rather than less difference between animal species and man in this area (see Chapter 3). There is little suggestion in animal communication of the 'systems' of paralinguistic effects postulated for man (see below); nor is there any comparison with the number and complexity

---

7 For general coverage of this field and related areas in the 1960s, see Birdwhistell (1961), Barbara (1963), Ostwald (1963), Kramer (1963, 1964), the papers by La Barre, Hayes, and Mahl and Schulze in Sebeok, Hayes and Bateson (1964), Crystal and Quirk (1964: Ch. 2), Austin (1965: 19), Diebold (1965), Ekman (1965), Crystal (1966a, 1969a), Egorov (1967), Abercrombie (1967: Ch. 6), Weakland (1967), Duncan (1969), Vetter (1969), Markel (1969b), the papers by Bateson, McQuown and Hockett in McQuown (in press), Heike (1969), Laver and Hutcheson (1972), Key (1970), Lehiste (1970). Poyatos (1970), R. Harris (1971).

of the phonetic variables which enter into the definition of human paralinguistic effects, and the nature of the semantic contrasts which they expound. The few broad similarities which do exist seem trivial by comparison.

(2) *Including non-vocal as well as vocal features of human communication.* This is the one normally implied by the use of the term 'non-verbal' in, for example, social psychology. Specifically, kinesics is brought under the heading of paralanguage. This is an influential sense, as it is the one used by Hill (1958: 408–9); and Abercrombie has given some reasons for his use of the term in this way in his 1968 paper (56). But, as Hayes suggested, in discussion at the Indiana Conference (Sebeok, Hayes and Bateson 1964: 153), this is a potentially confusing sense—and it is one which the title of the Conference carefully avoided. Despite the attempt to foist onto kinesics essentially linguistic categories, it is highly unlikely that kinesic behaviour has sufficient structural complexity, discreteness, or semantic organization to warrant its analysis in the same terms as linguistic behaviour; and spurious terminological identity is best avoided.

(3) *Including all non-segmental ('suprasegmental') features and some segmental ones.*[8] In this sense, Smith's vocal identifiers (1952), e.g. 'uh-uh', or Trager's vocal segregates (1958), including hesitation features, amongst other things, are allowed under the heading of paralanguage. Any segmental utterance not having the normal phonemic structure of a language (e.g. [ʊ] in English) is usually included. This is an unhelpful sense, it seems to me, as it is using the term 'paralanguage' in a catch-all, negative way, i.e. every vocal effect which *cannot* be accounted for in other, previously defined, more central (in some sense) linguistic categories. In fact, the boundary-line between the more generally-accepted paralinguistic features (in the sense of 4–6 below) and these segmental vocalizations is unclear, because of their functional overlap: durational variations which are non-segmental require reference to silence as a structural marker; but silence is linear (used sequentially and not concomitantly with segmental (verbal) utterance), and can also be used as an exponent of hesitation; hesitation, however, can be vocalized segmentally (cf. Blankenship and Kay

8 The generally-held distinction between segmental and non-segmental phonology is retained as a framework for discussion in this book (cf. p. 11). The former is defined purely in terms of vowels, consonants and their combinatorial properties. Non-segmental phonology comprises all contrastive sound-effects which have an essentially variable relationship to the segmental or lexical component of utterance, and which are not describable with reference to single segments (except insofar as single segments can be exponents of syllables); specifically, these are effects which operate continuously over a stretch of utterance, minimally one syllable (as in a pitch contour), or which are specified in terms of a number of segments, some adjacent, some not, all of which are affected by a single 'setting' or configuration of the vocal organs, to produce a single perceptual impression and a single semantic interpretation (e.g. labialization, velarization). 'Suprasegmental' features, in the sense of Trager, Smith, and others, thus comprise one subset of the totality of non-segmental features of a language. 'Intonation' and paralanguage' would be defined with reference to other subsets. It is not the purpose of this chapter to make any terminological decisions as to how non-segmental phonology may best be compartmentalized, however, for which see pp. 94–5.

(1964) and footnote 14 below); and once this is allowed in, then a wide range of formally similar utterances can equally well be called paralinguistic. But any such extension produces some terminologically bizarre situations, reflecting a conceptual confusion: for example, a segregate uttered on overhigh pitch would be a paralinguistic feature varied paralinguistically. It would seem to be clearer, as well as more consistent, to restrict paralanguage to the non-segmental component of utterance; though even here there are differences of opinion as to how much should be included under this heading, as the next three senses show.

(4) *Including voice quality as well as (all or most) non-segmental features.* The distinction between voice quality—in the sense of a permanently present background person-identifying vocal characteristic—and language is generally accepted in some form or other within linguistics, though the terminology for the former varies (e.g. 'timbre', 'voice set', 'personal articulatory setting').[9] Voice quality is considered idiosyncratic, biologically-controlled, irrelevant to the semantic interpretation of the message; language is considered to be shared, culturally controlled, the basis of semantic interpretation.[10] Paralanguage subsumes voice quality in, e.g. Cammack and Van Buren (1967: 7), where it is defined as 'variations in voice quality, tempo, register, and volume';[11] or Bronstein and Jacoby (1967: 83), where it is characterized as 'special qualities of voice or special changes in the tempo or in the loudness or softness that may accompany our speaking'.[12] Halliday, McIntosh and Strevens (1964: 96) seem

9 See, for example, Abercrombie (1967:91), Sharpe (1970), Laver (1968), and other references there. It is not the purpose of this chapter to survey research into voice quality; but insofar as paralinguistic analysis presupposes an ability to distinguish voice quality from other effects, then some awareness of current research in this area will clearly be helpful. Some recent papers on speaker identity, norms of articulation, etc., are the following: Fónagy and Magdics (1960), Kersta (1962), Siertsema (1962), Hargreaves and Starkweather (1963), Berger (1964), Floyd (1964), Voiers (1964), Akiyama and Yumoto (1966), Han (1966), Janota (1967), Laver (1968), Hollien (1974). Special emphasis on the physical analysis of voice quality (or some aspect of it) may be found in: Black (1961), Bowler (1964), Garvin and Ladefoged (1963), Laver (1964, 1967), and Wendahl (1966). A review of this literature, and a discussion of its relevance to non-segmental phonology, is to be found in Crystal (1969a).
10 For phenomena which might be considered as falling between these alternatives, see the discussion on sociolinguistic variation and paralanguage at the end of this chapter.
11 They further define it as 'all phenomena of speech that are not language', defining language as 'the phonological, morphological, and grammatical subsystems, together with the peripheral semantic and phonetic effects'.
12 'Qualities' here is not in Trager's sense, but is more like Abercrombie's (1967: 91), as Bronstein and Jacoby's discussion in Ch. 2 makes clear. The confusion this particular term can cause can also be seen in, for example, the title of Markel, Meisels and Houck (1964), 'Judging personality from voice quality'. Here, 'voice quality' *is* being used in Trager's sense; but the research they refer to in the 1930s, at the beginning of their paper, did not use the term in this way, but in the more general sense referred to at the beginning of paragraph 4 above. It would certainly help matters if Trager's voice qualities were always referred to in the plural.

to *identify* paralanguage with voice quality ('features, such as voice quality and handwriting, which do not carry formal contrasts'). Duncan (1969:118) also includes speech non-fluencies (defined as uncontrolled vocal effects) as paralanguage, and studies paralinguistic behaviour in psychotherapy inter-action, where the distinction between controlled, normal behaviour and its opposite ceases to be relevant for any definition of the term (cf. Rubenstein and Aborn (1960) for an interpretation in terms of language disturbance). But the theoretical importance of distinguishing between controlled, contrastive commu-nicative behaviour and uncontrolled, non-contrastive behaviour within a group is so central that there seems no advantage in putting them under the same label.

(5) *Including only non-segmental features, but excluding prosodic phonemes and voice quality.* This is the dominant sense of the term. In this view, the pitch, stress and juncture phonemes are considered linguistic; other functions of pitch, loudness and duration, and any other suprasegmental effects are con-sidered paralinguistic. Markel (1965) defines paralanguage as the 'non-phone-mic' aspects of speech; Duncan, Rosenberg and Finkelstein (1969) say, for example, 'paralinguistic intensity and pitch would be transcribed when these variables in speech exceed the range of variation necessary for conveying phonemic stress and pitch'; Austin (1972) talks of 'the signal system of the non-articulated vocal tract'. Ostwald (1964: 17), however, seems to allow intonation into his definition of 'paralinguistic acoustic cues', when he illustrates these by reference to 'variously intoned forms of "oh" and the nuances which support or belie overt meanings of words'. Scholars not working within a framework of prosodic phonemes either tend to call everything non-segmental paralinguistic, or (more often) talk about 'intonation and paralanguage'.[13] The distinction between phonemic and non-phonemic aspects of non-segmental phonology is of crucial importance in assessing paralinguistic studies; consequently it will be discussed further below.

(6) *Including only a sub-set of non-segmental features other than prosodic phonemes and voice quality.* Paralinguistic features here are defined with reference to a description of non-segmental phonology for a particular language, to produce a very restricted sense for the term, e.g. Crystal and Quirk (1964) and the work influenced by them. However, a requirement of any theory of paralinguistic phenomena, in whatever sense, is that they be defined with reference to phonetic criteria of a general nature (types of articulatory movement, etc.), and not solely from (in this case) English. The paralinguistic systems of Crystal and Quirk ultimately have to be seen within a more general framework, to allow for cross-cultural comparishns; and it would seem more useful to phrase one's

13 The distinction between intonation and paralanguage is, however, blurred in Aber-crombie (1967: 130), where paralinguistic phenomena are defined as 'features of voice dynamics such as continuity [*sc.* incidence of pauses], variation in loudness, in tempo, and in tessitura' [*sc.* a range of notes within which the pitch fluctuation of a speaker's voice falls during normal circumstances]. Intonation is part of paralanguage for Herriot (1970: 14), as is gesture and most other non-segmental features (cf. pp. 46–7, 151).

definition of paralanguage in these terms to begin with.[14]

(7) *Functional definitions.* Paralanguage does not seem ever to have been defined purely in functional terms, but there is usually a functional component in the definitions which are given. This normally amounts to no more than saying that these features are non-linguistic or extra-linguistic (cf. Abercrombie's definition (1968: 55) as 'non-linguistic elements in conversation', or Cammack and Van Buren's (1967: 7) as 'all phenomena of speech [that] are not language') —approaches which would be vacuous without any explicit definition of language. More specifically and positively, paralinguistic effects are said to be either expressive of emotions or personality (which is the standard account), or a means of identification of social groups (e.g. Lerman and Damsté 1969) or language varieties (e.g. Weeks 1971). Lotz's useful article on the structure of speech (1963) uses the term 'paraphonetic' (23) to refer to a channel of speech which gives information about emotion, attitude, etc., though it is not entirely clear to what extent there is an identity with another of his categories, the 'pragmatic' features of speech (17). Reference to a language-independent theory of emotion, personality or social groups is usually absent, however, and the useful work in this area is limited to experimental analyses of a fairly restricted order (see below). Suggestions as to paralanguage having any kind of structural or denotative function are on the whole absent—though if paralinguistic effects can enter into the exposition of certain types of intonation contrast (as stated in Charleston (1960: Ch. 1) and Crystal (1969a: 137)), then a potential structural function must be recognized.

The existence of this degree of terminological disunity among scholars, and the absence of any generally-recognized set of criteria for paralinguistic analysis, thus means that the most useful research is that which either explicitly relates its hypotheses to a specific model of paralinguistic behaviour (such as Trager's), or which concentrates on obtaining experimental evidence for some quite specific hypothesis, the terms of which are given a clear but *ad hoc* definition. The work of Duncan and others into psychotherapy interaction and related matters (1965, 1969) provides an illustration of this, as his investigations take

14 Also under paragraph 6 one might list the research into pausal phenomena, which has increased in quantity over the past ten years, and which is regularly considered to be paralinguistic. A critical account of this work is given in Crystal (1969a: 169–70) and Duncan (1969), and a general review of the research at University College London under Goldman-Eisler may be found in her 1968 book. Other recent papers are the following: Barik (1968), Bernstein (1962), Black, Tosi, Singh and Takefuta (1966), Blankenship and Kay (1964), Boomer (1963, 1965), Boomer and Dittman (1962, 1964), Dittman and Llewellyn (1967, 1968), Cook (1969, 1971), Cook and Lalljee (1970), Cook, Smith and Lalljee (1974), Goldman-Eisler (1961a,b,c,d,e, 1967, 1968, 1972), Grišina (1969), Henderson, Goldman-Eisler and Skarbek (1965a,b), Lay and Burron (1968), Levin and Silverman (1965), Levin, Silverman and Ford (1967), Livant (1963), Martin (1967, 1970), Martin and Strange (1968a,b), Matarazzo, Wiens, Matarazzo and Saslow (1968), Penge (1970), Simkins (1963), Suci (1967), Tannenbaum, Williams and Hillier (1965), Tannenbaum, Williams and Wood (1967), Hawkins (1971), Brown and Miron (1971).

well-recognized paralinguistic effects and examine their function in relation to clearly defined, specific social tasks. Duncan and Rosenthal (1968) provide evidence to suggest that the way in which an experimenter reads his instructions to subjects can be a determinant of their responses to an experimental procedure; and a subsequent and more rigorous experiment shows the relevance of paralanguage to the concept of experimenter bias more clearly (Duncan, Rosenberg and Finkelstein 1969). Duncan, Rice and Butler (1968) show that certain paralinguistic criteria are able to differentiate therapist behaviour in peak and poor interaction hours. In a different but comparably specific connection, Davy and Quirk (1969) show that paralinguistic behaviour is of relevance in assessing informants' judgments about the acceptability or otherwise of syntactic structure. Experimental work on the whole is lacking, however, and few of the projects which are currently examining aspects of paralinguistic behaviour on a larger scale, as part of a broader communicational framework, have as yet reported anything other than their first speculations: cf. Blasdell and others (1969) in relation to first language learning; Austin (1972), who relates his study to animal communication and other non-verbal activities; Lomax and others (1968), in relation to the cross-cultural study of song and dance style (cantometrics, choreometrics); the Tracor project (Pendergraft and Ziehe 1967) on developing a programming system for semiotics; and Ostwald (1963) in connection with psychotherapy interaction.

There is a marked lack of descriptive studies. English tends to be the language of illustration still, with very often the same examples cited over and over again. Novelty is provided by Austin's contributions (1965, 1973), by Vanderslice and Pierson (1967) on Hawaiian English (their term 'prosodic' subsumes some of what other scholars would call paralinguistic), by Lawrence (1971) on some aspects of Texan English, by Crystal and Davy (1969), who make frequent reference to paralinguistic effect in their study of occupational and other varieties of English, by Pellowe (1970) on Tyneside English, and by the work into English varieties by Osmers (1967), Davy (1968), Benyon (1969) and Kempson (1969). There is little on other languages, either explicitly or implicitly, under the heading of paralanguage, apart from Cammack and Van Buren's illuminating cross-cultural study of aspects of English and Japanese (1967), and Black, Tosi, Singh and Takefuta (1966). Lawendowski (1970), using a Pittenger and Smith (1957) framework, makes some reference to Polish; Fónagy and Magdics (1963) refer to Hungarian; Revill (1970) to Mbembe. Chapter 5 surveys the sociolinguistic literature from this point of view, and suggests that paralinguistic effect is of primary importance in the identification of several social categories (specifically age, sex, status, occupation, and speech function), though relatively little attention has been paid to this in the descriptive linguistic or anthropological literature.

It should be emphasized that most field workers, even in linguistics, do not make a systematic survey of paralinguistic effect a routine part of their investigations. People still seem unaware of the KIND of phenomenon which they are liable to come into contact with in this area of communicative activity, how they should describe what they hear, or how they should integrate this with other aspects of any linguistic description they may be making. The above references, as those in Chapter 5, are exceptional, and few of them actually use the term 'paralanguage'. Moreover, they are not readily comparable, as, in the absence of any generally-used theory, there is no guarantee that different scholars are using such terms as 'tone of voice' in the same way (it is often obvious that they are not[15]); there have been few attempts to transcribe utterances in order to indicate the frequency of occurrence and distribution of specific effects; and there have been certain methodological weaknesses (e.g. a failure to distinguish clearly between voice-quality and linguistic effect—a point I shall discuss further below—or to provide information about sampling of data or selection of informants). The sporadic, impressionistic nature of many of the above accounts is to be regretted, but the state of affairs is probably unavoidable at the present time, in view of the amorphous theoretical situation which characterizes fundamental research. There is after all little point in accumulating quantities of comparative detail which cannot, in the absence of an explicit theoretical framework, be compared.

Within paralinguistics, under the heading of the linguistic communication of emotion, there has been a considerable amount of discussion and experimentation, but once again, in the absence of consistent theoretical distinctions between such terms as 'controlled' and 'uncontrolled' (behaviour), 'emotion' and 'personality', 'trait' and 'stereotype', it is often difficult to compare the results of different groups. General reviews of this area are to be found in: Charleston (1960), Starkweather (1961), Dittman and Wynne (1961), Soskin and Kauffman (1961), Sychra (1962), Fónagy and Magdics (1963), Knapp (1963, especially Mahl's contribution), Davitz (1964), and J. Shapiro (1968). Kramer (1963) is a widely-read overview of work on 'nonverbal' properties of speech on the one hand, and personality and emotion characteristics on the other. Crystal (1969a: 62–77) provides another critique on similar lines. On the whole, experimental work has been geared towards determining the extent to which vocal effects are indices of different physical or personality traits or types as viewed 'from the outside', by obtaining reactions of sets of judges to stimuli. The work of Markel and others is of particular importance here. For example, Markel, Meisels and Houck (1964) is one paper which shows very clearly that specific impressions of a speaker's physical characteristics and demeanour are determined by qualities of voice (in Trager's (1958) sense). Markel, Eisler and Reese (1967) have indicated that regional dialect features in voice quality are significant in judging personality; and in a more comprehensive approach, Markel (1969a) finds further evidence to suggest that a formal profile of voice qualities is an index of personality types. The link between emotional and personality states is suggested in Costanzo, Markel and Costanzo (1969), where voice-quality profiles are viewed as representing modes of interpersonal orientation, which they interpret as constituting a bridge between

15 Few people would make a systematic distinction between 'tone', 'pitch', and 'melody', as in Adams (1957) for example: see p. 87.

personality dispositions and emotional states. Recent additions to the literature reviewed by Kramer are Ptacek and Sander (1966) on age recognition from the voice; Schwartz and Rine (1968b, but cf. 1968a also) on sex recognition from aspects of whispered speech; and Lay and Burron (1968) on hesitancy evaluation. Beier and others (1969) are working on the evaluation of cues (one class of which are paralinguistic in character) in judging emotional meaning, and showing that there is consistency in rating. Markel (1965) provides clear evidence of the reliability of rating some types of paralinguistic feature.

A major departure from the American approaches to paralinguistic study (cf. the second trend cited on p. 47 above) came in the work of various British scholars in the early 1960s, and provides the main source of theoretical comment on many of the questions raised at the beginning of this paper. A comprehensive bibliographical picture may thus be helpful. Crystal (1963) is an attempt to introduce paralinguistic studies to an audience which on the whole (apart from Abercrombie and Catford) had ignored it. Various criticisms were made and expanded in Crystal and Quirk (1964), which is largely concerned with the formulation of analytic principles, the definition of phonetic parameters for the description of paralinguistic features, and the development of a fresh notation for them. Crystal (1969a) is an attempt to develop an analysis of intonation for English within the framework of a more general theory of non-segmental phonology. This book incorporates discussion of the linguistic status of paralanguage (originally to be found in Crystal (1966a), and various experimental work (see Quirk and Crystal 1966), and Crystal's paper to the Tenth International Congress of Linguists, 1971). Further illustration of the approach is to be found in Crystal and Davy (1969), where different varieties of English are analysed in these terms, and a number of theses researched at University College London (Osmers 1967, Davy 1968, Benyon 1969, Kempson 1969, Penge 1970). The approach was also used in the Tyneside Dialect Survey at the University of Newcastle-upon-Tyne (see Pellowe 1970). There is a brief rejoinder to Crystal's original article in Trager (1964), and further comments on the points of difference are to be found in Rensky (1966) and André (1965, 1966). Further replies to the main criticisms which have been made of Trager's approach are so far lacking, but are expected.

The central question, which should have been raised years ago, and which has still no final answer, concerns the linguistic status of the vocal effects being labelled 'paralinguistic'. Trager's position is well-known, and is quite explicit, so I will not present it in detail here. As Trager says (1964: 23), 'the very essence of the analysis of paralanguage is in the recognition that paralanguage is NOT a part of language, and that therefore the statements about it are NOT linguistic statements.' This position follows naturally from the assumptions Trager holds: that linguistics proper concerns the analysis of phonological and morphological systems only (microlinguistics), pitch, stress and juncture phonemes being recognized as part of this description (Trager 1949, Trager and Smith 1951). The arguments against this position hinge on the question of criteria: on what grounds is the distinction between emic and non-emic phonological features based, and why should the 'proper' subject matter of linguistics be restricted to the former? These arguments are general ones, based on considerations of the nature of language as a whole. They assert that the microlinguistic view of language proper is an arbitrary preconception restricting one's view of other phenomena, which forces an analyst to make a binary 'yes/no' decision as to the status of certain features, where perhaps there is none, or where the analysis is of a 'more/less' kind. This point has been made in various places. Bazell (1954: 133) asked why phonemes should be the only criteria of relevance for intonation analysis, and his arguments apply *a fortiori* to paralanguage. Haas too (1957: 159) criticized the 'segmental principle' as being a major prejudice in linguistics. (Cf. also Halliday 1961: 252, 275, Crystal and Quirk 1964: 36, Crystal 1969a: 186, Bolinger 1949, and later discussion by him of 'gradience', and Sebeok 1962: 437–9 for a discussion of discreteness and gradience in relation to expressive language.) Stankiewicz also raised the question, at the Indiana Conference (1964: 266–7), but his point received no answer: 'it seems futile to approach language as a monolith and to exclude from it those phenomena which are not cut to the same pattern. . . . The linguistic status of certain features which signal emotion cannot easily be decided, since they do not lend themselves to the kind of systematization that linguists are used to, nor are they easily correlated with other linguistic elements.'[16] He suggests there may be a 'fuzzy periphery' to language, which scholars are now describing more consistently and in 'somewhat different terms from the cognitive or discrete elements of language'; but he leaves as open questions 'the systematicity of the expressive devices and their relationship to the cognitive elements of the code' and the 'grading' of expressive components, as opposed to the 'discreteness' of phonemes and morphemes (267). Crystal (1969a: 190) also argues that there is no reason for judging non-segmental phonological effect by phonemic/morphemic criteria:

The valuable discreteness of phonemic and morphemic definition, with their amenability to clear-cut substitutability tests of an either/or character, usually free from overlap, does not exclude the fact that there are parts of language which are not amenable to such treatment, but are more accurately and realistically covered by setting up scales of contrastivity, which are of a 'more/less' character. . . . There seems to be no real reason why these [prosodic and paralinguistic] features should be excluded from the field of linguistics proper, and why they should not be taken as wholly intralinguistic items, but of a different kind from phonemic and morphemic units, as these are normally understood.

(See also Lieberman 1973.)

16 Cf. Newman (1946:172), whose 'expressive prosody is not necessarily capable of the same type of systematization as that which is applicable to the usual kinds of morphemes'.
    Much of the trouble, it has been suggested (e.g. Kramer 1963, Crystal 1969a, 1971), is due to the uncritical and unsystematic use of vague descriptive labels (e.g. 'harsh', 'precise') in attempting to define the meaning of paralinguistic effects; it is not the effects themselves which are unsystematic and ambiguous, but rather the labels used to refer to them. For an analysis using a large number of such labels, see Voiers 1964.

The assumption underlying this argument is that any vocal effect which can be shown to have a systematic, shared, contrastive communicational function is by definition part of the overall sound-system of a language, and thus linguistic. In an experimental situation, if the substitution of one vocal effect for another in an utterance would lead judges consistently to rate the two utterances thus produced as 'different' in meaning—and moreover different in the same respect—then these effects are linguistically contrastive. (For reliability in rating paralinguistic features, see Markel 1965). This procedure is of course essentially the same as that used in traditional segmental phonology. But to restrict its application to segmental units only, or to a subset of the supra-segmental ones, is circular in that any such restriction presupposes the very distinction between linguistic and non-linguistic units which it was the purpose of the substitution test to establish. The procedure has to be applied to ALL vocal effects in the first instance, without introducing naive assumptions taken from early theories of meaning (e.g. suggesting that there is a non-arbitrary distinction between 'intellectual' and 'emotional' information in communi-cation). One then finds that there is certainly systematicity and discreteness in the paralinguistic area, though this is not as marked as in the case of intonation. It is therefore difficult to see what grounds there are for classifying some features of non-segmental phonology as phonemic (or linguistic), and some as non-phonemic (or extra-linguistic).[17] To avoid the arbitrariness implicit in this approach, then, it is suggested that a more appropriate model of the non-segmental sound system is to introduce the concept of a SCALE of linguisticness, ranging from 'most' to 'least' linguistic. At the 'most linguistic' polarity would be classified those features of utterance most readily describable in terms of closed systems of contrasts, which have a relatively clear phonetic definition, which display evidence of a hierarchical structure, which are relatively easily integrated with other aspects of linguistic structure (particularly syntax), e.g. tone-unit boundaries, nuclear tone type and placement, and other 'prosodic' features (in the sense of Crystal 1969a). At the other, 'least linguistic' end would be placed those features of utterance which seem to have little potential for entering into systemic relationships, which are relatively indiscrete, and which have a relatively isolated function and little integrability with other aspects of language structure, e.g. breathy or raspy vocal effects—effects which are often confused with voice quality characteristics on first hearing. Vocal effects lacking any semantic force would then be considered non-linguistic, and would

17 In addition to the arguments claiming considerable identity between suprasegmental phonemes and paralinguistic effects in general, one should also remember the arguments against extending the concept of the phoneme to *any* non-segmental effects—arguments which so far remain unanswered, though Bolinger's early strictures date back to 1949. The reasoning underlying these arguments is essentially the following: that if one examines the physical, structural and semantic characteristics of vowel and consonant (i.e. segmental) phonemes, on the one hand, and such features as intonation (or for that matter, paralanguage) on the other, one finds so little in common that to use phonemic terminology to describe the latter is to distort considerably their linguistic identity. For further details, see Bolinger 1949, 1951, Crystal 1969a: 196ff.

thus fall under the heading of either voice quality or physiological reflexes (such as coughing). It is, then, largely a terminological matter as to how parts of this scale are labelled: for a mixture of acoustic, linguistic and historical reasons, it is usual to separate off the effects based on pitch, loudness and duration, referring to these as prosodic features; but it is doubtful whether it is worth placing any great theoretical weight on such divisions.[18]

In a sense, the value of the above approach is not in the alternative analysis of paralanguage presented, as this might be totally misconceived, but rather in the attention it focuses on the need for analytic criteria to be made explicit. Far too much time has been spent on transcriptional matters and discovery procedures. Duncan (1969), for example, which is largely concerned with procedural matters, distinguishes three phases in research into non-verbal behaviour: the development of a notation, the analysis of structures between the transcribed behaviours, and the relationships between these and external variables. But the notational contribution of linguistics to paralinguistic study is very much a superficial one, and it should not be stressed at the expense of matters of analysis (a situation curiously reminiscent of the emphases in early discussions of phonemics in the thirties). It is clear from the critical discussion in Crystal (1969a: 75–7, 87–8) and elsewhere that there are a number of theoretical and methodological issues relevant to paralinguistic analysis which have hardly begun to be studied. Of particular importance is the need to develop a more sophisticated phonetic framework for the description of paralinguistic effects, in order to provide a more objective set of correlates for the notional categories of description that are regularly used. Lieberman and Michaels (1962) is one attempt to do this using acoustic criteria. Catford (1964) is another, using articulatory criteria: his study of phonation types is a preliminary survey of basic laryngeal activities in speech in terms of stricture-type and location, vocal-fold length, thickness and tension, upper larynx constriction, and vertical displacement of the larynx. It will also be important to correlate the phonetic 'basis' of paralinguistic effects with that of vowel and consonant phonemes. 'Secondary articulations' such as velarization, palatalization and labialization are regularly cited in both phonemic and paralinguistic studies, but there does not seem to be any generally recognized means of integrating this information, and there is a basic lack of knowledge about the 'facts'. For example, does a language which uses velarization as a normal phonemic distinctive feature also allow paralinguistic velarization? To what extent are paralinguistic effects reactions against regular phonemic tendencies in a language (cf. Stankiewicz's remarks (1964: 246) about the aversion of speakers of languages neighbouring on Russian to the Russian feature of palatalization when it was introduced into

18 For these reasons, I doubt whether analyses of paralinguistic behaviour in terms of a given pitch-phoneme framework can be valid (cf. Duncan, Rice and Butler 1968: 569, who make reference to their location in phonemic clauses). In view of the arbitrariness of the distinction between suprasegmental phonemes and paralanguage, it is not really surprising that paralanguage should be 'closely coordinated' with intonation (cf. Duncan, Rosenberg and Finkelstein 1969.)

speech, and similar examples) ? Further empirical studies are clearly necessary, as the amount of data on which generalizations about paralanguage are based is extremely small (as mentioned above, largely restricted to English, and moreover to fairly abnormal varieties of English, such as psychotherapy interaction).[19]

Similarly, there is a need for a more broadly-based view of the functional role of paralanguage and how it relates to non-linguistic effects. Functional definitions purely in terms of 'emotional' or 'affective' information are inadequate as they do not recognize the possibility of a structural role for these phenomena,[20] and a social function for paralanguage is only occasionally (and vaguely) referred to (see Chapter 5). In the latter case, the most important task is to ensure that the levels of abstraction in any social model are clearly defined and related to the linguistic variables. The situation is far more complex than appears at first sight. A person, while speaking, apart from his permanently present self-identifying vocal characteristic (his VOICE-QUALITY), simultaneously produces vocal effects which identify him as a member of a number of specific communities (e.g. belonging to a particular race, or nation, or class, or occupational group). Different sets of effects identify different communities, and each set may be said to form (in the absence of a better term) a COMMUNITY-QUALITY (e.g. British, upper-class, preacher, actor).[21] (The correlation between the various social abstractions and their corresponding linguistic ones (e.g. whether 'language' or 'dialect' best correlates with the concept of 'nation) need not concern us here.) The first point which has to be made is that the effects constituting a community-quality are not semantically contrastive within that community—for example, a working-class Yorkshire Englishman does not notice that any features of his voice are (a) English, (b) Yorkshire, or (c) working-class, as long as he is talking within his own community, i.e. to other working-class Yorkshire English people. The situation is complicated, however, by the fact that any of the community-qualities can be seen 'from outside', and some or all of the vocal effects from it used by speakers from outside the community in their speech, e.g. in telling a joke. All community-qualities may be affected in this way; and even an individual voice quality may be given an institutionalized role (e.g. 'He's talking like a Churchill'), though this is less common. Moreover, a community may respond collectively to another community, as in the case of people's reactions to the community-qualities of racial minority groups, or in the examples given by Stankiewicz (cf. above). A second complication is introduced by the fact that most people, not being phoneticians, get their facts

19 Blasdell (personal communication, 1969) is conducting a series of pilot studies on the acoustic characteristics of paralanguage in spontaneous conversation.
20 It is normal to talk of a grammatical function for intonation, but paralinguistic effects can expound intonational categories (e.g. whisper (cf. Trim 1970) or creaky voice), and this has to be allowed for.
21 There is unfortunately no generally-agreed term for 'voice-quality of a community', hence the above coinage. Honikman's 'articulatory settings' (1964) might do, but the phenomena being discussed above should not be viewed as having a solely articulatory definition.

wrong when they are attempting to imitate another community or individual, and instead of (or as well as) introducing vocal effects which are indeed there, produce imagined features ('stereotypes'). Often, in fact, the stereotyped features have more of an evocative effect than the real features (cf. 'You hardly sound like an American at all', and the like; see further, p. 79). Lastly, there is also the point that, while speaking, a person is using his language system with its normal range of contrasts, and this includes paralanguage. But each community may have its own paralinguistic features (analogous to regional dialect features in segmental phonology, syntax, etc.), and distinctions therefore have to be made between those paralinguistic features which belong to the language as a whole ('common-core' features, used by all speakers, whatever their class, occupation etc.), and those features which identify specific sociolinguistic categories within the language.

We can summarize the set of socio-paralinguistic possibilities in the following way.

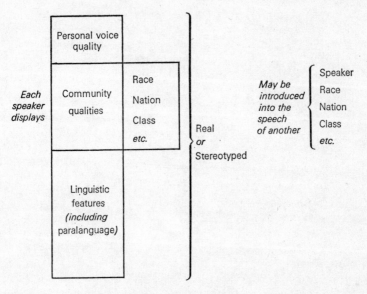

Fig. 6 Sociolinguistic dimensions of paralinguistic variation

It is unlikely that the above outline covers the whole range of sociolinguistic variables involved, but at least the factors mentioned have to be distinguished and assessed. I am not of course suggesting that these factors are all thoroughly understood. It is by no means clear, for example, whether the contrastive use of community-qualities by another community is legitimately or usefully classifiable as paralinguistic, or whether it ought to be called something else. And in the absence of both data and a consistent theoretical approach on the part of either linguists or sociolinguists,[22] the questions can hardly be resolved at the present time. It is to be hoped, however, that the recognition of these irritating complications in paralinguistic study will act as a stimulus, and not as a deterrent, to subsequent fundamental research.

22 Some discussion of these matters is to be found in Hammarström (1963, and in subsequent writings, including his paper to the Tenth International Congress of Linguists, 1971): he distinguishes between 'idioprosodemes' (features of particular speakers), 'socioprosodemes' (features of particular groups within a society), and 'diaprosodemes' (features of groups of speakers from a particular geographical area). See also Webster and Kramer (1968), Chreist (1964), Cohen and Starkweather (1961), and the work being done on evaluation of regional accents, where the notion of stereotype needs reference to features of paralanguage: Giles (1970, 1971a,b, 1972), Cheyne (1970), Strongman and Woosley (1967), Lambert (1967).

3
Paralanguage in animal and human communication

To both layman and scholar, 'tone of voice' is held to be a significant point of overlap between human and animal communicative systems. One does not need a batch of references to support the assertion that factors such as pitch, loudness and speed of speaking are relevant in the elicitation of differentiated responses by many domestic pets; and the implication that this is accordingly an area of communicative behaviour that animals and man share is widely found in the literature on zoösemiotics and communication. Sturtevant, for example, expressed the general view (1947: 45) that 'the exclamatory parts of language, like many animal cries, [are] characterized by extreme variations of pitch and loudness. . . . There is abundant proof that other animals of the same species respond to these calls roughly as men respond to the highly emotional features of languages.' This area, generally labelled as paralanguage in the context of human communication (see Chapter 2), is considered analogous to the expressive vocalizations of various animal species. Abe (1967: 55), for instance, talks about 'the universality of animals' use of symptomatic signs which belong to the field of paralanguage', and Thorpe uses the term 'paralinguistic' to refer to both human and animal communication (1972: 27, 33). In the search for continuities between animal and human communication, then, it would seem that paralinguistic phenomena provide evidence of a particularly compelling kind. It is the purpose of this chapter to suggest that positive conclusions on this topic are probably false, and at best premature.

As the basis for discussion, I propose to use a broad linguistic definition as in sense 5 (p. 54): in other words, paralanguage is defined as meaningfully contrastive institutionalized non-segmental phonation. This therefore excludes kinesic and other non-vocal phenomena—a desirable distinction, in my view, until such time as it can be shown that there are sufficient parallels between paralinguistic and kinesic structures to warrant a conflation. Likewise, this sense postpones any discussion of whether intonation and related features are sufficiently different from other non-segmental linguistic behaviour to warrant their being given a totally different theoretical status. The point at issue is whether sense 1—the conflation of non-human and human vocalization—is legitimate, and it is upon this that the present chapter hopes to throw some light. A systematic distinction between prosodic and paralinguistic features is maintained throughout the rest of this book, but it seemed unnecessarily cumbersome to insist upon it in the present instance, as such distinctions are not generally made in the literature on animal communication.

The question is: Given this range of phenomena in man, to what extent is it a major area of overlap with animal vocal behaviour? Certainly, if we are speaking in operational terms, there does seem to be an overlap. While accepting that there is an absence of comprehensive descriptive studies (cf. the lament of Sebeok, Altmann and others, e.g. Altmann 1968: 501), the partial accounts we do have are couched in terms that are remarkably similar to those used for the study of human paralinguistic behaviour. Brief examples are the tentative functional classification of neighing in terms of height, loudness and length (Tembrock 1968: 379), and later in the same paper, the identification of a wide range of vocalizations in terms of pitch direction and range, loudness, rhythm, tonal quality, and various laryngeal, spasmodic and other contrasts (see especially the discussion of *Felidae*, 367); and of course there are the classical analyses of bird vocalization by Thorpe (1961 and elsewhere). In this area, as in human paralinguistic studies, a great deal of effort has been expended on the problem of terminology, both for formal labelling (e.g. croak, grunt, hiss, shout) and its semantic interpretation (e.g. happy, surprised, intention to frighten)—though it is strange that such 'human-orientated' terms as 'intonation' and 'para-language' receive no attention at all in the otherwise admirably full terminological preamble and index in Busnel (1963). From a functional point of view, the threefold classification of paralinguistic phenomena into emotional, social and grammatical roles also has parallels in zoösemiotics (the first two are obvious: by grammatical, I am referring to the view—held, for example, by Thorpe (1972: 33, 54)—that certain animal vocalizations display a definite 'syntax'). For such reasons, then, one might expect the notion of paralanguage to be readily applicable to both human and animal vocalization, and a conclusion about continuity made accordingly.

But I think we would be wrong to draw such a conclusion—at least, for the present. I wish to argue that any suggestion of a real similarity between human paralinguistic phenomena and animal vocalization is premature, and in the present state of our knowledge, misleading. The essence of the argument is that paralanguage was given an inadequate analysis, when the question of its potential relevance for the study of animal communication was first raised—namely, in the design-feature approach to language of Hockett (1960; see also Hockett and Altmann 1968). In terms of the criteria used there, paralanguage did seem to be intermediate between human language (in the sense of phonemes, morphemes, syntax etc.) and the various kinds of animal communication illustrated. Now that a great deal more paralinguistic study has taken place, it is possible to re-evaluate its status vis-à-vis human and animal communication, and to conclude that paralanguage is much closer to the rest of language than was originally anticipated. The overlap with animal communication is minimal and trivial.

In terms of the sixteen design-features of human language recognized by Hockett, paralanguage emerged as follows:

Clearly positive
(1) broadcast transmission and directional reception
(2) rapid fading

(3) openness (new linguistic messages are coined freely and easily)
(4) tradition (language conventions are passed down by teaching and learning)
(5) prevarication (ability to lie or be meaningless)
(6) learnability (possibility of foreign-language learning)

Query positive
(7) specialization (the direct-energetic consequences of linguistic signals are biologically unimportant; only the triggering consequences are important)
(8) semanticity (the existence of a denotative relationship between signals and features in the world)

Partially positive
(9) vocal-auditory channel
(10) interchangeability (adult speakers are both transmitters and receivers) .
(11) complete feedback (speaker is able to perceive everything relevant to his signal production)
(12) arbitrariness (no dependent physical interrelationship between signals and referents)
(13) discreteness (repertoire not continuous)
(14) displacement (can refer to things remote in time and space)

Negative
(15) duality of patterning (meaningless signal-elements combine into meaningful arrangements)
(16) reflectiveness (or reflexiveness) (ability to communicate about the system itself)

The design-feature listing has its weaknesses, as is readily admitted (Hockett and Altmann 1968: 64). In particular, not all the features have the same degree of importance, and thus establishing the status of a type of behaviour, such as paralanguage, becomes difficult. But there are certain specific problems with this characterization of paralanguage as it stands, such that it is possible to argue that most of the negative points (9–16) arise from an inadequate understanding of the formal complexity and functional significance of paralinguistic effect. This is very clear in relation to points 15 and 16.

Of all the design-features, duality of structure (or 'double articulation') seems to be the most important, as regards the specificity of its claims about linguistic structure (cf. Lyons 1970: 12). This is the property whereby a set of signal elements, themselves meaningless, when used in patterned combinations produce meaningful results. Language, therefore, has duality of patterning, and the same is said of various animals, including primates, *Canidae* and birds. But paralanguage is said to have no duality. This seems unreasonable. Whatever definition of paralanguage one takes, Thorpe's comment about birds would seem to be equally applicable to it: 'a bird's song may . . . be made up of anything from half-a-dozen to several hundred "notes". . . . Most of these "notes" are quite meaningless if sounded alone; but grouped in the correct pattern of the song they can convey a great deal of information both as to the species and the individual involved' (1972: 33). For example, it is well-known that the non-segmental characteristics of a single syllable (e.g. a pitch, a stress, a duration, an instance of nasalization, a whisper) are uninterpretable until they are put into sequences and related to the voice norms of individuals in specific contexts. In intonation, the fundamental concept of a 'contour' or 'tone-unit' is recognition of the fact that, characteristically, semantic interpretations can only be assigned to 'complete' syllable sequences; and the same applies to variations in tempo, loudness, rhythm, and other effects. In each case, the minimal variable element is generally meaningless. (The qualification 'generally' is important because there are usually a few cases within a language where—assuming a known speaker—there are effects which can be interpreted semantically on the basis of minimal occurrence: in other words, the signal elements are meaningful, and their sequential combinations do not produce a different kind of meaning. Examples would be the 'voice qualifications' of Crystal and Quirk 1964: laugh, giggle, tremulousness, sob, and cry. But there are not many examples of this kind in language.) The need to take into account rules of sequence and of hierarchical structure is well-recognized in intonational studies (e.g. Halliday 1967; Pike 1944); and one needs to adopt a similar point of view in accounting for the meaningfulness of most other paralinguistic phenomena.

'Reflectiveness' is the property of language by which we can communicate about the system in which we are communicating. (It is a better term than 'metacommunication', used for instance by Altmann (1967), as this is readily confusable with the linguists' and philosophers' use of the term 'metalanguage'.) Reflectiveness is in effect the recognition of context-dependence in language—the fact that certain signals alter the significance of other signals. In their recent discussion, Hockett and Altmann (1968) illustrate 'metacommunication' in the following way: it is

> communication that is some sort of commentary on other communication. . . . In human speech we can have 'primary' communication and metacommunication in the same system, as when we interrupt what we are saying with 'You're not listening!' or with 'I guess I expressed that badly'. But we also carry on, in paralinguistic and kinesic form, a virtually uninterrupted running commentary on what we are saying in words. Something much like this seems to be the case with many other animals: virtually all social messages are accompanied by contextual or "framing" cues that affect the interpretation or response. (67)

But this approach gives rise to problems. I do not wish to go into the question as to whether reflectiveness operates in animals, about which there is difference of opinion (e.g. Thorpe, following Hockett, says there is not (1972: 33), whereas Cullen cites cases to the contrary (1972: 108)). Purely on the human side, one must ask: How valid is this notion of 'commentary'? To what extent is it possible to take an utterance in a given situation, and determine what within it is 'central' and what 'modulation'? As Birdwhistell says (1970: 86), and see further, 188–9): 'It is all too easy to assure ourselves that there is in any social interchange a *central*, a *primary* or a *real* meaning which is only modified by a redundant environment. . . . Our temptation to classify certain aspects of a transaction as the central message and other aspects as serving only as modifiers rests upon untested assumptions about communication.' I would agree. To say that X alters Y to Z presupposes that we have criteria for isolating X as 'basic' or 'primary'. And how does one make such a distinction in practice? The more one examines speech in its full interactional context (and not simply in its written representation), the more one finds examples of utterance where the primary determinants of the speaker's identity and purpose, and of the listener's response, are paralinguistic ('Say it as if you mean it', 'You don't *sound* as if you're a clergyman', and the unavoidable 'It wasn't what he said, but the way that he said it . . .'). In such cases, paralanguage has played a central, not a peripheral role. Another example would be the phonological exponence of emphasis: the emphasized word in 'He *never* said that' may be produced in a variety of ways—with very high pitch range, very low pitch range, fortissimo loudness, pianissimo loudness, extra-long duration, whisper, husky, or creaky voice—and it is difficult to see how any of these effects in this context can be said to be 'merely modulating' in function (this phrase being taken from the discussion of J. M. Cullen's paper in Hinde 1972: 124).

If we grant paralanguage a communicative status in its own right, it follows that we must alter our opinion about its ability to display reflectiveness. But we must first take account of the objection of Lyons (1972: 54), who considers it debatable whether intonation has this property, 'since the repetition by the listener of some part of what the speaker has just said with a different and distinctive intonation (and stress) may have the effect of querying, not what has been said, but the appropriateness of the words chosen to describe it'. This ambiguity does exist; but it can be avoided, with the contrastive intonation involved having a clearly reflective function. One example is in the use of high pitch range (↑) plus rising tone to express echo-utterances (Quirk *et al.* 1972: 408 ff.), as in:

A John's ˋCOMING.   B He's ↑ˊCOMING?

A It's ˋJOHN on the phone.   B ↑ˇJOHN?

Another example is the intonation which indicates the use of a 'softened' connecting phrase (cf. pp. 6, 19) where the phrase in the appropriate intonation conditions the stylistic force of the accompanying sentence, and contrasts with the 'literal' meaning of the words, as in:

you ↑ˊKNOW / I think he's ˋRIGHT (= let me tell you, I think . . .)

you ˋKNOW I think he's right (= you are aware that I think . . .)

Examples using other paralinguistic effects would be the use of husky or whispered voice on the word 'not' in the following:

A John's coming to the meeting.   B He's not?

On grammatical words, it seems unlikely for anything other than a reflective function of paralinguistic effects to be present. And as a final example, there is the allegro tempo used on a phrase to indicate that the preceding structure was an error, as in the italicized phrase following:

You're not getting the bus *getting the train* are you?

Now given such examples, I think we must argue that the reflectiveness involved is a property of the paralinguistic system itself. It would be misleading to relate the marked intonational or speed contrasts involved directly to the verbal context preceding, as the 'commentary' notion suggests, viz.

John's COMING.◄——— John's COMING?

Rather it should be:

John's COMING.   John's COMING?

This seems to be typical of intonation, where the 'meaning' of a tone cannot be judged in isolation. It is of course partly dependent on the nature of the verbal language accompanying, but it is also very much dependent on the perceived contrast with the intonation of the previous utterance. I do not know how much of intonation is a commentary on previous (or subsequent) intonation in this way, but the potential importance of this function must surely be recognized. The same applies to paralanguage in general.

If we now move on to the design-features which are said to be *partially* positive in respect to paralanguage, it also seems possible to indicate a rather more central role for the phenomenon than in the original analyses. The question of *vocal-auditory channel* is clearly a matter of definition, which I have excluded from consideration by the definition adopted in this chapter. (A comparison of the structural differences between paralinguistics and kinesics warrants a separate study). *Interchangeability*—whereby adult speakers are transmitters and receivers of the same range of linguistic signals—would seem to apply almost totally to paralanguage, as long as we realize that by linguistic signals here we are referring to relative, and not absolute contrasts. The fact that a female voice is higher in terms of fundamental frequency than a male is not a relevant consideration: the point is that the relative differences between, say, high and low pitch contours, or between normal and allegro speed, are isomorphic between men and women (see further, Chapter 4). *Complete feedback* states that the speaker is able to perceive everything relevant to his signal production. If the emphasis is on *able*, I can see no difference between para-language and language here. *Displacement* is the ability to refer to things remote in time and space. This property, as Hockett and Altmann accept (1968: 64) is not clear, as it not an all-or-none matter, but one of degree. 'Just how far away from the site of a communicative transaction must the topic of the message be before we will speak of displacement? And . . . do we measure the distance of the topic from the transmitter or the receiver?' There is no intrinsic reason of course why pitch, and the other variables, should not be used with a dis-placed, cognitive role: witness the use of tone in some languages to distinguish between present and past tense, for example (as in Twi). But even with respect to paralanguage in general, it is perfectly possible—and perhaps even normal—if someone has been frightened, for instance, for the vocal indications of the fright (e.g. tremulousness, high pitch-range, short tone-units) to remain for some time after the event. *Contra* Lyons (1972: 54), then, it would seem that intonation, and probably paralanguage as a whole, is in principle capable of displacement. We are therefore left with *discreteness* and *arbitrariness*, as partially positive design-features—and these are more debatable.

The question of the arbitrariness of paralinguistic features is nowhere near solution, but one thing is clear—that there can be no total dependency of paralinguistic effect on the nervous state of the organism. The view that there is an endogenous basis derives from the widely-held assumption that the sole function of paralanguage is emotional, and that such features are, as Bastian puts it, 'linguistically insignificant' (1964: 144). But the existence of numerous 'structural' or 'cognitive' uses of paralanguage, especially of pitch, loudness and speed, demonstrates the contrary (see Chapter 1), as does the range of social or stylistic 'roles', where paralanguage is introduced into a discourse in a controlled manner (as when one 'adopts' a persuasive tone of voice, or an authoritative voice: see the classification of social roles in Chapter 5). But even in relation to the purely emotional role, there are considerable differences between the paralinguistic norms of various languages, and the function of the formal contrasts found. Comments about the 'liveliness', 'monotony' or 'speed' of different languages suggest the former; misinterpretations of abrupt-ness or sarcasm in learning a foreign language suggest the latter. There are, of course, cases where the paralinguistic effect is certainly correlated with nervous tension, e.g. degrees of increasing intensity of excitement correlating with increased pitch height; degrees of increasing intensity of disparagement cor-relating with increased pitch depth or huskiness. But to what extent these are universal remains unclear. Certainly, when one considers the range of functions which paralinguistic effect enters into, and the range of difference which cross-linguistic comparisons have already indicated (e.g. in Sebeok *et al.* 1964), it would seem premature to be talking of universals. Referring to paralanguage as 'partially positive' in respect of the design-feature of arbitrariness thus seems to be reasonable—though it is perhaps something of an understatement, as there is far more arbitrariness involved in paralanguage than in other modes of semiotic behaviour.

The question of discreteness has been clouded somewhat by a tendency to confuse physical and linguistic notions of discreteness. As Altmann points out (1967: 341), it is not enough to claim that a communication takes place analogically rather than digitally by showing a continuous gradation in a signal: there must also be functional continuity—a one-to-one mapping of the signals onto a continuous array of denotata—and the difficulty lies in demonstrating this. Thus to say that a falling and a rising tone are at opposite ends of a continuously graded scale is true in a trivial, physical or perceptual sense, but by no means self-evidently true in a semantic sense, and it is in fact extremely difficult to state the 'meaning' of the contrasts in terms which demonstrate a continuous semantic gradation. Even with examples in context, judges tend to give semantic interpretations of paralinguistic features using a wide range of labels (e.g. a rise in pitch may be understood as 'sympathetic', 'interested', 'puzzled', 'ironic' . . .), and these labels often have little in common with those used for the interpretation of the other features with which they are supposed to be in continuous gradation (e.g. a drop in pitch *may* be interpreted as 'unsympathetic', 'uninterested', etc., but one will also find a fresh set of labels used, such as 'serious', 'matter-of-fact', 'sad' . . .). It is clearly a complicated situation, which will only be sorted out once the semantics of the various labels have been given some separate clarification—establishing the meaning-relations (of antonymy, hyponymy etc.) which operate between them, for instance. And meanwhile, all one can safely say about paralanguage, from the point of view of discreteness, is that while it is obviously not discrete in the same sense as the phonemic and morphemic systems of verbal language, it is not at all obvious that it is analogic either, in Altmann's sense.

My own view is that the amount of discreteness to be found in paralanguage has been seriously underestimated, due to an assumption that the only kind of discreteness which matters is that associated with phonemes and morphemes (see Chapter 2). The arbitrariness of this demarcation is but one criticism among many which have been made of the phonemic model of intonation; and the dangers of defining significant contrastivity in language solely in terms of a model set up for the analysis of one kind of linguistic patterning only (i.e. the phonemic kind) has been criticized by others (e.g. Sebeok 1968: 9). The point is that to show that paralinguistic features lack phonemic-type discreteness is not to say that they have no discreteness at all. Discreteness is itself a 'more/less' phenomenon: some contrasts—even within phonemics—are more discrete than others. In paralanguage, one may show that certain features are highly discrete, others not, and between them one may plot a gradient of linguistic contrastivity, along which the various systems of features can be placed—this, at least, is the approach of Crystal 1969a. But whether this approach as a whole is valid or not, what is important for the present argument is the recognition of the existence of a wide range of prosodic and paralinguistic contrasts that are quite comparable to the morphemic or syntactic discreteness operating elsewhere in language (see Chapter 1). I am not denying the difficulty of setting up discrete units in the area of paralanguage, of course (cf. Diebold

1968: 544–5), but admitting this is very different from denying paralanguage any discreteness at all. It might be, then, that future discussion of this issue would fare better if more attention were paid to our techniques of measurement, and other aspects of our research design. If, as Saussure said, it is the point of view which creates the object, then it is about time we looked more closely and critically at the former. (See further Sebeok 1962, especially on the questions of gradience and expressiveness in language.)

On the basis of these remarks, it seems that at best paralanguage in its general sense can be disassociated from language only in respect of a partial difference under the headings of discreteness, arbitrariness and duality. There are therefore little grounds for considering it to be 'midway' between human language and other modes of communication, human or animal. It may be that a comparable structuring will emerge in animal vocalization, with further study; but in the meantime I would agree with Marler (1961: 303) that the notion of paralanguage is not readily applicable to animals. It is as potentially misleading to talk about animal vocalizations in terms of pitch tunes etc. as it is to talk about vowels and consonants, unless it is made clear that the descriptive terminology has a quite different status. (An identical problem faces the student of infant 'pre-linguistic' vocalization: see Chapter 8.) There seems to have been a pendulum swing in comparative studies, whereby an original emphasis which attempted to make a complete differentiation between language and animal communication (e.g. Hebb and Thompson 1954) has now moved to one where there is a desire to show as much in common as possible. To go into the relative merits of these approaches is hardly a matter for linguists; but it is important that in any such discussion we should keep the limitations of our theoretical constructs clearly in mind. The loose use of the term 'paralanguage' provides an illustration.

4
Relative and absolute in intonation analysis

Most intonation analysts would consider it a truism to insist that any model of the formal properties of a language's intonation system has to be relativistic in character. By this one would mean that the linguistic constants in the system are the contrasts between the features involved (pitch, loudness or whatever) and not the values of the features themselves, as defined in any absolute, physical way. The point hardly needs quotation to support it, but it will be useful to refer to one person's formulation of the relativity claim as a reminder of how the position is typically presented. Abercrombie, for example, says (1967: 107):

> In the phonological analysis and description of the patterns of speech melody of both tone and intonation languages, it is not *absolute* pitch that is of importance . . . it is the position of the points in the pattern *relative to each other* that counts, not their frequency in terms of number of vibrations per second . . . the *intervals* between the points in the pattern are absolute and constant in the patterns of musical melody, but they are relative and variable in the patterns of speech melody. Thus a pattern in speech melody can be either compressed or expanded in the dimension of pitch and still remain the same pattern, although in one case the intervals are smaller and in the other larger . . . the voice may rest on any one of an infinite number of points (within its possible range). . . .

I have been brought up to believe this view, and I think I still hold it, more or less as an article of prosodic faith. But I am not at all sure what I have committed myself to by this belief, nor does it seem to explain everything in intonation that needs to be explained. In this chapter, then, I simply want to ask exactly what is involved in, and what follows from, maintaining that intonational features (or prosodic features in general) are relativistic in character, and to speculate, in a devil's advocate kind of way, about whether all aspects of an 'absolutist' view are as heretical as they are usually made out to be.

It is perhaps best to begin by eliminating from the discussion various features of the 'standard' relativistic argument which are either false or unnecessary. Firstly, I think we have to be clear that the main theoretical opposition with which we are presented (relative v. absolute) is not the only way of seeing the situation. There is no *a priori* reason why all aspects of a language's intonational system should ultimately derive from the application of a single principle, whether this be relative or absolute in its claims. It is perfectly conceivable that an intonation system should display various properties, some of which can be explained through a relativistic principle, others through some concept of absolute pitch—and I shall argue below that such a view is indeed preferable. At the very least, claiming that intonation is relative should not commit one to excluding any kind of absolute reasoning in an attempt to explain phenomena.[1] Rather the reverse (as I shall argue below): claiming that intonation is relative makes sense only if some kind of absolutism is introduced into one's analysis from the very beginning.

Secondly, there is no *a priori* reason why the concept of absolute pitch should be given a definition solely in terms of fundamental frequency. I am not referring here to the well-known fact that other acoustic dimensions enter into the specification of pitch judgments, but rather that a useful definition of absolute pitch might well emerge in terms of articulatory or neurological norms on the one hand, or auditory, perceptual norms on the other. 'Absolute' is however invariably restricted to acoustic definition, and this is theoretically misleading. A good example of a misleading emphasis arising out of this view is the standard argument which attempts to justify a relativistic approach by reference to 'voice-types' (e.g. soprano, male, cf. Luchsinger and Arnold 1965: 101–2 or 'voice-qualities' (person identifying vocal effects, cf. Crystal 1969a: Ch. 3). Because successful linguistic communication between people of different voice-types or voice-qualities is self-evidently the case, it is argued that intonation features cannot be defined absolutely. For example, concerning voice-types, one can quote Pike (e.g. in his discussion of tone languages (1948: 20): 'Thus the "high" tonemes of a bass voice may be lower in absolute pitch than the "low" tonemes of a soprano.' But the relevance of this kind of argument diminishes as soon as a non-physicalist sense of 'absolute' is taken.[2] One could for instance hypothesize that a voice-type (and thus a pitch level), in any individual, is the result of a basic neurological pattern, common to all speakers, which can only manifest itself through a set of obligatory 'hormonal transformations'. The point is undemonstrable, at present, but theoretically possible. More obviously and usefully, one might argue for absolutism on *auditory* grounds, that each individual makes use of certain perceptually 'stereotyped' norms, a point I shall return to below.

Thirdly, and arising out of this, one must also query the implication of precision which attaches to the idea of absolute definition in terms of fundamental frequency—at least as far as connected speech is concerned (which is what we should be interested in). Any suggestion that a pitch point in a linguistic pattern

1 Cf. the use of speech synthetic techniques as validation procedures, where mean physical (e.g. formant) values are accepted in an otherwise relativistic model.
2 Voice-types are in any case linguistically uninteresting. Their study, like that of voice-quality, establishes the 'background' against which linguistic structure manifests itself, but does not readily produce further hypotheses about phonological structure. Voice-types and voice-qualities are extremes of vocal effect, the former being one of the most 'universal' kinds of phonetic effect there is, the latter being by definition the most idiosyncratic. The interesting phenomena of language fall in between. And the relativity covered by these concepts is probably only of minor significance anyway: I take Pike's point about 'high tonemes', but the operative word in his statement above is '*may* be lower'. Most people surely have their high tonemes (or tones, or pitch phonemes) at a higher fundamental frequency than other people's (or their own) lower ones most of the time; and if so, then any theory ought to reflect this point prominently, and not over-emphasize extreme cases.

can be given an accurate specification in terms of a single figure of fundamental frequency (or, perhaps, a constant range between two fixed values) should be carefully avoided as being both technically unrealistic, and also unnecessary for linguistic purposes. A weaker notion of 'absolute' is required. A single figure for any syllable is very much an acoustic simplification, in view of the unsteadiness of the fundamental in speech: at best such a figure could be only a mean value, dependent for its validity on a variety of theoretical and methodological considerations, e.g. analytical decisions about syllable boundaries, the extent of intrasyllabic sampling, decisions about the particular acoustic analytical method used (e.g. whether the instrument measures one cycle and converts its period to frequency, or whether a certain minimum number of cycles is required for a readout), and, of course, the usual technical limitations on available instrumentation, where for most practical purposes an error rate of 2 per cent or more has to be allowed for. This last point needs to be stressed. It is of course possible to reduce the error factor, for the analysis of simple waveforms under laboratory conditions; but for the analysis of *linguistic* data, 2 per cent is an underestimate, bearing in mind the well-attested difficulties in obtaining recordings of conversation etc. of high quality (the results cited by Miller (1970) are particularly impressive, however). In view of all these variables, it would be a perfectly reasonable question to ask whether a view of absolute pitch measured solely in terms of fundamental frequency is in fact particularly meaningful for speech, or whether the range of actual or potential physical variation subsumed under any one frequency figure is not so large as to make the notion vacuous. In any case (one might continue to argue), even if it could be accurately shown that a syllable's fundamental was x Hz, such information would not be of any *direct* value as far as understanding intonational principles was concerned. For one thing, different fundamental frequency values would have to be interrelated, and this would involve a theory of pitch perception. For another, frequency would first have to be related to the other acoustic factors necessarily simultaneously present in speech. In other words, a view of absolute pitch defined solely in terms of frequency is both artificial and unhelpful, or, to put it charitably, misconceived.

This point also relates to my earlier argument about the irrelevance of voice-types and voice-qualities. It is trivially true that different voice-types and qualities manifest different fundamental frequency ranges, but why should frequency be singled out in this way? A voice-type or quality is an extremely complex acoustic phenomenon, involving the use of many other parameters than frequency; and it may well be that some *combination* of features (perhaps other than frequency, but more probably including it) are used in a fixed, absolute way. To be specific, there may be a fixed ratio between frequency and other dimensions of the speech signal which is standard for all people, regardless of voice-quality or type—in other words, what is absolute is not the individual parameters, but their combinatorial properties. This seems to me to make a quite plausible hypothesis in articulatory terms: the articulatory conditions operative in the vocal tract of an individual (e.g. thickness of vocal folds) will clearly condition other vocal effects than range (e.g. various kinds of pharyngeal friction, use of creaky voice, falsetto) and will contribute directly to voice timbre.[3] For instance, as a soprano speaker moves from a low pitch to a high one, it is likely that she introduces concomitantly into her voice the same kind of effects as would be produced by a tenor speaker moving between the same two points. We all know when two such speakers are 'straining at the top of their ranges': how do we know? I should not be surprised if there were clear correlations between frequency and other kinds of vocal effect which turned out to be constant throughout the whole of a person's range. Putting this another (albeit loose) way, we might plausibly argue that a soprano is 'doing the same kind of thing' as a bass speaker in producing a particular pitch contrast (or more generally, intonational contrast); and if this is so, then we have here a legitimate notion of 'absoluteness' which might usefully be regarded as a basis for the understanding of intonational contrastivity. Each of us (one might hypothesize) perceives, holistically, an intonation contrast within its background of timbre features, and we use the latter to 'allocate' certain values of frequency to an appropriate linguistic category. It is not possible to explain the experimental results below without some such hypothesis, and there are other theoretical arguments in favour of it, as we shall see.

So far, I have been looking at some of the implications of the term 'absolute' as it seems to be used in the standard discussions. The term 'relative' also has to be examined carefully. Firstly, it is not in fact true, nor is there any need to assert, that the range of pitches expounding intonational features is in principle infinite, as Abercrombie suggests; yet the point has been made over and over again since Pike. 'Apparently there is no specific number of general height levels, but an infinite variety of possible ones . . .' (1945: 76); and, on the same page, concerning pitch intervals, he claims 'an infinite variety of possibilities'. The fact of the matter, of course, is that it is just not possible to hear unlimited variability in pitch within an individual or group: since the work of Stevens and others, it has been generally recognized that the number of discriminations possible at any given reference level is extremely restricted (see for example Stevens and Davis 1938: 94–5). There are not all that many points for a voice to be heard as resting on (or starting from, or modulating through); and any theory of intonation should take account of this.

Secondly, and more important, we must ask exactly what the principle of relativity is being invoked to explain. Presumably the primary variability relevant to the issue is that which is assumed to exist within a speaker which does *not* affect the linguistic interpretation of the utterance. If we take a (simplified) situation such as the one illustrated on page 78, where a rising tone AB is different in meaning from the tone CD, then the question is to determine how high A or B or AB as a whole can be produced without the utterance taking on the meaning of CD or some other meaning (and conversely). The point at which AB 'becomes' CD is the upper limit of AB's variability (X in the diagram), and

3 See Crystal 1969a: 122ff. for the notion of timbre, and 1969a: Ch. 4, for that of creaky voice, etc.

one can similarly imagine a lower limit, Y. XY thus comprises an area of 'free variation' for a particular intonational feature. Now if this is so—if, that is, the relativity hypothesis is restricted to explain pitch (etc.) variations which do not affect the meaning of utterances—then the point has to be made clearly in any discussion; and generally speaking, it is not. How much compression or expansion can a melody pattern take and still be 'the same' pattern (a similar query might be made of Bolinger's configurations, cf. 1951: 208)? Exactly how much variability does the relativistic argument commit us to?

This is a familiar question, for it was raised twenty years ago by Bolinger in his (so far unanswered) critique of pitch phonemes: 'Unfortunately we are not enlightened on *how* relative these relative pitches are supposed to be' (1951: 199). He shows very clearly in this paper the kind of muddle one can get into without clear criteria to handle overlapping. But the question has to be asked of *any* kind of relativistic intonation system, not solely of a pitch phoneme one. Obviously there have to be limits on the amount of variability subsumable under the heading of any linguistically significant pitch level (or sequence of levels). But how are these limits to be defined? One cannot simply argue that 'differences in pitch levels are relative to one another' (Bronstein and Jacoby (1967: 48); cf. Abercrombie above), for any such definition of relativity is ultimately vacuous, and any intonation system based *solely* on such a view would in principle be impossible to apply consistently to data (as Lieberman has shown regarding the Trager-Smith system (1965)). Of course the fact that different scholars on different occasions *can* transcribe different voices with relatively little disagreement (using a tonetic system, at any rate; cf. Lieberman 1965: 51, Crystal 1969a: 15–16) suggests that we do as a matter of course introduce some kind of phonetic consistentizing principle into our analyses. But it is possible to argue the point theoretically, and assert that any intonation system claiming consistency and objectivity (and they all do) *has* to assume some kind of standardizing ability on the part of the analyst in his task of identifying and classifying intonational features. It is all very well to assert, as do Bronstein and Jacoby, that 'Levels are merely higher or lower than other levels. Each speaker uses these relatively different pitch levels within his own pitch range. The listener automatically translates them into correspondingly relative levels within each speaker's range. There are no absolute levels' (1967: 48). But *how* is this mapping of one set of values onto another done? What explanatory principle can be involved? And does it necessarily follow from what has been said that there are no absolute levels?

The answer to the last question seems to be 'on the contrary'. Rather, the only kind of hypothesis which can account for this isomorphism is one which claims that there is something in the intonation system of a language which is *not* relative, which provides a consistently recognizable invariant basis from person to person. So how is this claim best reflected in any model of an intonation system?

There are two ways in which we can make the relativity hypothesis work. We can make the range of conditioning factors absolutely explicit—that is, we clearly answer the question 'relative to what?'—and/or we can postulate an absolutely defined pitch level (or more than one), to which pitch variations can be related independent of context. In the present state of the science, the former solution seems unlikely; not all the factors are known, few of the ones which are have been empirically investigated, and there is no 'socio-psycho-linguistic theory' capable of integrating them. Pitch relativity is usually discussed in relation to the overall *voice-range* of the speaker, or his physiologically-determined *voice-type* (see above): but there are clear indications that other factors affect pitch-range norms and variations. For instance, there is the nature of the *participation* situation in which a speaker is involved (whether monologue or dialogue, and if the latter, how many people are involved); the voice-type of the person(s) being addressed;[4] the *variety* of language being used, defined in terms of stylistic constraints imposed by occupation, status, purpose etc. (see Crystal and Davy (1969) and Chs. 5–7); the ability of the listener to hear pitch differences, which varies markedly in terms of age, personality, emotional state, etc. (cf. Shepard 1964: 2350); the basic emotional state of the speaker, affecting norms of pitch-range, as illustrated by the literature on functional voice disorders (cf. Murphy 1964: 5 ff.); the non-linguistic context, affecting both speaker and hearer (e.g. the size of the room, temperature, location of the frequency stimulus, cf. Black 1950 on rate and intensity variations of this kind); and the voice-quality as a whole (i.e. not just the pitch-range) of an individual speaker. Pitch-range variations between languages (language or dialect A using a higher overall range than B) might also be relevant. Most important of all, however, there is the evidence from *voice stereotypes*.

This concept is fairly commonly cited in the social psychology literature, and is discussed by Kramer (1963) and Crystal (1969a, and above, p. 63). A stereotype is an individual's or group's conventionally held, oversimplified mental picture of some aspect of reality (e.g. of a person, or a race); it corresponds in some respects to the reality of a situation, but distorts or ignores others. The 'northern' accent, which a comedian might adopt on stage for a joke, could be (and usually is) a stereotype: it would not be a minutely accurate rendering of any one northern accent, but would simply select a sufficient number of phonetic features to give the impression of northern speech. Now for obvious reasons (namely, that we have personal knowledge of far fewer people than we have cause to come into auditory contact with), people more generally and more readily attempt to classify voices into types than to identify them individually, and their classification tends to be in terms of stereotypes (of occupations, personality

4 Cf. Lieberman (1967: 44–6), showing that a child's absolute fundamental frequency varies in terms of the relative height of the voice of the parent. This 'vocal empathy' seems a normal adult phenomenon also.

traits, etc.). 'That sounds like a lawyer/undertaker/politician . . . ,' 'He sounds very authoritative/persuasive/mature . . .'. It would seem that all voices are capable of classification in these ways (though we lack a complete list of all the classificatory parameters involved), that non-segmental factors are dominant influences on our identifications, and that there is considerable consistency in judges' reactions to voices (though one has to analyse the judges' descriptive labels fairly carefully, e.g. to determine whether such labels as 'mature' and 'authoritative' would be viewed as synonymous)[5]—these points clearly emerge from the reviews of the literature by Kramer and Crystal above. Moreover, we seem to carry out this process in an almost automatic kind of way: it is normal to make snap, stereotyped judgments about people on the basis of their vocal effect on us (cf. 'posh', 'forceful', 'domineering' etc.), and very often we subordinate our person-identifying knowledge to a stereotype, as in:

I can |never 'take 'John SERIOUSLY|—he |doesn't ''SOUND 'like a LAWYER|.

Our ability to classify voices in such ways is little understood, but the most likely explanation seems to be that we are extremely selective in this task; that is, we extract certain dominant perceptual values from the voice and match these against a learnt standard of stereotyped norms. In other words, just as we do not hear unlimited variability within an individual (cf. above), nor do we hear unlimited variability *between* individuals. Speakers learn a finite set of standardized perceptual values, derived from a selection of the available range of vocal effects (including pitch), which combine in various ways to produce a set of semantic stereotypes; and, if this is so, there are clear implications for the theory of relativity in intonation. Imposing a perceptual 'grid' on utterance means *inter alia* that a person's intonation system will be interpreted within the vocal stereotype people have of him on any given occasion; and if the stereotype is fairly constant, then the interpretation of any linguistically contrastive pitch features will be fairly constant also. This would be particularly so, if pitch features were being used as part of the stereotype, for these would form a perceptually standardized, or absolute, base, to which the intonational features would be related. If pitch features formed *no* part of the stereotype, then the non-pitch standardized features would act as a grid within which we could 'place' the pitch system, because of our awareness of the common articulatory basis of pitch with many of these other features (as argued above). Either way, the same conclusion is reached, that our perception of pitch variability in utterance is constrained by the application of perceptual norms, and that analysis of intonation can only begin after the perceptual norms of pitch height have been recognized (in practice, one listens to the whole of a speakers' output in a dialogue before beginning to transcribe the first sentence). All of which is tantamount to saying that intonational contrastivity is explicable only within a framework of absolute values.

5 One may also 'condition' people to react to voices in certain ways, by presenting different contexts previously: e.g. a voice can evoke the reaction 'leadership' or 'masculine' depending on the context given to judges (e.g. insurrection v. love-making).

One could arrive at this conclusion on quite independent grounds, by arguing that some kind of perceptually absolute level in intonation study is an indispensable foundation for any kind of intonation theory, and that in fact all current models do use such a foundation, though not usually making their reliance on the notion explicit. To begin with, there is the regularly cited, and intuitively quite clear concept of an individual's 'natural speaking level'—a concept which Pronovost, for instance, defines as 25 per cent of the way up a person's total singing range, including falsetto (1942)—though this is hardly a practicable viewpoint for the linguist, where total singing range is not a concept which is readily deducible from tape-recorded data. There is clear evidence (especially in the literature on organic voice disorders) that this level has a neurophysiological basis: the occurrence of vocal nodules, contact ulcers and the like are unambiguous indications of disorders which it is the purpose of the therapist to eradicate by a return to 'norms' of pitch, loudness, etc.—the 'most natural, relaxed' kind of speech. Such concepts may be imprecise, but they should not be ignored by the phonetician working in this area. A related point would be to refer to the changes in average speaking level readily noticeable in general conversational interaction, which correlates with such 'marked' attitudinal states as excitement, depression. These have been fairly well studied (see the review in Crystal, 1969a: 62–94), and pitch-range seems to be of major diagnostic significance.

For the linguist, any such reference-level, to be useful, has to be defined in such a way that it helps to provide an illuminating model of (non-segmental) phonological structure, and a workable transcription. This is usually casually done by reference to the 'middle' of the voice-range, or in (say) interlinear transcription, placing the dots on average midway between the 'highest' and the 'lowest' points in range. In Crystal (1969a: 143, 227, and elsewhere), the pitch-range distinctions for English are more systematically isolated and interrelated by hypothesizing a pitch constant for any speaker, and this is taken to be the first prominent syllable (or 'onset') of any stretch of utterance definable as a tone-unit. This syllable is taken as providing the most consistent approximation to a pitch level towards which a speaker automatically tends to return for the commencement of a new tone-unit—unless a specific attitude on his part requires extra pitch-height or depth at this point to make a particular contrastive semantic effect (this happened about once in every 200 tone-units, in the data in Crystal 1969a). Average speaking level, in this sense, is explicitly related to the phonological constructs of tone-unit and syllable; and it is then used for the definition of other prosodic features of pitch-range, thus (it is argued) simplifying the overall description of the tone-unit. In other words, I would claim that the explicit recognition of a norm of pitch level in one's intonation description is both economical and a means of relating otherwise unrelatable observations about linguistic structure and semantic effect. The question remains open whether the norm onset syllables, which were determined in the above approach on the basis of auditory agreement, can also be defined with reference to a norm of physical variability, whether in terms of fundamental frequency, or whatever. It is likely that this *is* possible, i.e. that most speakers (within a voice-type) on most occasions produce most onset syllables within a narrow band of frequencies, which can be considered an absolute physical norm. If this could be shown to be so, then this would be central empirical evidence bearing on the question of consistentizing ability, cited above. As far as I know, however, no research of this kind has been done, presumably because of the vast amount of work involved.[6] Meanwhile, we should not underestimate the empirical question: pitch levels are variable in principle, but are they in fact? The untested assumption is that they are; but I wonder.

For a variety of reasons, then, I would argue that the hypothesis of at least one absolute level in intonation is not ruled out by the relativity hypothesis, and that postulating such a level might be shown to be necessary on physical, physiological or perceptual grounds. The question now follows of how much absoluteness one can establish, and whether there is any empirical evidence for it, other than the scattered and rather indirect points already mentioned. One kind of evidence emerged from a recent pilot experiment, which suggested that people act, in some respects, as if they were using some absolute norms. Thirty students of linguistics were asked to rate various falling tones in terms of three categories, 'high', 'mid', 'low'. The nuclear syllables were extracted from connected speech of the 'educated discussion' type, using a segmentator. Three male and three female speakers were chosen, each with a different overall voice-range, and all speakers of 'modified RP', and six tones were extracted from each speaker. The tones were judged auditorily to cover various pitch-ranges (in terms of the system of syllabic pitch-range outlined in Crystal (1969a: 144ff.), namely, two tones with 'high booster' beginning, two with 'drop' beginning, and two with 'middle-range' beginning). In no cases were tones chosen from utterances involving attitudinal extremes. The 36 tones were arranged randomly and presented to the judges. The results were clear: tones which my previous analysis had classified as high and low were consistently assigned to the categories 'high' and 'low' respectively in 90 per cent of cases, and the remaining 10 per cent were all assigned to 'mid' (never to the opposite pole). 'Mid' assignments were consistently made less often, but still 60 per cent agreement obtained: the remainder were spread over the other two categories. This suggests that people have a definite predilection to identify two ranges of pitch independently of voice-type and voice-quality, high and low, and there is some indication of a middle range. I would not want to claim very much for these preliminary findings, but I think they are sufficiently promising and un-expected to justify a more precisely-controlled study of the problem, over a wider range of varieties.

6 It would mean obtaining a statistically viable sample of onset syllables from utterances which had already been transcribed, and classified in terms of voice-type, determining the fundamental frequency and other relevant factors, and analysing these using some multivariate technique. At Reading, a new model of speech segmentator has been developed to try to get round the time-consuming problem of extracting syllables from continuous speech.

My conclusion from the above mixture of facts and speculations is naturally extremely tentative, but it would seem, at the very least, that an unqualified relativistic view of intonation is just as untenable as an unqualified absolutist one would be; and that a blend of both notions is required, if existing assumptions and methods in intonational analysis are to be given any single, coherent explanation. If pressed to be more constructive and specific, then I would propose a model in which pitch relativity is constrained by the existence of absolute levels, and would hypothesize that people operate with at least three pitch reference-areas (norm, low, high), within which any system of intonation analysis must be accommodated.

5
Prosodic and paralinguistic correlates of social categories

Research into the linguistic correlates of social categories has been almost exclusively based on the study of lexical, grammatical and segmental phonetic and phonological characteristics. What are generally referred to as 'speech styles', i.e. modes of speaking restricted to or primarily associated with a particular social group, are illustrated solely with reference to restricted usage of items of vocabulary and of grammatical inflections or structures, and to differences in the articulations of vowels, consonants and vowel–consonant sequences. As pointed out in Chapter 2, the non-segmental phonetic and phonological characteristics of utterance have been little studied in relation to the linguistic definition of social categories. For example, Labov (1964: 166, and 176 n.7), while allowing the importance of non-segmental phenomena in language, considers them to be essentially unquantifiable at the present stage of study, and therefore omits them from his own work on the ground that 'we lack the large body of theory and practice in codifying intonation which we have for segmental phones'. Goffman (1964: 133) looks at this area from a different viewpoint, referring to the expressive aspects of discourse which cannot be clearly transferred through writing to paper—he refers to them as the 'greasy' parts of speech!

More recently, linguists have begun to examine non-segmental vocal effect in detail, but earlier chapters have shown how limited has been the attempt to describe systematically the range of non-segmental features which are in principle operative in a language, or to work out a theory that will define and interrelate them satisfactorily. Yet little of this work has so far been used in sociology or anthropology. The very important collection of papers on the ethnography of communication edited by Gumperz & Hymes (1964) provided a move in the right direction. Hymes in his introduction to the volume demonstrates very clearly the need to develop an 'ethnography of speaking'—informally defined as a specification of what kinds of things one may appropriately say in what message forms to what kinds of people in what kinds of situation, and, given a set of alternatives, what consequences stem from selecting one rather than another—and refers to the need for semiotic and other studies. Most of the contributors to the volume underline this point at various places. Albert, for example, refers to the training in tone of voice and its modulation, *inter alia*, for men in Burundi, and shows its relevance to age, sex, kinship and other relationships, referring to certain highly conventionalized speech patterns such as those used in visiting formulae, petitioning situations, rules of precedence and respect patterns. Distinctions are made, many of them non-segmental, according to the social role of those present, the degree of formality (especially relating to whether the situation is public or private), and the objectives of the speech situation. 'Together, social role and situational prescriptions determine the order of precedence of speakers, relevant conventions of politeness, appropriate formulas and styles of speech, and topics of discussion' (1964: 43). But despite this much-needed emphasis on theoretical principles, neither Albert nor any of the other contributors to the volume present any detailed account of the non-segmental phonology involved: the references stay at a maximally general level.

It should be emphasized that this collection of papers is quite exceptional in its orientation in this area. On the whole, most fieldworkers, even in linguistics, are still unaware, in principle, of the *kind* of linguistic phenomenon they are liable to come into contact with in this part of language, how they should label phenomena that they hear, or how they should integrate these with other aspects of any linguistic description they may happen to be making. The present chapter is therefore an attempt to outline this area of study, so that the functional range of non-segmental features in a social anthropological context may be more readily recognized. But first I ought to indicate the extent to which non-segmental features *have* been noted in the description of social categories, either by linguists or by anthropologists, as this may help to clarify the nature of these features and underline the need for research in this area. A partial survey of the literature in this respect is not all that meaningful, in fact, because, in the absence of any generally-agreed theory, there is no guarantee that different scholars are using such terms as 'melody', 'tone', and 'stress' in the same way (cf. p. 57); and there have been few attempts to transcribe utterances in order to indicate the frequency of occurrence and distribution of specific effects. But at least some of the references used here may help to provide a context of situation for those not too familiar with the subject.

I have divided the main references into five generally recognized categories (though there is, of course, some overlapping): institutionalized non-segmental correlates (or indications, depending on the point of view) of *sex*, *age*, *status*, *occupation*, and *functions* (*genres*). I shall add some references to English in order to indicate further the kind of information involved.

Sex

It is probable that there are important non-segmental differences between the speech habits of men and women in most languages, though very little data have been analysed from this point of view. Cf. such informal remarks as 'Stop clucking like an old woman', or references to 'sexy' voice and the like (see Laver 1968: 49). Intuitive impressions of effeminacy in English, for example, partly correlate with segmental effects such as lisping, but are mainly non-segmental: a 'simpering' voice, for instance, largely reduces to the use of a wider pitch-range than normal (for men), with *glissando* effects between stressed syllables, a more frequent use of complex tones (e.g. the fall-rise and the rise-fall), the use of breathiness and huskiness in the voice, and switching to a higher (falsetto) register from time to time. (This provides an interesting

contrast with Mohave, for instance, where a man imitating a woman (or trans-
vestite) does not change to falsetto, but uses his normal voice, and rather
imitates verbal and segmental effects (see Devereux 1949: 269).) According to
Ferguson (in Sebeok *et al.* 1964: 274), velarization in Arabic indicates, among
other things, masculinity, whereas avoidance of velarization indicates the
opposite. In Darkhat Mongol, women front all back and mid vowels (see
Capell 1966: 101). In Yana, men talking to men 'speak fully and deliberately',
whereas when women are involved (as either speakers or hearers) 'a clipped
style of utterance' is used (see Sapir, in Mandelbaum 1949: 212). Also in Yana,
to express interrogation, women lengthen final vowels, whereas men add a
segmental suffix, *-n* (Sapir, *op. cit.*: 179–80, cf. also 211), though it is a descriptive problem whether the length should be interpreted non-segmentally or not.
In Chichimeca, where male and female names in the same family may be
identical, it is reported that 'tone' may be used to differentiate the sexes being
addressed (see Driver & Driver 1963: 108). Syllabic tone differences may
distinguish between sexes in Koasati (Haas 1944). Sex differences, moreover,
sometimes correlate with age. According to Garbell (1965), many female
speakers over seventy of Urmi, a dialect spoken by Jews in north Persian
Azerbaijan, replace practically all 'plain' words by 'flat' words, i.e. words
consisting of 'flat' phones, which in Garbell's metalanguage means such
features as the strong velarization of all oral consonants, the articulation of
all labials with marked lip protrusion and rounding, and pharyngealization.
Again, *responses* to non-segmental vocal effects can be a valuable part of a
description, e.g. in Mohave, the breaking of the male voice in adolescence is not
considered an important, or even a relevant, indication of puberty (Devereux
1949: 268), whereas, of course, in English it is a feature that is regularly re-
marked upon. And, as a last example, one could note the training in voice
modulation that Burundi men receive, but women do not (Albert 1964: 37).

Age

References to the non-segmental correlates of age are very sporadic indeed in
the sociolinguistic literature, though this was one of the most readily demon-
strable correlations in the early work in social psychology (see Kramer 1963;
Allport & Cantril 1934), and one has a perfectly clear intuitive impression of
'old', 'young' voices, and the like. In fact, the only regular references are to
baby-talk (i.e. the speech characteristics of adults addressing babies). Kelkar
(1964), under the heading of *paraphonology*, refers to the extended pitch and
loudness characteristics, and the relatively slow and regular speed of baby-talk
in Marathi, and mentions certain general vocal effects, such as pouting and
palatalization. Ferguson (1964), with reference to English, also cites the higher
overall pitch of baby-talk, the preference for certain pitch contours, and
labialization, but does not discuss it further. Ervin-Tripp (1964) refers to some
general characteristics of children's play-intonations, and Burling (1966) shows
that broad rhythmic similarities exist between samples of children's verse from
a number of languages. It is highly likely that older groups are also discriminated

by non-segmental features (and not just by grammar and vocabulary, which are the only areas generally cited), but there is no published evidence on the point, apart from a few general remarks, as in Albert (1964) and Garbell (1965). Children's non-segmental phonology is discussed further in Chapter 8.

Status

Non-segmental phonology is frequently used to indicate the social identity of the speaker on a scale of some kind (his 'class dialect', as many would say), or the identity of the receiver in these terms. Certain tones of 'respect' might be conventionalized indications of a particular kinship or caste relation, for instance, or may indicate different social roles. John Boman Adams (1957: 226) mentions the importance of stereotyped pitch patterns and tones of voice in order to establish status between participants in one dialect of Egyptian:

The villager is ordinarily conditioned to give and receive communications whose content is so stereotyped that he pays little attention to it other than to note that it conforms to the norms of traditional utterances and that the speaker is socially acceptable. . . . These statuses are often established in the exchange of stereotyped expressions of esteem and concern that are obligatory whenever two or more persons meet. Since the same expressions are always uttered, interpretations of 'friendliness' or 'enmity' depend upon meanings conveyed by subtle qualities of tone, pitch, and melody. These qualities, in their different modes, are interpretable to one who is acquainted with their culturally defined meanings.

In Cayuvava, a rapidly-disappearing language in Bolivia, there is a set of nasal phonemes, but nasalization also occurs with 'honorific' stylistic function (according to Key 1967: 19): an individual of lower social or economic status addresses one of higher rank with a prominence of nasalization for all vowels of the utterance; and similarly with a woman being polite to her husband, or a man asking a favour. Albert (1964) refers to a number of similar examples, also instancing a typical sociolinguistic use of silence in this respect: in Burundi conclave, the silence of the highest-ranking person negates the proceedings, indicating total disapproval (whereas silence of lower-ranking people would have no comparable effect) (41). Gumperz (1964: 144) distinguishes between two forms of the vernacular in Khalapur, 'moṭi boli' and 'saf boli', the former being used primarily within the family group, the latter being used in external relationships, and refers to particular distributions of pitch glides occurring in the former but not in the latter. Longacre (1957) notes a very restricted formal third person enclitic in Mixtecan, which adds length and nasal quality to the syllable. What M. Shapiro (1968) calls 'explicit' and 'elliptical' codes in Russian are generally distinguished, *inter alia*, by tempo, the latter being faster. Bernstein (1964) makes some reference to intonation in his distinction between restricted and elaborated codes in English. Raffler Engel (1972) discusses the prosodic distinctiveness of black and white children.

Many of these oppositions imply a distinction between formal and informal (non-casual and casual etc.) kinds of speech, which has been frequently referred to in English (e.g. by Joos 1962). Speed of utterance is presumably one of the features that would distinguish formal from informal speech; and there is, as usual, a fair amount of informal evidence for the existence of status styles in English, e.g. 'How dare you talk to me like that! I'm not one of your employees/students/secretaries . . .', and reference to 'la-di-da' voices, 'talking down', and so on. Hoenigswald (1966: 19) makes the point that in this field it is important to study the *ideals* of speech behaviour cherished by a group as well as the actual speech behaviour used, and an interesting area of research will be the systematic examination of elocution handbooks—not to condemn them, as linguists generally do, but to view them descriptively, as data concerning the desired (real or imagined) correlates of genteel, educated speech and the reverse. Non-segmental effect is regularly referred to here: see, for example, the influential work of the American elocutionist Rush (1827) in this respect. One should also note the vocal effects used, sometimes as mocking forms, when addressing a member of a stigmatized group, e.g. Sapir refers to the 'thickish' sounds of s and ʃ 'pronounced with the lower jaw held in front of the upper' when talking to hunchbacks in Nootka (see Mandelbaum 1949: 183), and to the way of satirizing cowards in this language, when either addressing them or referring to them, by 'making one's voice small' (i.e. using a 'thin, piping voice') (184). Cf. children's sing-song cat-calls in English, using the tune:

Gumperz, finally, mentions the importance of sentence speed and pause (as hesitation) in the analysis of status, and suggests that it is about time that scholars broadened the range of their linguistic investigations to take account of these matters (in Bright 1966: 46). The points mentioned in this section are certainly only some of the possibilities. There are hardly any data to illuminate the question of the covariance of change in social status with change in tone of voice (e.g. after marriage, or after some initiation rite), though the existence of such phenomena can hardly be doubted.

Occupation

In English we are all familiar with the 'tone of voice' that is generally attributed to people acting in their professional capacities, such as the clergyman, lawyer, and undertaker. Phrases such as 'you sound like a clergyman' are conventionally meaningful, and would be interpreted (e.g. in an attempted imitation) as referring to a vocal effect in which pitch-range movements were narrowed, there was frequent use of monotone, rhythm was regular, tempo fairly slow, and overall pitch-height and resonance of the voice were increased. There are many occupations that would be recognized primarily on the basis of the non-segmental features involved, e.g. the disc jockey, barrister, preacher, street vendor, parade-ground commander, sports commentator, and many other kinds of radio and television announcer. Certain of these roles naturally overlap with status to some extent. Miller (1956: 181) talks about *authority roles*, by which he means 'a conceptualized position within a system of interpersonal relations whose incumbent is authorized to perform designated regulative functions for a designated action group during designated activity episodes', and many of those he cites (perhaps all?), e.g. drill sergeant, coxswain, foreman, cheer leader, involve the use of non-segmental features. The notion of a 'professional voice' is commonplace, if ill defined. Lecturers are generally aware of the kind of feature they have to introduce into their voice in order to awaken enthusiasm or promote participation in an otherwise dead class or audience.

Many of these matters have been given some experimental support, and it is not difficult to plan tests in order to verify one's impressions. A great deal of work has already taken place in the related area of defining personality traits, usually in the form of presenting judges with various non-segmental patterns (the verbal side of the utterance having been removed, e.g. by using nonsense-words, or acoustic filtering devices, or by articulating the different patterns on a single, neutral sentence—see Kramer 1963), and asking them to rate the function of these patterns in terms of various traits. ('Trait' is fairly broadly defined in such work, and subsumes age, sex, and certain occupational characteristics.) This research, largely reported in psychology journals between about 1935 and 1950, is methodologically unsatisfactory in many respects (e.g. insufficient attention was paid to the backgrounds (i.e. the preconceptions) of the judges, and there was a blurring of theoretical concepts which should have been kept apart—the difference between voice-quality and linguistic contrasts, for instance, which I shall discuss further below), but certain correlations between non-segmental patterns and features of extra-linguistic situations did emerge—and were generally referred to as *voice stereotypes* (see Chapter 4, and Crystal 1969a (Ch. 2) for a review of this literature). An important theoretical distinction which was not made in this work, but which must be made in future research, is that between *recognition* and *production* stereotypes (cf. the distinction between passive and active in vocabulary study); for example, it is part of our competence that we can discriminate various kinds of radio and television styles of speech, but I would agree with Labov that few speakers are ever directly influenced by such patterns as far as production is concerned (see 1967: 74).

There seem to be few occupational differences involving non-segmental features mentioned in foreign-language descriptions. The only area that receives a regular mention is religious and magical language, and this really overlaps my next category, speech functions.

Speech functions

Particular modalities, or genres of speaking, are generally signalled through the use of non-segmental characteristics, as elocutionists are well aware. In the context of oral literature, one would also expect frequent use of these features, as they would provide an important means of adding further variation to the very restricted, stylized scope of a poem or story (see, e.g. Meese 1968). Jacobs (1956: 127) emphasizes that

stylized devices such as connectives, pauses, and vocal mannerisms, to effect transitions from Scene to Scene or Act to Act in a longer story, are invariably discernible in its dictation in the native language. But publications infrequently if ever preserve evidence of these devices.

In Mohave, when a traditional, memorized text is being uttered, it is delivered in a staccato, rapid manner, which the speakers find very difficult to slow down (sometimes impossible, when the utterance is in front of other people from the same tribe—Devereux 1949: 269). Henry (1936: 251) refers to changes in force, pitch, vowel quality, aspiration and pharyngealization as Kaingang story-telling devices which were commonplace rhetorical forms in the language, e.g. 'the Kaingang always raise their voices when they are describing some long drawn-out activity, and their voices even take on what might be to us a complaining tone' (which tone, incidentally, 'was the usual tone to describe the slow climbing of a hill'!). Sapir talks of *styles of recitative* in Paiute, referring to the speech of certain mythological or traditional characters designated by certain sounds and tones of voice (in Mandelbaum 1949: 186, and cf. 465). Related to this is the tone of voice adopted by a community when imitating another: cf. Sapir's remarks about the Nootka's imitations of other tribes, e.g. adopting velar resonance (speaking 'in a rumbling fashion') for the Uchucklesit (Mandelbaum 1949: 193), or speaking in a 'drawling' manner (i.e. 'a somewhat exaggerated rise in pitch towards the end of a sentence') for the northern Nootka (194). The vocal stereotypes adopted by comedians, stage villains and certain traditional pantomine characters in our own culture would be further cases in point.

Distinct genres also exist in conversation in some languages. In Shiriana, different types of conversation can be distinguished on a non-segmental basis. Migliazza and Grimes differentiate between 'one-sided' and 'balanced' types (1961: 36–7). They illustrate the former by reference to 'myths' and 'narratives', and their distinction is worth quoting at length because of its detail:

Phonologically a myth is characterized by an initial period in which only lento pause groups occur, a body in which combinations of lento and andante pause groups occur, many of which contain ideophonic feet[1] and a termination in which one or two lento pause groups occur, with extra length on the vowel of the final stressed syllable in the contour and at times a voiced breath intake after the end of the final pause group . . . four pitch levels [adequate for normal speech] do not handle the pitch patterns, which range over a wide area and move largely in long glissandos.

1 An ideophonic foot is a highly conventionalized effect, referring to a rhythm unit 'accompanied either by an anomalous pitch pattern . . . or by a voice quality that stands out in contrast with that of the rest of the utterance (usually laryngealized or breathy in relation to the overall voice quality).' (Migliazza and Grimes 1961: 35). *lento* and *andante* are differentiated partly in terms of speed and partly in terms of the number of contours involved.

As an example of 'balanced conversation', the authors cite the *bargaining dialogue*, which is

delivered at night by a trading partner from one village to his partner from another in the presence of all hosts and members of a trading party, in which each partner's speech has the general characteristics of a monologue, except that the intonation is replaced by a chant form. (38)

They also mention the relevance of *crescendo*, *decrescendo* and laryngealization for the definition of certain speech styles.

Another well worked-out example is Conklin's (1959) study of ways of modifying normal speech patterns for purposes of entertainment or concealment (most frequently as part of voice disguise in customary courting behaviour) in Hanunóo, a language of the Philippines. There may be both segmental and non-segmental aspects of this, but the latter vary independently of the former. There are four types: *yanas* (barely audible whispering), *paliksih* (utterance involving clipped pronunciation, greater speed, greater glottal tension, expansion of the intonational contours and shortening of the long vowels), *padiqitun* (falsetto), and *paha·gut* (any sequence of articulations during which the direction of air flow in normal speech is reversed, i.e. inhalation).

Malinowski often implies the relevance of non-segmental phonological effect in *The language of magic and gardening* (London, 1935), making explicit reference to it in his notes about 'modes of recitation' of magical formulae. Fischer (1966: 180–81) refers to the variation in the recitation of magical formulae between Ponape and Truk: the repetitions of the former are as exact as possible, but the latter make great use of expressive variations. Genres of religious speaking are regularly prosodically distinctive. Conwell & Juilland (1963: 30) refer to the distinctive rhythmicality of prayers in Louisiana French, which is apparently very similar to the rhythmicality of litanies and other liturgical languages in English (see Crystal and Davy 1969: Ch. 6 and Chapter 6 below). West (1962: 90) reports that in Mikasuki, the language of the Seminole Indians in Florida, stress and tone differences are minimized in sermons. The introduction of song and chant characteristics into Welsh preaching (*hwyl*) involves markedly different pitch, length and speed characteristics, as well as such paralinguistic effects as resonance and tremulousness.

A typology of speech functions in language has not yet been established, though there have been numerous attempts at it. The scattered comments collected in this section clearly indicate that non-segmental effect will be a major part of the definition of the physical basis of these functions. In English, phatic communion, routine requests, avoidance ploys, routine format (sports results, weather forecasting, etc.), public-speaking, official announcements, ceremonial language, sports commentary, telephone conversation, television advertising (and other forms of persuasion): these are just some of the areas where intonational and related phonological features are markedly different from those used in spontaneous utterance. For further references to speech functions, see Stern (1956, esp. 382–3) and Frake (1964).

There has, then, been considerable sporadic, impressionistic comment as to the sociolinguistic function of non-segmental effects, though the utility of this has been marred by lack of an adequate theory, inexplicitness of definition and certain methodological weaknesses. As an example of the latter, it is sometimes difficult to know the extent to which the description of a given effect is intended as referring to a linguistic feature of an individual, a group, or the language as a whole. When data are restricted to the output of one or two speakers of a language, there is always the danger of a lack of perspective causing mis-interpretation (a problem that takes an extreme form in the Cayuvava language mentioned above, where there were apparently only six living speakers at the time the description was made). Also, too little reference is made to voice-quality norms for the languages as wholes, e.g. establishing overall pitch-range, loudness, speed, and so on. But enough has been done to show clear lines of research, and the links that exist between linguistics and related, non-linguistic, semiotic fields. Here one might instance the importance of *speech surrogate* systems, such as the use of conventionalized whistling patterns, which may reflect intonational or paralinguistic patterning in the language (cf. wolf-whistles and rise–fall intonations in English), or the co-occurrence of kinesic features with speech (cf. La Barre 1964), or the relationship between intonation and primitive music (cf. Herzog 1934). Stankiewicz (1964) provides further comment on this point.

It is possible that an 'integrated theory' of all the observations made in this area may prove as valuable to social anthropology as Trager's framework has been in stimulating and helping to codify psychiatric research in America (see the references in Sebeok *et al.* 1964). The descriptive framework outlined in Crystal & Quirk (1964), and developed in Crystal (1969a) and used throughout this book, allows for the incorporation of all the effects noted in this chapter, and groups them into systems on the basis of shared formal characteristics. The following conceptual stages need to be distinguished:

Non-linguistic vocal effects

(A) VOICE QUALITY

Speech (or any act of communication) takes place against a personal and en-vironmental background, which has to be identified by the analyst, in order to be discounted. Voice quality is the idiosyncratic, relatively permanent, vocal background of an individual, which allows us to recognize him, as opposed to other members of the group. It may be both segmental and non-segmental in character, but the latter is usually the dominant factor. It is a physiologically-determined activity, over which most individuals have little or no measure of control. For a useful model of voice quality, see Laver (1968). In the present chapter, I have been concerned only with those non-segmental features which display—to however small a degree—a group-identifying function.

(B) PHYSIOLOGICAL REFLEXES

Physiological reflexes, such as coughs, sneezes, or husky voice due to a sore throat, may also occur along with speech, and must also be discounted as background 'noise'.

Semiotic frame

A model of an act of communication in semiotics is generally viewed as a bundle of interacting events or non-events from different communicational subsystems, or *modalities*, simultaneously transmitted and received. This communicative activity has been variously called a 'signal syndrome' and a 'communication configuration' or 'network'. It is distinct from the personal and physical background in that (a) it is variable with reference to the biological characteristics of the individual communicator, but is a pattern of behaviour shared by a group, and (b) the activity has always some culturally determined, relatively conventionalized value, or 'meaning'. The subsystems are five in all, corresponding to the five senses, vocal/auditory, visual, tactile, olfactory, and gustatory; but only the first three are regularly used in normal communication (the latter have little potential structure, but are none the less of some importance as carriers of information to such people as doctor and chemist, e.g. in analysing body odours). The study of patterned, conventionalized, visual human bodily behaviour (facial expressions and bodily gestures) is known as *kinesics*. Non-vocal communicative subsystems have not been the subject-matter of this chapter: their relevance to anthropology is discussed in La Barre (1964).

Vocal-auditory component

The vocal-auditory component in communication can be broken down into the following categories:

(A) SEGMENTAL-VERBAL

This, the traditional centre of linguistic attention, would in its widest definition cover segmental phonetics and phonology, morphology, syntax, and vocabulary. A sub-set of verbal items is usually distinguished in semiotic literature: these, generally referred to as *vocalizations*, cover such items as 'mhm', 'shhh', 'tut tut', and the like, which are articulated using sounds outside the normal range of phonetic resources in the language. These overlap, formally and functionally, the next category.

(B) PAUSE PHENOMENA

These comprise the various degrees of silence and 'voiced pause' (e.g. the 'ers' of English) that exist in a language. These features are clearly segmental, from the formal point of view, but functionally silence overlaps non-segmental features, as it enters into the physical definition of such effects as rhythmicality and intonation contour (and is partly subsumed under the notion of juncture, by some scholars).

(C) NON-SEGMENTAL FEATURES

These are aspects of the phonic continuum which have an essentially variable relationship to the phonemes and words selected as defined by (a) above (see p. 52). Detailed illustration of all features is provided in Crystal (1969a). They may be grouped into two general categories:

Prosodic features

These are meaningful contrasts due to variations in the attributes of pitch, loudness, and duration (which have a primary, but not an identifying, relationship to the fundamental frequency of vocal-cord vibration, amplitude of vocal-cord vibration, and speed of articulation respectively), either singly or in combination. Some values from these three variables permanently characterize speech. Prosodic features sharing a similar formal basis and displaying some mutual definition of contrastivity are grouped together into *prosodic systems*. The following systems have been distinguished:

(i) *Pitch*. There are two systems of pitch, *tone* (referring to the direction of pitch-movement in a syllable, as when it falls, rises, or stays level, or does some of these things in rapid succession) and *pitch-range*. By pitch-range, I mean the distance between adjacent syllables or stretches of utterance identified in terms of a scale running from low to high. Speakers and groups have a normal pitch-level and range, and they may depart from this in different ways to produce extra-high or low speech, either in a sudden step-up or down, or gradually. The normal distance between adjacent syllables may be narrowed (perhaps reduced to monotone) or widened, and different languages display different kinds and degrees of pitch-range variation. The patterns of pitch-movement that occur in a language are referred to as the *intonation*. Connected speech is considered as analysable into a series of *units* of intonation (variously called *tone-units* or *tone-groups*), which have a definable internal structure, and which function in sequences to produce melodic contours of a more general nature. (See further, Chapter 1 above.)

(ii) *Loudness*. Degrees of loudness which affect single syllables are referred to as degrees of *stress*. (*Accent* refers to a syllable which has been made prominent owing to a combination of both loudness and pitch factors.) Speakers and groups have a norm of loudness, which they may depart from in different attitudes, styles of speech, etc. Over stretches of utterance, there may be *forte* or *piano* loudness, to various degrees. As with pitch-range, the change from one level of loudness to another may be sudden or gradual (as with *crescendo* and *diminuendo* utterance.)

(iii) *Tempo*. Single syllables may be shortened or lengthened (clipped and drawled respectively); stretches of utterance may be faster or slower than normal for a speaker or group, to various degrees (*allegro*, *lento*), and, as above, the change may take place suddenly or gradually (*accelerando*, *rallentando* speech).

(iv) *Rhythmicality*. Combinations of pitch, loudness and duration effects produce rhythmic alternations in speaking, distinct from the rhythmic norm of the language, e.g. increasing the perceived regularity of a sequence of stressed syllables in an utterance, or decreasing it; clipping certain syllables to produce staccato speech, or slurring them, to produce *glissando* or *legato* utterance. There are numerous possible contrasts here, and of course the physical correlates of each would have to be carefully defined in any description.

Paralinguistic features
Non-segmental variations *other* than those caused primarily by pitch, loudness and speed, i.e. where other physiological mechanisms in the oral, nasal or pharyngeal cavities are being used to produce an effect, are referred to under this heading. Prosodic features, being permanent features of utterance of course enter into these effects, but they are variable in respect of their definition: any of the features listed below can be uttered with variable pitch, loudness, and speed (with one or two minor restrictions). Paralinguistic features are discontinuous and relatively infrequent in speech. They do not display such clear-cut formal and functional contrasts as do prosodic features, consequently the systemic nature of their function is more difficult to demonstrate. One possible system would group together the different kinds of tenseness that may occur in a language, e.g. tense, lax, slurred and precise articulations; others would involve degrees and kinds of resonance of articulation, contrasts in register (e.g. falsetto, chest), degrees of pharyngeal construction (e.g. huskiness), types of whisper and breathy articulation, spasmodic articulations (i.e. the pulsations of air from the lungs are out-of-phase with the syllables of an utterance, as when one laughs or sobs while speaking, or says something in a tremulous tone), general retraction or advancement of the tongue (e.g. velarization), distinctive use of the lips (labialization), and various kinds of nasalization. A complete description of the possibilities here has not been written, but this cannot really be carried out in the absence of reliable data.

If one examines the data discussed in the first half of this chapter in the light of the categories outlined in the second, it will be seen that all the vocal effects cited (or, at least, plausible interpretations of all these effects) can be described in terms of one or more of these categories. A great deal more work is needed before such an approach could be formalized as part of any general sociolinguistic theory; meanwhile, it may be the case that even a tentative formulation could stimulate fieldworkers to look more closely at this aspect of language, thereby providing the reliable and wide-ranging data that this corner of linguistics so badly needs.

6
Non-segmental phonology and sociolinguistic distinctiveness: an illustration from religious language

In order to clarify the relevance of the study of religious language to socio-linguistic theory and practice, it seems to me necessary to make a preliminary, broad identification of those foci of attention which are conditioning our ideas about priorities in contemporary sociolinguistic thinking. As perspective for what follows, then, I wish to isolate three current emphases, which I loosely label empirical, methodological and theoretical. By an 'empirical' task within sociolinguistics, I mean the establishment of a detailed formal description of systematic covariation between linguistic features (of whatever kind) and social context. By a 'methodological' task, I mean the establishment of explicit criteria and techniques, which will enable us to assess the factual validity of our observations about covariation, and provide a basis for comparative analysis and research consistency. By a 'theoretical' task, I mean the establishment of explanatory principles as general as possible, capable of accounting for the range and kind of covariation observed, in terms of some sociolinguistic model of patterns, categories, rules and the like. If the study of religious language is to be fruitful, it should be able to contribute to the advancement of any or all of these tasks. I feel that a threefold contribution of this kind is perfectly possible; and in the present paper I will indicate one area of religious linguistic studies in which this might be done.

I will concentrate on the empirical, for this seems to me to be the area in which the most urgent claims for sociolinguists' attention lie. The current literature displays ample theoretical speculation, and some well-developed methodological routines; but there are precious few facts. Hypotheses abound; but few have been adequately tested. The paucity of facts is best reflected by the limited answers we can give to the question 'What exactly constitutes the linguistic distinctiveness of the sociolinguistic category X?'—where X refers to any of the usually recognized range of social functions (ethnic, regional, class, professional, purposive etc.). Or, putting this another way, one might ask, 'What features in the physical form of an act of communication lead us to identify (to a stated degree of certainty) this act as a token of a particular sociolinguistic type?' Apart from a very few detailed surveys, this question cannot be answered for most sociolinguistic contexts, even in English. It is doubtless this dearth of evidence which makes so much of our present-day output seem like theorizing rather than theory; for there are some very important types of linguistic evidence which so far have been little investigated. Indeed, in the case of non-segmental phonology, the evidence has sometimes been ruled out as irrelevant on *a priori*, 'general' grounds. If one holds the view, still widely maintained by structuralist-inclined linguists, that paralinguistic features and related features are not 'language proper', then one will be unlikely to introduce them as parameters on which to plot sociolinguistic distinctiveness; and many studies have ignored them as a result. But a critical examination of the grounds on which the concept of 'language properness' was set up in the first place (see Chapter 2) might lead one to disregard this premiss, and suggest instead that considerable attention be paid to the potentially highly significant use paralinguistic features have in constituting the sociolinguistic identity of a spoken text.

The model of language presupposed by this discussion, in broadest outline, sets up three levels, or components—phonological, syntactic, and semantic (this latter subsuming both lexicon and semantic discourse relations). Clearly, a sociolinguistically distinctive use of language might make use of features which could be analysed in terms of any or all of these levels; and we are all familiar with papers that deal with the 'syntactic' analysis of say, scientific English, or the distinctive 'lexis' of class-variation in English, and so on. The research literature, however, displays a remarkable concentration on the syntactic level alone; apart from the recent work into segmental phonological matters (as in the work of Labov and others), and a few scattered studies of lexis, the general feeling seems to be that most of the sociolinguistic distinctiveness of spoken language is syntactic in character. This feeling almost certainly derives from recent preoccupations with syntactic models of analysis. If one is told to investigate the sociolinguistic distinctiveness of a text, but given only a syntactic knife and fork to do it with, then naturally one's overall conclusions are going to be syntactic in character. I want now to argue that in fact the basis of most sociolinguistic distinctiveness in speech is phonological in character, and non-segmental phonological in particular. My hypothesis is that the distinctiveness of a spoken variety of language lies primarily in its use of prosodic and paralinguistic features. (A parallel hypothesis, arguing for the graphological distinctiveness of written texts in terms of layout, type-contrasts etc. might also be made, of course.) As evidence, I shall look at the non-segmental properties of certain categories of religious language, illustrated from English.

There are a number of reasons why religious language makes an excellent area for testing sociolinguistic hypotheses. Firstly, it presents a well-institutionalized area of sociolinguistic experience. Because of its formalized dependence on linguistic traditions (e.g. certain texts of old viewed as sacred or dogmatic), and the regularity and high frequency of repetition of the linguistic situations involved, it should be possible to make representative samples of usage much more easily than in many other areas of sociolinguistic behaviour, and to make a description of the 'facts' of the variety relatively quickly. Indeed, the chimerical notion of an 'exhaustive' analysis may, in such restricted linguistic areas as this, turn out to be a real possibility. Secondly, religious language, although institutionalized, is by no means homogeneous, but displays a number of well-recognized categories of linguistic variation—sermons, litanies, prophecies etc. Accordingly, it permits an investigation of the classic theoretical question, 'Are the following usage samples tokens of the same type (i.e. do they belong to the same variety) or are they not ?' Or, putting this another way, 'Can all these samples be generated by the same set of rules, or not ?' Moreover, in this connection, it must not be forgotten that the social conventions operating to produce this category of sociolinguistic behaviour impose severe limitations upon the length of texts and the range of variability of the language they contain. Interesting questions about the generalizability of rules, the economy of descriptions and the like, may thus be more likely to receive a satisfactory answer, with such data, than in the case of many other sociolinguistic categories, as there is less material, quantitatively and qualitatively speaking, to be accounted for. Thirdly—and very clearly in the case of English—the features of religious language are by no means restricted to the analysis of religious behaviour. While the basis of religious language obviously lies in the specific practices of particular groups, the *effect* of religious language transcends this, affecting the community as a whole. Religious linguistic effects enter into other areas of sociolinguistic experience, and give rise to questions requiring more general explanations. One may see this most clearly by the regular use of features of religious language in literature; but it is also apparent in the various kinds of humour within a culture, especially satire and joke-telling. There is, in a phrase, a 'national consciousness' about the features (or at least, about the most important features) of religious language, and this is far more marked than in the case of other linguistic varieties. There are at least three reasons for this. There is, to begin with, the length of the historical traditions of religious practice, stemming from the common Christianity of English-speaking cultures, which manifests itself in such matters as obligatory Bible instruction in state schools. Religious linguistic behaviour is regularly taught, albeit not always practised. Second, religious language has had a peculiarly pervasive influence on the development of the literary language, and indeed the language as a whole (see, for instance, Brook's study of the language of the Book of Common Prayer from this point of view, 1965). And thirdly, there is the high degree of personal relevance to the language's purpose, and the domesticity of much of its subject-matter, which makes it much more likely to enter into everyday life than, say, the forms of legal language, which display a comparable historical tradition. As a result of such factors, there is a clear stereotype of religious language in the community as a whole, part of the linguistic equipment of believers and non-believers alike. This seems to be far more marked than in the case of any other variety, and would seem to constitute an additional reason for investigating the properties of this particular use of language.

All sociolinguistic investigation commences by assuming on intuitive grounds that a particular category of language-situational covariation exists: the subsequent analysis is then intended to verify this intuition (or perhaps, more strictly, to falsify it). In the case of religious language, general intuition of the categories operating within this area would lead one to recognize several distinct 'genres', or *modalities* (to use the term introduced in Crystal and Davy (1969))—for instance, sermons, litanies, biblical readings, blessings, invocations, spontaneous expressions of various types, individual and group liturgical prayer, and so on. For this paper, I shall restrict myself to four modalities which were intuitively identified in a Catholic Church in England over a period of two weeks—the only ones regularly used (excluding the confessional, in view of the marked reluctance of the participants to permit the presence of a tape-recorder!). They were: unison prayer, individually-read liturgical prayer, biblical reading and sermon. One hour of each category was recorded, transcribed and analysed. A short example of each type is given below. (In passing, I should like to emphasize that each sample was given a rating for 'typicality' and 'success'. A number of participants were asked to say whether they felt that the samples were 'abnormal' or 'poor' in any respect, these labels not being further defined. Only utterances about which there was a consensus of 'normality' were included in the final samples. The reason for this procedure should be clear. There is little point in trying to discern general linguistic patterns if one's selection of data is felt to be misleading, e.g. if a sermon was felt to be too informal or too intellectual by the congregation. Some safeguards of this kind seem to be prerequisite for satisfactory sociolinguistic generalizations. But they seem to be rarely reported on in the literature, and they often seem to be ignored, analysts assuming, invalidly, that any selection of data—e.g. of scientific language, journalese, or religious—is bound to be satisfactory merely because it has been used. The point is discussed at length in Crystal 1972).

There is no space here to report other than the main findings. Briefly, the following four points emerged:

(i) Vocabulary was of little diagnostic significance. The range of vocabulary used in the course of the hour-samples overlapped considerably between the different modalities. On the basis of a straight frequency count of items, or of item-combinations ('collocations'), it would be impossible to make valid predictions of a type-token kind with any great accuracy.

(ii) Nor was syntax particularly helpful. The main syntactic features of religious language of this kind have been outlined elsewhere (see Crystal and Davy 1969: Ch. 6), and classified in terms of sentence-type, sentence-connection, clause structure, group (noun-phrase, verb-phrase etc.) structure and word-structure. Many features emerge at each 'rank' in the analysis—for instance, the use of extensive vocative structures, archaic verb morphology, and other well-known characteristics. The point which has to be made here is that all of the important features of syntax and morphology are to be found in all modalities. Frequency and distribution of syntactic patterns display few important differences across the samples; and the differences which do emerge are not those which one would intuitively consider to be the defining characteristics of religious language. (The syntactic parallelism of litanies would presumably be exceptional, but analogous sequences to those used there may be found in other modalities too, e.g. in many Old Testament passages, and in sermons (cf. the metrical phrasing noticed in certain types of sermon, e.g. by Rosenberg 1970); in such cases, phonological distinctiveness still obtains, as argued below.)

1 *Sample of unison prayer*

|I be'lieve in 'one GŌD| . the |Father ALMĪGHTY| .
|maker of 'heaven and ĒARTH| . and of |all 'things
'visible and INVĪSIBLE| - |and in 'one 'Lord 'Jesus
CHRIST| the |only be'gotten 'Son of GŌD| - |born of the
'father be'fore 'all ĀGES| - |God from GŌD|. |Light from
LĪGHT|. |true 'god from 'true GŌD| - be|gotten not
MĀDE|. |consub'stantial with the FĀTHER| through |whom
all 'things were MĀDE| -

2 *Sample of individual (priest's) prayer (read aloud)*

"narrow"   "O |God the 'King of GLŌRY|" - who hast ex|alted
thine ↑only *n*SON| |'JESUS CHRIST| with |great TRIUMPH
unto thy 'Kingdom in *n*HEAVEN| - we BE|SEECH thee|
|leave us not COMFORTLESS| . but |send to 'us thine
↑Holy 'Ghost to ↓COMFORT us| and ex|alt us 'unto
the ↑same PLĀCE| |whither our ↑Saviour 'Christ is

"descending" ↑gone BEFORE| - "who |liveth and REĪGNETH| with
|thee and the 'Holy *n*GHOST| |one GOD| |world without
END| A|MEN|"

3 *Sample of sermon (with notes)*

"high narrow"   the "|book of the 'prophet ISAĪAH| - |thirtieth"
"high precise"
"narrow   "*n*CHAP'TER|" - "the |fifteenth 'verse of the CHAP'TER|"
  diminuendo"
"narrow"   - "I|SAĪAH|" |chapter ↑thirty 'verse FIF"TEEN|" --- in
"tremulous"
                      =
"resonant"   "re|turning" and REST| - ye |shall be SAVED| -- in
                      |quietness . and in ↑CONFIDENCE| - shall |be your
"piano"
"allegro   " ↓STRENGTH|" - "in re|turning and 'rest ye shall be"
  diminuendo"   =
"diminuendo
  tremulous"   "*n*SAVED|" in |quietness and "in *n* CONFIDENCE| -
"piano"
"allegro" |shall be ↑your ↓STRENGTH|" --- "|this is a 'story of
"tense"   a 'man who was in a" "HURRY|" - and who |travelled .
"tense"   too "FAST|" -

4 *Sample of biblical reading*

the |scribes and 'Pharisees brought a ↑WŌMAN along|

"narrow" who had been |caught com'mitting ADULTERY| . "and
|making her 'stand THÉRE| in |full 'view of ÉVERYBODY|"

"descending" they |said to JĒSUS| . "*h* MĀSTER| |this 'woman was
↑caught in the ↑very 'act of com'mitting ADÚLTERY| .
and |Moses has ŌRDERED US| |in the LÁW| to CON|DÉMN
'women like 'this| to |death by STŌNING|" - |what

"low descending" have ﹒you to SAY| -- "they |ASKED him 'this as a
↑TEST| . |looking for 'something to 'use AGÁINST
him|" -- but |Jesus 'bent DŌWN| and |started 'writing
on the 'ground with his FINGER| --

Conventions (for further explanation, see Crystal 1969a, Crystal and Davy 1969)

.   ⎫
-     ⎬   increasing degrees of pause length
--   ⎭

ˋ falling tone   ˊ rising tone   ˇ falling-rising tone

-	level tone
|	onset syllable of the tone-unit
∥	tone-unit boundary

SMALL CAPITALS indicate the word carrying the tonic syllable

'	stressed syllable stepping down in pitch
↑	stressed syllable stepping up in pitch
↓	marked step-down in pitch
" "	indicate that the passage within is to be read according to the marginal indication
=	lengthened syllable or sound
n	following syllable narrowed in pitch range
h	following syllable at high level

(iii) Segmental phonology for individual speakers (three in all), on all occasions of recording, was identical. All used varieties of Received Pronunciation, and the vowel/consonant systems used displayed no significant variations of a regional, class or temporal character. There were certainly no grounds for discriminating between the modalities here.

(iv) This leaves the non-segmental phonology: and this, it emerged, was fundamentally different within each sample. The above extracts give some indication of this, but the main differentiating characteristics may be summarized more generally, as follows:

Unison prayer, with text available as a cue. Each punctuation group is a prosodic unit, but it is a prosodic unit of a rather different kind from the tone-unit (or primary contour) found in all other varieties of spoken English, as it requires only two obligatory prosodic features—a most emphatic syllable, and stress conforming to the distribution of lexical words within the unit. The introduction of variation in nuclear tone-type (e.g. rising, falling-rising tunes) or in pitch-range (e.g. high falling or low falling) is optional, and usually not introduced. Any participant in a congregation may, if he wishes, articulate his words with as much feeling as possible, introducing a wide range of pitch patterns; but as far as the total, cumulative auditory effect is concerned, such effort is unnecessary, and few speakers bother. A congregation— or any speakers in unison—has very much one voice. When a group speak an utterance together, differences in the phonology of their articulation become blurred, and the outside listener is left with a 'single voice' impression, consisting solely of variations in emphasis. The pitch level on the whole is low and monotone, though towards the end of a longer stretch of utterance than normal there may be a noticeable descending movement. This is absolutely predictable at the very end of a prayer, where the 'Amen' (and often the words immediately preceding it) is given a marked drop in pitch. But otherwise pitch contrasts are regularly reduced to zero, leaving monotone and rhythmicality as the defining characteristics of unison liturgical prayer.

Individual liturgical prayer, whether spontaneous or cued by a text, is marked particularly by a narrowness of pitch-range, which affects all types of nuclear tone; level tones are more frequent than in other modalities of speech by individuals; there is a gradual descent of pitch towards the end of the prayer (as above), and a strong tendency to keep tone-units short and isochronous. Of particular importance is the absence of the usual range of prosodic and paralinguistic variations (e.g. of speed, loudness, rhythm, tension), and the avoidance of any prosodic variability that might be construed as idiosyncratic. There is also the related point that this is one of the few cases where one is allowed to speak with little or no significant kinesic accompaniment: we find a minimum of facial expression and bodily gesture in this modality, a marked contrast with sermons.

Biblical reading. The important point to note about this modality is the expected effect of the written language on the individual recitation, which obtains whether the person actually follows the text as he reads, or whether he has learned it off by heart (either in advance, or from some oral tradition). The regularity of the speed and rhythm, the tendency of intonation to follow the punctuation, the predictable occurrence and length of pauses, the avoidance of prosodic and paralinguistic features which express extremes of attitude or characterization (even where the narrative might justify them), the use of lengthy tone-units and pitch-range 'paragraphs' which impose structural organization upon the text (cf. the prosodic organization of radio news-reading): these are the main features which place this modality at a considerable remove from individual prayers and sermons.

Sermons. Whether learned, much-rehearsed or spontaneous, sermons display considerable prosodic and paralinguistic variation, as the brief extract shows. At times the variability is so marked that the utterance takes on some of the characteristics normally associated with a different communicative medium, song or chant (see, for instance, the reports of Rosenberg (1970), Marks (1972)). Different degrees of prosodic expressiveness exist; but even the most 'reserved' kind of sermon analysed presents a considerable prosodic range. The point needs no labouring.

Even from these sketchy generalizations and the few pieces of illustration, it should be clear that non-segmental features are easily able to demarcate the four modalities. There is very little overlap in terms of either selection or frequency of use. One might display a similar non-segmental distinctiveness within other modalities also, e.g. the litany, or the confessional interchange; and the point has been noted in the analysis of other rituals and other traditions. One would point to the centrality of metrical and pausal systems in Rosenberg's analysis of the qualities of certain kinds of spontaneous sermon (1970); or Fitzgerald's (1970) listing of twelve outstanding characteristics of prophetic speech in Gã, nine of which fall within my definition of prosodic and paralinguistic features; or Goodman (1969) and Samarin (1972), who pay particular attention to intonation and related features in their analysis of glossolalia. There now seems to be an increasing body of evidence to support the view that non-segmental factors are crucial in identifying the distinctiveness of religious modalities (and of course for other sociolinguistic categories too—see Chapter 5); but as far as I know there has been no attempt to formulate any corresponding general hypothesis as an explanatory principle of widespread applicability, and points of methodological and theoretical importance have not been made. I conclude with a mention of three more-general points, one theoretical, one methodological and one 'rhetorical'.

First, the range of non-segmental variation manifested in such modalities as the above would seem to be better accounted for by postulating a concept of prosodic 'code-switching' rather than attempting to bring together these usages under the same set of rules. One may see this also in the non-linguistic background that accompanies these samples. In each modality, the speaker tends to adopt a fresh 'articulatory setting' (see Honikman 1964; cf. the 'voice-set' concept of Trager 1958). One can see this, for example, in the larynx-raised articulation of a preacher, or the laxness and low pitch-range of the unison speaker, or the variations in tone-unit length, which ultimately relate to breath-group and emotional role. It would seem difficult to handle all these modality-differences within a single description of non-segmental phonology. The system seems radically different in each case. But to what extent is it theoretically acceptable to set up a 'multi-glossia' situation solely for one linguistic level? Diglossia situations as usually outlined normally assume that the linguistic distinctiveness operates throughout the whole of the language system; which is very far from being the case here.

The basic methodological point is to ensure that analysis of non-segmental variability does not continue to be ignored or minimized in sociolinguistic investigations of speech: its explanatory power seems to be considerable. Religious language makes the point clearly, in my view, but it could also be shown to apply to other categories of speech (as Crystal and Davy (1969) argue). In addition, there is the methodologically-central question of ensuring that some psycholinguistic verification is provided for our sociolinguistic analyses—dealing with such matters as the perception of sociolinguistic distinctiveness, the rating of descriptive labels, and so on. But this goes beyond the bounds of the present topic.

Finally, there is the rhetorical point that research of the present kind indicates very clearly the interdependence of sociolinguistics with other aspects of linguistics. In the process of selecting samples, obtaining popular reactions to them, evaluating intuitions, investigating perceptions and determining how to label what we perceive, we are much in need of the expertise of psycholinguistics, as already mentioned. In the objective statement of text similarities, we may need the help of statistical linguistics, with its suggestions for multi-variate analysis, improved techniques of significance testing, and the like. In our search for descriptive generalizations, we need to use the concepts developed by such fields as literary criticism (especially in work on metrics, oral literature etc.) and musicology. And of course there is the ultimate reliance on a meta-language whose validity it is ultimately the purpose of general linguistic theory to assess. It is fashionable to talk of sociolinguistics as if it were a separate field, and attempt to define its boundaries. But its success is crucially dependent on progress in related fields, and attempting to isolate it too far can ultimately only be stultifying.

7
Intonation and metrical theory

In this chapter, I want to examine the nature of the non-segmental variation found in oral performance in poetry, and the way in which aspects of this variation have been and can be considered to be identifying features of this genre. My feeling is that certain important kinds of variability (in particular, the kinds of patterning generally referred to as 'intonation') have been under-estimated or ignored, and my hypothesis is that if these factors are given a proper role in any discussion of 'poetic identity', a more adequate account of the phonological basis of poetic effect will be obtained. Put briefly, this is yet another exercise in metrical theory—a topic which has received considerable discussion in many linguistic and critical journals over the last few years. Mr Thomas Barham put it—a trifle optimistically—in a paper to the Philo-logical Society in 1860, that metrics is not difficult, simply neglected. These days, metrics is no longer neglected, but its true complexity has begun to be better perceived, and it is, most assuredly, difficult!

The linguistic discussion of metre[1] seems to have produced considerable agreement about its nature and function; but any agreement is to a great extent obscured in the various publications by differences in terminology, an absence of definition of central concepts, and a failure to suggest procedures of analysis capable of producing anything empirically verifiable. This point may be seen if we look briefly at the common conception of the nature of metre, as presented in this literature. There is almost total agreement that metre, however defined, should not be identified with the psycho-physical analysis of utterance, as displayed in any reading of a text.[2] Metre is held to be an abstrac-tion, in some sense, and is not to be identified with performance.[3] But in which

1 By this I am referring to the discussion which has been taking place over the past ten years or so, stimulated largely by the articles in *The Kenyon Review* 18 (1956), 412–77, by Whitehall, Chatman, Stein and Ransom; and by the articles and discussions in the Indiana University Conference on Style held in 1958 (see Sebeok 1960). A thorough discussion of most issues considered relevant at this time is to be found in Chatman 1965; and most of the important articles are to be found in Chatman and Levin 1967, Freeman 1970 and Gross 1966. In this chapter, references to articles will where possible refer to these volumes, using the conventions 'in Freeman, 14', etc.
2 An apparently physicalist sense of metre may be found in Shapiro and Beum 1965: 63, or Fussell 1965: 5.
3 For representative statements on the point, see Chatman 1965: 103ff., Wimsatt and Beardsley (in Chatman and Levin, 95–6), Fowler (in Freeman, 348) and Jakobson (in Sebeok, 366–7). (One must, I think, disregard Jakobson's loosely-phrased comment, on p. 364 of Sebeok, that the metre that underlies the structure of poetic lines is *not* 'an abstract, theoretical scheme'. The context suggests that he is using the adjectives in a derogatory sense of 'abstruse'.)

sense? The various possible interpretations of the term 'abstraction' are well represented in this literature, but the word itself is not, as far as I am aware, ever defined. There is, for instance a fairly widespread interpretation in terms of 'regularization' or 'normativeness'. Metre is a 'normative fact' to Wimsatt and Beardsley (in Chatman & Levin 92), and almost the same words are used by Lotz (in Sebeok, 207) and Hollander (in Sebeok, 402-3, cf. 302), amongst others. This use of 'normative' is not too clear, but it seems to mean that metre is the underlying principle governing the formal characteristics of the poetic text in some regular way.[4] It is objected to by some—for instance, by Chatman, who prefers to see metrical analysis as 'the process of summing the scansions of all intelligible recitations', and who thus sees metre as 'a consensus, not a normative formulation' (*op. cit.*, 105). Alternatively, one may see metrical abstraction in a general sense of theoretical construct (as Hrushovski, in Sebeok, 179); as idealization (Whitehall, in Sebeok, 201); as mental construct of the author (as Chatman, in Sebeok, 158) or of the reader/native speaker also (Beaver, in Freeman, 445); as perceptual effect (Thompson, in Freeman, 342); as potentiality (Chatman, in Sebeok, 158); as derivable solely from poetic performance (Wells, in Sebeok, 199) or requiring additional knowledge (Beaver, in Freeman, 439); as linguistic systematization involving only phonology (as most people) or phonology plus grammar and lexis (Fowler, in Freeman, 348) or this plus non-linguistic events (as Jakobson, in Sebeok, 365, 367); or defined explicitly with reference to a particular linguistic framework (such as that of Trager and Smith, as in Epstein and Hawkes 1959) or linguistic theory (as in the generative concept of metrical 'competence', seen in Halle and Kayser (in Freeman, 367) and in Freeman's own work in this volume, 481). Doubtless one could make further discriminations, if there were any purpose to be gained by doing so.[5] Agreement over any one interpretation of 'abstraction', however, does not necessarily produce an agreed definition of metre. One has still to consider whether the normative role, for instance, of metre is aesthetic in function, or structural, or both. Or again, if a text displays deviations from some postulated norm, are the deviations to be considered as distinct from the poem's metre, or are they part of it in some way? As Bateson put it, in an editorial postscript to Hawkes (1962b), 'I want a definition of metre that includes the *discordia* as well as the *concordia*' (423). This is one position: if it is taken, then how much deviation, or 'license' is to be permitted? As Halle and Kayser

---

4 This point may be more readily appreciated through the idea of divergence from a norm, which is a major theme of structuralist metrics. Expectancies are established, which may be broken at specific points to produce effects. 'Ordinarily the audience knows the pattern, or the poet makes his pattern known to the audience by repeating it clearly in his language as the poem begins' (Thompson, in Freeman, 340). 'Poets seem to adopt strict forms and meters *in order that* they may proceed to violate the normal or canonical "we" of that form or meter' (Hollander, in Sebeok, 403).

5 I am not of course suggesting that the labels in the previous sentence are in any way a satisfactory summary of the theoretical position of any of the scholars cited at any one time. I simply want to indicate the widely different emphases which may emerge from a single term.

say, we want a 'principled basis' to explain the fact that only certain devia-tions are tolerated and not others (in Freeman, 371). When a set of definitions are systematically examined and such questions asked, it is clear that a defini-tion of metre has to do with a great deal more than talk solely of abstraction.

Distinguishing the notion of an underlying system from its actualization in any discussion of metre is however crucial. As Morris Halle puts it (1970: 64), it is fundamental 'to bring out the distinction between the *meter* of a poem, which is a sequential pattern of abstract entities, and the *mapping* or *actualiz-ation* of this meter by concrete sequences of words, syllables, or sounds that make up the lines of the poem'. (Cf. Freeman (in Freeman, 489).) The terms of the definition of metre must be independent of the terms used to define its actualization; hence any definition which introduces a term like 'stress' or 'prominence' (and most definitions do) is confusing levels of abstraction, and should be avoided. I would accordingly define metre as the hierarchic system of continuous recurrent non-segmental phonological equivalences which con-stitute the organizing principle of a poetic text. The idiosyncrasy of this defin-ition will emerge in due course, but I would make a few comments by way of clarification here and now. First, hierarchy refers to the taxonomic relationship operating between the notions of 'text', 'stanza', 'line', 'foot' and 'syllable', as manifested phonologically; in my account, as we shall see, only text, line and syllable are obligatory members of the hierarchy. 'Continuous', secondly, refers to the fact that a metrical pattern, defined at a particular level in the hierarchy, is not interrupted, except insofar as a set of permitted deviations from a norm of equivalences may be recognized. Thirdly, concerning the definition's restriction to phonology: if a more general view was required, e.g. allowing syntactic or lexical recurrence, one could substitute the term 'lin-guistic' for 'non-segmental phonological' here. But on this point, I agree with Wimsatt and Beardsley (in Chatman and Levin, 103), who argue that 'To get a meter, some other kind of equality has to be added to the succession of syntactic entities. . . . The meter . . . is some kind of more minute recurrence.'

We may now move on to the question of actualization. What expounds the equivalences referred to in the definition? Here too we find an area of apparent agreement in the linguistics literature. Here it is said that English metre uses the syllable as its primitive unit of measurement, and stress as parameter of contrast.[6] This is the traditional view, and on the whole the linguists do not

6 It is a pity that the linguistic discussion concentrates so much on English to the exclusion of other languages. The absence of any regular reference to the detailed discussion and analyses of the Russian and Czech metrical literature (see below, p. 114) is particularly unfortunate. Over-concentration on a single language inevitably leads to premature generalizations, and these abound in metrics. In the absence of any large-scale typological work, statements such as 'the iambic measure is particularly suited to English', which are common, are largely meaningless. The prematurity of such state-ments is reflected in the naivety of rhythmic typologies in general, e.g. the distinction between syllable-timed and stress-timed languages, cited by Pike, Abercrombie and others, which is very much a simplification, and misleading in the sense that it tends to blind one to the existence of languages which manifest rhythmicality of both kinds, or

depart from it. It stays remarkably uncriticized, in fact—perhaps because of the way in which stress was lauded as a 'better' explanation of metre than quantity, in the traditional debate. There is considerable discussion about how many degrees of stress are required in metrical analysis, as one might expect for this period of linguistic history; but the nature of stress itself seems largely to be taken for granted. Apart from a detailed discussion in Chatman's *Theory of meter*, there is little attempt to define what is involved; and as every author uses the term, agreement is sometimes more apparent than real. All the different approaches to stress, familiar from the general phonetics literature, are to be found here—physical, physiological and auditory views, and senses which seem to be based on combinations of criteria under these headings (cf. Crystal 1969a: 113ff.). Particularly confusing (in view of the care most phoneticians take to keep the terms apart) is the loose interchangeability of the terms 'stress' and 'accent'. For instance, Wimsatt and Beardsley say, 'for our discussion of English meters, stress is the thing', and then immediately refer to 'stress or accent' (in Chatman and Levin, 103). Another common confusion is between 'stress' and the more general notion of prominence. Since the work of Fry (e.g. 1958) and others, the complexity of prominence variation in language has been abundantly clear, with pitch, duration, and other factors being involved as well as loudness; but all too often one finds authors using the notion of prominence (e.g. in the definition of 'ictus'), equating this with variations in stress, and equating this with variation in loudness.[7] Fortunately a considerable measure of agreement is imposed upon the use of the term by the majority of authors' using the Trager/Smith framework of analysis. Here, as is well known, stress is viewed phonemically as an independent variable from pitch and juncture, based on perceptual variations in degrees of loudness (Trager and Smith 1951: 35–6). In other work using the concept of stress, also, there is usually no incompatibility in the approach taken with a view of stress seen in terms of loudness. For such reasons, then, it seems fair to assume that when metrists talk of stress, they are referring to a pitch-independent variable of which the primary perceptual correlate is loudness; and it is such a view of

of a totally different kind (cf. Mitchell's (1969: 156) review of Abercrombie 1967). Similarly, why should there be only a triadic typology of metrical systems, viz. quantity v. tone v. stress (cf. Jakobson, in Sebeok, 361; Lotz, in Sebeok, 140)? Systems involving other variables, or combinations of these variables, are perfectly conceivable, and probably common (e.g. Anglo-Saxon, Welsh).

7 The notion of 'metrical stress', as most authors use the term, illustrates this confusion. It is sometimes used to refer to syllables whose prominence is primarily due to loudness, sometimes to those where pitch is the primary perceptual correlate. More subtly, one should note the way in which the fairly general notion of syllabic prominence is oriented towards stress through the use of a terminology of 'weight', e.g. in Lotz (in Sebeok, 203): 'The only thing that matters in English meter is the differentiation between the two types of syllables: the heavier and the lighter.' Fowler is very clear about the need to define prominence generally (1968: 300): 'A prominent syllable may be so by reason of any or all of . . . quality of the syllabic vowel, length, stress, pitch'; but even he cites examples of 'metrical stress' where it is difficult to see how the contrastivity involved could not primarily involve pitch.

stress as the only important factor in English metre which I shall take as the basis for discussion in the rest of this paper.

One of the irritating things about published versions of conferences is that they never put discussants' comments in phonetic transcription. The tone of voice of many an interjection, accordingly, remains no more than an intriguing possibility. At the Indiana Conference on Style, Voegelin's comment, I feel, is particularly intriguing: 'I don't want to introduce a new topic, but I do have a question: I miss a discussion of intonation patterns' (in Sebeok, 203). So do I. Indeed, I miss a discussion of the relevance or otherwise of the whole range of prosodic and paralinguistic features of language in relation to metre.[8] On the whole, apart from a few worthy exceptions which I shall discuss below, intonation is dismissed as being irrelevant to the discussion, without any reason being given, e.g. Lotz (in Sebeok, 138), 'intonation patterns are not metrically relevant in English', and also Wimsatt and Beardsley (in Chatman and Levin, 93), Wells (in Sebeok, 198–9), and Hollander (in Sebeok, 203). Or again, 'Intonation in English is a variant feature [i.e. not relevant for the metric structure]; we can have a line with any intonation pattern and the line remains metrically the same' (Lotz, in Sebeok, 203).

It is not difficult, in retrospect, to see why stress was emphasized so much, and intonation discounted in this way. The label 'stress' had a long and revered metrical history, and to analyse metre was for many people to trace a historical tradition (cf. Hollander's comment on this point, in Chatman and Levin, 125); the fact that the one label obscured a multitude of senses and ignored other linguistic factors was not appreciated. Or again, a common gloss for intonation was 'speech melody'; but musical notions were too close for many metrists' comfort to the traditional view of quantitative metrics, which was often presented in a quasi-musical format. But by far the most important reason lay in the uncritical acceptance of the Trager/Smith framework of analysis, which gave prior treatment to stress, and relegated many aspects of intonation to the extra-linguistic darkness of metalinguistics. It is important not to underestimate the influence of this framework on other disciplines. Within linguistics, we know, their approach is no longer in vogue, and it has been severely criticized.[9] But

8 There is some discussion of features other than stress and intonation (which I shall discuss separately below), usually in the context of performance. See for instance Fowler 1968: 318–20; Chatman 1957: 252–3 and 1965: 185–6; and Levin 1962: 368. H. L. Smith (1959: 68), rather ambiguously, talks of English metre 'drawing on' paralinguistic features. He refers to pause and drawl features, and after emphasizing that 'stress is not the whole story' (70), he goes on to say, 'The necessary placing of terminal junctures contributes both to meter and to rhythm as do the required occurrences of pitch phonemes within intonation patterns' (74). But 'contributes' and 'required' need to be amplified before we can interpret this sentence. (Against this, however, one should note Hawkes's (1962a: 39n.) reference to an unpublished paper of Smith's, where apparently 'paralinguistic pause' was not considered part of prosody, but of performance.)

9 Cf. above, p. 59. I do not mean to imply, of course, that the neglect of intonation is *solely* due to the Trager/Smith approach. The neglect is more widespread: Abercrombie, for example, does not mention intonation in his discussion of line-end

in such other fields as anthropology, psychiatry and semiotics, it is still widely used (see Sebeok *et al.* 1964), and its phonological approach is still the basis of such widely-used teaching handbooks as Gleason (1961) and Hockett (1958). It was this model which provided the first really systematic attempt to apply linguistic ideas to metrical analysis, and it was accordingly used with an authority and definitiveness which certainly Trager and Smith themselves never claimed it possessed. As usual, the disciples were more dogmatic than the discoverers. Thus there was continual reference in the late 1950s and early 1960s by literary scholars to the approach of 'the linguists'. Repeatedly, scholars outline the Trager/Smith system and then apply it to the analysis of some piece of text (the best-known example being the book by Epstein and Hawkes (1959). The various assumptions about four levels of stress, pitch and so on, are consistently referred to as 'facts' by many (e.g. Hawkes 1962a: 36ff.), instead of what they are, hypotheses. A few writers, it is true, seem to be aware that the Trager/Smith model is precisely that, an artefact—and, moreover, one whose theoretical presuppositions had not been questioned—but not many. For instance, McLoughlin, replying to an article by Chatman in the *Quarterly Journal of Speech* (1958: 176), points out that this system should not be taken for granted; a similar point is made by Pace (1961: 413n.), and Chatman himself hints at the point (in Sebeok, 205): 'I also do not believe that intonation is relevant to English metrics, at least not in terms of the present analysis of English which separates stress and intonation as different phonemic entities.' But on the whole these comments do not attract attention, and remain unamplified. And as a result, the stress phoneme principle, with its associated problems (e.g. which phoneme should be assigned to which syllable), became the sole focus of phonologists' attention.

The main objection I had to the metre-as-stress approach when I first read this literature was to its dogmatic tone. The question demanding to be answered is Why? On what grounds, other than tradition, has stress been singled out from the other phonological features of verse and been identified with metre? What experimental evidence is there to justify the priority of stress in this way? None has been provided; the assumption is axiomatic. Even Lotz, for instance, in his valuable article on metric typology, while accepting that in principle any prosodic feature can be used in a metrical system, denies all but stress to English (in Sebeok, 138), but gives no reasons. Or again, he argues (*ibid.*, 204) that a well-established metrical scheme must be present before intonation can be called into play, as a modifying factor. But on what grounds was intonation excluded from the metrical scheme in the first place? None are given. Or, as a third example, Whitehall points out that 'higher pitches usually occur at points of primary stress and reinforce the stress peaks in both the metrical and isochronous line even as they help to cut the line into its syntactical segments' (1956: 419). But if this is so, then why was stress singled out at the expense of pitch in the first place?

markers (1965: 25). But the majority of linguistic metrical discussions adopt the Trager/Smith model, at least for the purposes of argument.

It seems to me that there are both general and practical grounds for adopting an alternative approach, in which intonation is considered a constitutive factor in English metre (or, indeed, metre in general). I shall discuss some empirical evidence bearing on the point below. Here, I should simply like to note that such an approach is likely to provide a much more integrated theory of poetic form. Any account of metre in terms of syllabification and stress alone is bound to lead to the recognition of two formal categories of poetry—a distinction difficult to maintain on semantic or critical grounds, and usually not sought. So-called 'free verse', for instance, will have to be defined in some such way as 'poems which have no consistent metrical scheme' (thus says Hrushovski, in Sebeok, 183; cf. Thompson, in Freeman, 342). If, however, one can show that features of intonation (or some other factor) are in common to both 'standard' versification and the more 'esoteric' kinds,[10] and are organized in such a way that they satisfy a general definition of metre (see below), then such unilluminating dichotomies might be avoided. In other words, instead of an analysis of

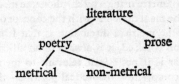

we have

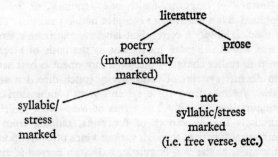

Taking a fairly simple-minded view of poetry (e.g. the material collected in our library shelves under that heading), the latter model is more powerful because it accounts for more of what we want to call poetry. As Halle and Kayser state (in

10 Free verse is suggested as being based on intonation and pause by Jakobson, in fact, in Sebeok, 360. A detailed presentation of this position is to be found in Mukařovský 1933. He analyses cases of free verse in French, Czech and German, and claims that in each the same principle of rhythmic organization manifests itself: 'une intonation spéciale, caractérisée surtout par une formule mélodique très marquée, à la fin de chaque vers; le canevas rythmique y est donné rien que par cette intonation' (155).

Freeman, 369ff.), metrical theory must account in a principled way for most
lines of poetry. It may not be possible to develop an absolutely clear distinction
between poetry and prose using a definition of metre as the only criterion (cf.
Lotz's notion of metre as the 'distinctive characteristic' of verse, in Sebeok,
135); but if we have a criterion which will handle most cases, then the 'metrical
grammar' we set up can be left to determine the status of the unclear cases.[11]
Hammond, referring to the problem of free verse (in Sebeok, 207) says: 'If
we could find a formula based on some general principle of equivalence in
poetry, we might arrive at a broader vision of our subject.' My suggestion is that
this general principle is primarily intonational in character.

Of course, it depends what one means by intonation. This is yet another
term which is rarely defined in the metrical literature, and when it is, it is sometimes given a very specific sense (e.g. pitch variation only), and sometimes a
more general sense.[12] Moreover, one would want to avoid the highly restrictive
account of intonation, as presented by Trager and Smith, for instance, as their
description is inadequate in many respects (see Chapter 2): it would indeed be difficult to develop an account of metre using a pitch-phoneme model of intonation,
as I shall argue below. But the main difficulty with the concept of intonation with
which we are presented in the metrical discussion is that it is an oversimplification. Whenever intonation is raised, it is always in an all-or-none way. Is it
a feature of performance, or is it not? Is it relevant to metre, or not? The
possibility of there being a compromise theoretical position—that some aspects
of intonation may be relevant and others not—does not seem to have been
raised. But it is surely time we moved away from the simplistic position that
intonation is a single 'feature' of language, which one 'acquires', or 'makes
errors in' (see p. 11). Intonation is a much more complex notion than this. The
term, as it is generally used, is simply a convenient label summarizing a large
variety of formal patterns which use pitch movement as the basis of identification. As I have argued in earlier chapters, the pitch movement is best seen
as being organized into distinct systems of contrastivity (pitch-direction and
pitch-range, in particular); features from these systems work combinatorially
to produce specific configurations (described in terms of tone-units, tonicity
etc.); and the configurations have a variety of functions, ranging from a
centrally linguistic grammatical function, through various kinds of conventional
attitudinal and social function, to the non-linguistic, indexical, person-identifying features.[13] The various features, and combinations of features, display a
clear hierarchical structure, as has often been pointed out (e.g. by Halliday

11 The reason for the difficulty of making a clear distinction is discussed below, p. 123.
As De Groot pointed out, the discussion is sometimes blurred by people assuming that
the opposition poetry : prose is parallel to that of poetic : prosaic, which is by no means
the case. Prose can be poetic, and poetry prosaic, but poetry cannot be prose, and vice
versa. (Cf. De Groot 1968: 534.) What makes a theoretical distinction unclear are the
perceptual difficulties involved in rating the amount of equivalence between the various
units of a poetic text.
12 Cf. Chatman's definition as 'an amalgam of stress, pitch, and juncture' (1956: 422).
13 The term 'indexical' is used by Laver (1968) and taken up by Lyons (1972).

(1967: 12ff.), Pike (1963), Jakobson, in Sebeok, 374). What has not so often been pointed out is that the features of intonation are not equivalent in terms of the amount of linguistic contrastivity (or 'valeur') they expound. Elsewhere, experimental evidence has been presented to suggest that tone-unit boundaries, nuclear tone placement (tonicity) and tone-type (falls, rises etc.), along with other features, are graded in the amount of contrastivity they expound (Quirk & Crystal 1966). This view of the various features of intonation in terms of 'graded contrastivity' is part of a more general model of non-segmental phonology as a whole in terms of a scale of linguistic contrastivity. It is discussed at some length in Crystal 1969a (129ff.):

Some non-segmental features have a very high degree of internal patterning and contrastivity, similar to the segmental contrasts and duality implicit in the rest of language; others are substantially less discrete in their definition and less systemic in their function, being much closer to the range of completely non-linguistic vocal effects. . . . At the 'most linguistic' extreme [of the scale] would be placed those prosodic features of utterance, describable in terms of closed systems of contrasts, which are relatively easily integrated with other aspects of linguistic structure, particularly grammar, and which are very frequent in connected speech. . . . At the other, 'least linguistic' end would be placed those paralinguistic features of utterance which seem to have little potential for entering into systemic relationships, which have relatively little integrability with other aspects of language structure, are very infrequent in connected speech, and are much less obviously shared, conventional features of articulation, being more frequently confusable with voice-quality or physiological vocal reflexes than any other non-segmental features. . . .

A concept of graded contrastivity in non-segmental phonology, and particularly in intonation, is of considerable relevance to metrical analysis, as it permits us to recognize that different non-segmental features make a varying contribution to the metrical identity of a text: it does not force us to assume that all intonational features, say, are equally important from the metrical point of view. Some intonational features seem to have a central, obligatory role to play (see below, p. 120); others have a negligible role, from the viewpoint of establishing the underlying phonological system of a text, and would seem to be needed solely in relation to a description of performance.[14] The question of how and

14 Such features (e.g. the pitch-height of unstressed syllables, or the direction of syllable movement in the 'tail' of a tone-unit), along with various paralinguistic features (such as tremulousness, resonance) are sometimes cited as performance features in this way; but of course it does not follow that all intonational contrasts operate in the same way.
Brief references to the possibility that indices of metricality might best be seen as organized in terms of a scale have been made, e.g. by Lynch (1953: 211–24), who refers to a 'scale of relative values', and distinguishes between metrical stress, syntactic stress (which subsumes certain intonational features), and 'prominence due to repetitive utterance' (reduplications, such as alliteration). Pace (1961: 418) also argues that 'the search for a norm requires a weighting of rhythmic significance', and suggests that stress and terminal junctures are always significant, pitch is sometimes significant, and plus juncture occasionally is. His approach seems correct in principle, though I would disagree with his ordering. Cf. further Jakobson's view that there are both obligatory and highly probable features of metre (in Sebeok, 361).

where to draw the boundary-line now raises itself, and this is a separate topic which I shall discuss further below: at this point, I simply want to emphasize that when I argue for intonational relevance in metrics, I am not committing myself to seeing all aspects of intonation as having a metrical role to play, or all aspects as having the same metrical role.

In passing, one should note that the 'graded contrastivity' concept is quite contrary to the phonemic approach of Trager and Smith, of course. There, the assumption is that the various non-segmental variables can be analysed into two clearly distinct types: phonemic (microlinguistic) and non-phonemic, which in terms of their analysis are non-linguistic (strictly, metalinguistic). There is no gradation. For me, 'the principle of linguistic significance in phonetic difference' (Wimsatt and Beardsley, in Chatman and Levin, 93) covers far more than phonemic contrastivity. Tempo variations, for instance, are meaningful, though they are not as linguistically central as, say, pitch-range variations. Attitudes to this point are unclear in the literature, because of a failure to be specific about what is idiosyncratic in an utterance (i.e. linguistically unimportant) as opposed to what is shared. There is a tendency to suggest that anything which is not clearly phonemic is 'merely' expressive or individual. For example, Wimsatt and Beardsley (*ibid.*, 98) refer to dragging and clipping syllables as individual features which sound 'odd, affected, or funny'. But these features *can* 'change the meaning', and there *can* be a 'public pattern' for them (as they put it).

It would be a rash man who attempted to argue for such a change of view as that presented here without looking for *some* support in the previous literature. There are in fact a number of comments suggesting that intonation may be metrically relevant—though little discussion of what intonation is, how it correlates with stress, or how fundamental the relationship of intonation to metre might be. It is always a relief to find Jakobson on one's side, for instance. 'No linguistic property in the verse design should be disregarded. Thus, for example, it would be an unfortunate mistake to deny the constitutive value of intonation in English meters' and 'Whatever is the reciter's way of reading, the intonational constraint of the poem remains valid' (in Sebeok, 365). *Why* it would be a mistake, and what such terms as 'constitutive' and 'constraint' actually mean, is not explained further in his paper; but from his other writings one can see what he means,[15] and of course Jakobson here is but one voice among many in the Russian formalist metrical tradition and in Prague School metrics. In the work of Mukařovský (1933), Tomaševskij, Kuryłowicz (1966: 164), Kopczyńska and Pszczolowska (1961) and others, we can see a firm insistence on the relevance of intonation for metrical analysis. For example, Zhirmunski (1966: 232) says, 'The complicated rhythmic pattern specific to accentual verse is based on the peculiarities of [this] intonation'; and Mukařovský, using Karcevski's view of intonation as a basis, argues at length for an

15 For instance, his discussion of certain types of line in Slavic verse in terms of intonation, in 'Slavic epic verse', *Selected writings of Roman Jakobson IV* (The Hague, 1966), 414–68; see esp. pp. 454–5.

underlying recurrent intonational pattern in a poem (cf. p. 107 above), and concludes at one point (155), 'C'est donc du côté de l'intonation qu'il faudra diriger nos recherches.' De Groot maintains this also, but without amplification: 'It should not . . . be overlooked that some indications that may seem to concern recitation are actually a matter of linguistic form, especially so-called emphasis, indicated, e.g. by underlining or italicizing, which is actually a matter of sentence intonation' (1968: 537)[16] More recently, Taglicht (1969) has argued that intonation is metrically relevant in English, illustrating his views with reference to the function of tone-unit boundaries and tonic syllables in segmenting and distributing prominence within utterances; and Faure (1970: 35—see especially Ch. 6) argues that intonation is the 'decisive element' in metre. (For other brief mentions of the relevance of pitch, see Hendren (1961: 305), Pace (1961: 415, 416) and Leech (1969: 125).)

As I have suggested, intonation is rather ignored than argued against in the metrical literature: the papers cited in the previous paragraph are exceptional in the extent of their references. I know of only one place where a case is made against bringing intonation in, and that is in the otherwise very useful article by Fowler, 'What is metrical analysis?' (1968). Here (298), he argues that intonation can make little contribution. 'Suprasegmentals do not uniquely specify syntactic structures in a systematic way, are not reliably diagnostic for syntax except in some very broad distinctions, and are manifestly not indispensable (written language exists) . . . conscious reference may be made to intonation contours in rare cases where context is inadequate', and he refers to Hultzén for support. But Fowler is considerably underestimating the structural significance of intonation in speech (or in poetry, for that matter) when he adopts this position. I would not wish to interpret the notion of intonation as grammatically as, say, Halliday (1967) does, for reasons explained in Crystal 1969b, but there is still far more to the grammatical function of intonation than Fowler seems to allow. Not only sentences (which he accepts), but also clauses and elements of clause structure regularly have their boundaries indicated by intonational criteria; and where the elements of clause structure are at all complex, intonation may be used to demarcate elements of group structure (especially in the noun phrase) (see Chapter 1). There are many more cases of intonationally-resolved ambiguities in syntactic structure than he seems prepared to accept, particularly using tonicity and tone-type contrasts: there are relatively few syntactic structures involved, certainly, but each potential ambiguity is of very frequent occurrence in the language, and problems of an intonational kind thus turn up often in everyday speech. It is in any case premature to minimize the role of intonation in these matters, in view of the fact that one of the areas of grammatical structure most likely to display intonation as an ambiguity-resolving factor, namely discourse structure, has hardly been studied at all from this point of view at the present time. Also, broadening one's

16 In passing, he notes (542) that 'An interesting problem is whether in English verse the metre . . . has features of pitch. Unpublished experiments by Buiskool [which I have not seen] seem to point in this direction.'

view of intonation to include both pitch-range contrasts over polysyllabic stretches of utterance and tone-unit sequences allows a much larger number of possible contrasts of a grammatical nature to be expounded under this heading, e.g. the marking of parenthetic utterance by means of pitch-range. The necessity of punctuation in writing, or other graphic cues (such as colour or type-size), in order to avoid ambiguity, seems to dispose of Fowler's parenthesis. Moreover, in his examples, and in his citing of Hultzén, Fowler seems to be confusing the very different prosodic systems of two varieties, conversation and poetry. Whatever the intonation system of poetry turns out to be, it is undoubtedly far more complex, and permits far more discriminations in meaning, than does conversational language, about which most of the intonation analysts, such as Hultzén, talk. If the criterion of relevance for intonation to be considered metrical is the extent to which it can disambiguate utterances, as Fowler suggests (298),[17] then one can readily argue that in poetic performance it is used in precisely this way most of the time. Where one places the tonic syllables, where the tone-unit boundaries, where the subordinate and superordinate contours, and so on—all these decisions, and others like them, are being continuously made in the performance of a text, and a large number of these decisions *must* be made if intelligibility is to be retained and the 'correct' meaning expounded. The potential semantic discriminations found in a poetic text are extremely fine—much more so than in conversational English, where subtle contrasts and nuances are on the whole absent or ignored—and the role of intonation as disambiguator thus becomes more crucial (as for instance in the way in which it is used to distribute emphasis in a line via the placement of tonic syllables, or lines in a verse, by the use of polysyllabic pitch-range contrasts). On any criterion of disambiguation, then, intonational contrasts cannot sensibly be excluded from metre. The reasoning that is applied to show that stress is relevant metrically seems to apply equally to intonation.[18]

But perhaps the most important reason for the over-concentration on stress at the expense of intonation lies in the syllabic orientation of traditional and

17 This criterion is widely accepted, though little understood. The question of the nature of poetic ambiguity in metre has been given some discussion, for instance by Chatman (in 1957, and in Sebeok, 206); but in the absence of any clear theory of meaning within which to work (which would provide criteria for synonymy, specify the relationship between cognitive and affective meaning, and so on), the discussion is largely unintelligible or vacuous, e.g. Wells' comment (in Sebeok, 198), that 'the inadequacy of any inadequate record [of a poem] lies in its being ambiguous', adding that it may happen that 'the ambiguities . . . are resolved by appeal to the general principles of the language'.

18 Fowler seems to accept this point in practice, but does not make the appropriate theoretical generalization. Three of his four rules which enable one to discover the distribution of ictus and non-ictus in an English poem require intonation to work, most of the time (see 300–02) and, as he says, the notion of intonation contour is 'central' to any discussion of caesura and enjambement (302). In the light of such statements, I find it difficult to understand why he wants to play down the role of intonation so much. But perhaps I am being confused by his terminology: a crucial term in his paper, ictus, is not defined, and his use of the term 'contour' is oddly restricted (311).

linguistic metrics. As many of the quotations used so far in this paper make clear, the syllable is considered to be the primitive unit of measurement for metre, in terms of which a typology of combinatorial possibilities (i.e. the types of feet) is developed. As stress is generally considered to be a feature of syllables (or words, cf. the notion of 'lexical stress'), whereas intonation is a feature of phrases or sentences, the two notions of syllable and stress are viewed, accordingly, as complementing each other. A clear statement to this effect is found in Chatman (1965: 58). 'Stress is a fundamental property of full vowel mono-syllabic words, and of one syllable in polysyllabic words, which in any environment, accented or not, can serve to distinguish them from what are otherwise homonyms. . . . Accent, on the other hand, is the prominence which one syllable in an uttered phrase receives when it is the center of the pitch contour.'[19] But while a distinction between stress and accent is undoubtedly of value, one wonders why the 'center of the pitch contour' has been recognized in the theory, whereas the contour as such has not. W. Haas has made the point, with which I agree, that the recognition of a contour in one step 'cannot be avoided' (1957: 155–6). The historical reason for the omission I have suggested above: intonation patterns are not given primary significance in the model used by linguists, nor are units of measurement larger than the syllable.[20] In other words, this seems to be a clear case of a particular model of analysis being retained and applied further than its insights warrant. It is always difficult, of course, to throw away a carefully-constructed model that has proved illuminating; but one must also be aware that models are little more than analogues whose validity is temporary, and evaluated very largely by the nature of the insights they provide (see further, Chao 1962). In the present case, I am suggesting that the stress phoneme/syllable unit model has far outlived its usefulness in metrics; and in attempting to apply it to the analysis of *all* categories of poetry, one very quickly comes up against many problems, which are solely by-products of weaknesses in the model. It has a value in the partial description of some kinds of poetry still, of course: I do not in fact want to throw away this model altogether. But in order to handle problems such as free verse, there seems little point (and a great deal of harm) in trying to force them into a syllable stress/foot framework (into which they will not go) when one could be trying to devise a fresh model which will handle these categories of poetry as well as the traditional ones equally readily. And the model I am suggesting uses the notion of line,

19 The influence of Bolinger (1958) is acknowledged. See p. 6 above.
20 Cf. Lotz (in Sebeok, 138). To be fair, there have been a few references to the possibility of alternative models. The most well-developed of these is Nist's view that word-groups are 'the basic building blocks of English rhythm' (see Nist 1964: 76). The basic unit of metrical structure is a *cadence* which (for English) is 'that rhythmical pattern of accentual collocation which occurs between the actualized major junctures' (77). Stress is still the basic phenomenon involved, however, though he does mention that pitch and 'prolongation' are important. Cf. also Bateson's views, fn. 21 below; and for early (and very forceful) opposition to a foot/stress model, and support of a view in terms of 'accent-groups' ('tones', 'accents', 'cadences', and 'extensions'), see Skeat 1898: 484.

expounded by reference to the intonation contour and related prosodic features, as its basic element.

The line, indeed, has been suggested before, though the concept is not usually defined. To De Groot (1968), in fact, the *only* formal distinction between prose and poetry is that 'a poem has a strong continuous correspondence between successive series of words, called "verses" or "lines" '.[21] Now while I agree with De Groot's general emphasis here, I would not wish to argue that the line is the *only* criterion of difference—there are other phonological distinctions operating too. But it is in my view the fundamental criterion. The concept of line should not be viewed as the incidental result of a process of syllable arithemtic. A much more illuminating and powerful model is obtained if the line is taken as a primitive unit of metrical theory—in De Groot's terms, as an initial Gestalt, whose total 'weight' is the unit of measurement for poetic organization.[22] What, then, is a line? I take it as axiomatic that any metrical theory must be capable of accounting for oral poetry, on the one hand, as well as poetry seen from the viewpoint of the hearer (as opposed to the author, or reader): in other words, a purely visual notion of line must be avoided. 'Line' for me, therefore, is a term for a unit in a phonological hierarchy. It enters into larger phonological units (e.g. verses), and consists of smaller units (e.g. syllable prominences). While it may conceivably be given some definition in segmental (e.g. syllabic) terms, in my view its identifying exponence is non-segmental, a *prosodic contour*. A prosodic contour is a perceptual unit primarily organized using variation in pitch, but sometimes using phonological features from any of the other non-segmental systems in the language (loudness, tempo, rhythmicality, pause, paralinguistic). This definition is not particularly helpful unless the rules governing the nature of the pitch-variation and the use of these 'other' features are made explicit; but it at least indicates clearly the direction in which I want the argument to go. On this basis, a number of more specific hypotheses can be formulated, e.g. that the (non-segmental) phonological system of poetry is different from that of prose; that the normal exponence of a line is a single tone-unit; that this is usually sufficient to provide unambiguous indication of line-end boundary; and that deviations from this are tolerated only if other non-segmental features are introduced to act as structural markers. What evidence, then, can be brought to bear?

Originally, my impressions of the intonational organization of poetry were based solely on what seemed to me to be the most obvious features of individual performances. There have been few experiments to try to go beyond this.[23]

21 Bateson also suggests 'that this basic pattern [i.e. the underlying metre] is not to be found in the foot but in the line—and that the necessary element which is the distinguishing characteristic of English verse . . . is the *total stress-weight of the line*' (see his editorial postscript to Hawkes in *Essays in criticism* 13 (1963), 200–01).

22 The term 'Gestalt' is also used by Mukařovský (1933), who warns against the distortions of an atomistic approach, and asks, 'Quel est le facteur essentiel et indispensable pour la formation de la forme-figure ('Gestalt') du vers?' (154).

23 The few suggestions for experiments which were made in the early period of metrical discussion (e.g. Osgood's in Sebeok, 208–9) do not seem to have been followed up.

I have, accordingly, tried to obtain some experimental information bearing on the above hypotheses. Presumably, any such evidence would have both productive and perceptual aspects, and so far I have concentrated on the former. Two experiments have been carried out. In the first, a number of poetic texts were read by people of different degrees of experience: professional actors/readers; colleagues and students from my own department, none of whom had had experience of reading aloud; and non-academic friends. No speakers who had speech markedly deviant from RP were included. The texts were: Wordworth's lines composed upon Westminster Bridge, the first verse of Gray's Elegy, an extract from T. S. Eliot's *Prufrock*, and an extract from the same author's *The Dry Salvages*. The first two were chosen because they displayed a fairly simple metrical pattern (in the traditional sense), and would be relatively familiar to most readers, thus not presenting much in the way of a textual problem; the Eliot for the opposite reason.[24] Another reason for including some straightforward pieces of text right at the beginning was that there seemed to be little point in developing a theory which might be able to handle the difficult cases if it were unable to handle the easy ones (the majority)! Each speaker was asked to read aloud the extracts; the order of presentation of the extracts was varied. The readings were then transcribed using the system of analysis outlined elsewhere (1969a). I also had the readings rated for 'success' by colleagues in the English Department using a 7-point scale, the poles being identified, without further definition, as 'good reading' v. 'bad reading'. The tentative generalizations below derive from an analysis of readings which were allocated to all but the bottom three points.

In a second productive test, there were two groups of informants. One group was presented with two texts of poems that they did not know, and were asked to read them aloud. The other group was presented with the same texts set out as prose. A conventionally metrical text and a sample of free verse were chosen. Then the reverse procedure followed. A piece of prose was read as such, and then set out as poetry, with the line-endings corresponding to grammatical boundaries, various possible lineations being tried.[25] The results were transcribed, as above.

The analysis produced the following information, valid for all texts used.

(i) All lines were coterminous with tone-unit boundaries, with the sole exception

24 Specifically, the first extract was the passage beginning, 'The yellow fog. . . .' and ending '. . . and fell asleep', eight lines in all; the second was the extract beginning 'The sea howl . . .' and ending '. . . Clangs the bell', 22 lines in all.
25 One example being (from the opening chapter of A. Warren and R. Wellek's *Theory of literature* (London 1949)):

> We must first make a distinction
> Between literature and literary study.
> The two are distinct activities:
> One is creative, an art;
> The other, if not precisely a science,
> Is a species of knowledge or of learning.

of cases that would traditionally be called 'enjambement'.[26] Also, additional polysyllabic prosodic features (such as allegro, low pitch-range, forte) tended not to overlap line-endings, again with the exception of enjambement.

(ii) 80 per cent of all lines consisted of a single tone-unit. A number of lines contained more than a single nuclear tone, but in almost all cases, a subordinate tonal relationship existed (see p. 27 above). In other words, one of the nuclear movements is maximally prominent within a line, this usually occurring (as has often been pointed out) towards the beginning or towards the end of the line. In the few cases where a subordinate relationship did not seem to be operating—i.e. the various tone-units involved seemed to be of equal status (e.g. before and after what is traditionally termed a caesura)—usually a prosodic cohesion is superimposed upon the line, for example by saying the line using a descending pitch movement, as in

|Ships| |towers| |domes| |theatres| 'and |temples lie|'

(' ' indicate crescendo, = a drawled syllable) or by introducing a marked rhythmic movement into the line.[27]

26 In these cases, the prosodic contour is interrupted, and completed on the next line (cf. Leech 1969: 125). But not all cases of enjambement are like this. Often a tone-unit boundary does occur, and the enjambement is signalled by the use of other non-segmental features which 'override' it, particularly common being an increase in tempo and loudness as the end of the run-on line approaches, and the use of a 'holding' articulation which anticipates the initial segment at the beginning of the next line (cf. Crystal 1969a: 153–4). For example, in the line 'This City now doth, like a garment, wear/The beauty. . .', the end of the line displays increasing crescendo, the phrase 'like a garment' is spoken allegro, and the closure for the initial 'th' of 'the' is heard immediately after the vowel of 'wear', and held for an instant. There is far more to enjambement even than this, though. In some cases in the second test, cases of enjambement occurred where there was little clear prosodic cue, but line-ending was correctly assigned by the majority of informants. In such cases, the informants may have been relying on their knowledge of the previous structure of the poem, i.e. awareness of line-units which did display clear boundaries. But this does not always work. The one case of utter confusion in my informants was caused by the penultimate line of the extract from *The Dry Salvages*, which was put in largely to see what would happen here:

> And the ground swell, that is and was from the beginning,
> Clangs
> The bell.

Even with pauses before and after 'clangs', extra loudness, and drawled 'ng', the dominant tendency was to see the last two lines as one.
27 Rhythm, interestingly, was not an unambiguous criterion of poeticality in the above tests. Both prose and poetry versions in Test 2 retained certain features of any rhythmic identity the text had. The readers did not try to make the prose text scan, when it was printed as poetry; and the traditionally metrical poetic text retained its rhythm to a great extent in its prose 'counterpart'. Rhythm seems to be a prosodic feature which can be introduced into a poetic line for a particular effect. Many categories of poetry do make regular use of it, in addition to intonation; but it cannot be taken as a primitive, because (a) it is inessential to many kinds of poetry, as we have seen, and (b) it is much

(iii) Within lines, points of prominence were usually pitch-contrastive, not loudness-contrastive. Readers read the Wordsworth text using between 35 and 40 prominent syllables; of these, about 90 per cent in any reading would be tonic, or use marked features of syllabic pitch-range, viz. perceptible stepping up or down in relation to the previous syllable (see Crystal 1969a: 144–6).

(iv) The range of features needed to transcribe the contrasts made use of in the poetry readings was much greater than that needed for prose. For example, in earlier work on conversation, spoken prose etc. (Crystal and Davy 1969), it was found necessary to postulate but one degree of pitch-height on either side of a norm, in order to account for any semantic contrastivity expounded by pitch-range, e.g. the notion of parenthesis. A transcription of 'low', 'high' and 'zero' was adequate to identify any contrast, and degrees of height or depth were disregarded, on the grounds that they did not correspond to meaning differences which could be established with any kind of consistency or agreement by judges. In the transcription of the poetic texts, however, it proved easy to distinguish two degrees of pitch-height on either side of a norm, and sometimes the need for a third suggested itself.[28] Similarly, it proved essential to allow a further degree of pause contrastivity into the poetry readings than was necessary for prose, and also there was the need to develop a much more refined rhythmic typology (to handle the perceptual phenomena associated with traditional typologies of trochaic rhythm etc., which are generally not found in prose). Further, much greater use was made of fixed configurational patterns, extending over more than one line, and identifying larger units in the phonological hierarchy, such as the couplet or the verse.[29] A greater range of subordinate tone-unit configurations was needed, for instance, and there was considerable use made of complex patterns of loudness, pitch-range and speed. I have not gone into this in any depth, but for instance there seems to be a fairly rigid constraint on the patterns of ascending and descending pitch-range used in a four-line verse, such as those of Gray's Elegy, the lower height of the final line being the most obvious feature. Or, to take a clear, if trivial example, prosodic constraints on a limerick are probably total—a 'prosodic idiom'.

In other words, in poetry we seem to be dealing with a distinct non-segmental phonological system, and the range of distinctiveness is best described by

---

less able to maintain a structural function (segmentation etc.) than intonation. (Interestingly, the better the reader, the more likely he is to *avoid* making his reading rhythmically 'pat'.)

28 This was particularly so in those readings by the professional actors, on the whole those which were rated highest for 'success'. Incidentally, it seems to be the case that better performance correlates with better 'control' of pitch features, especially tonal subordination. But the extent to which metrical and other training can condition performance ability is very little understood at the moment. Conversely, a reading is much more likely to be labelled pejoratively, e.g. 'doggerel', when there is minimal use of pitch variation, the prominence in the line being expounded by stress alone.

29 Cf. the 'tonal paragraphs' of radio newsreaders. Hrushovski (in Sebeok, 189) points to such patterns in the organization of Whitman's lines.

reference to the unit line. I do not know the full extent of the systemic differences from prose. For some of the more subtle prosodic contrasts, especially those which seem to have a solely aesthetic function (such as variations in the pitch-height of unstressed syllables), it proved impossible to get judges to agree on a transcription.[30] But it is not necessary to have a complete inventory of systemic differences before concluding that the systems are different. And in fact, for the prosodic features which seem to be centrally diagnostic, such as tone-unit, tonicity, nuclear tone-type, syllabic pitch-range type and placement, and polysyllabic pitch-range type, there was almost total consistency in identification. These are some of the features which seem to contribute obligatorily to the identification of a prosodic contour ('line'), and which, I would claim, are thus constitutive factors in metre; but they are probably not the whole story.[31]

(v) However, to define line as a prosodic contour is not to achieve an account of metre. The line is simply the unit which can be used for establishing equivalences, and the specific contour identifying any one line could in principle occur in prose reading too. In metre, however, the equivalences themselves are the thing, whereas in prose these are very few, they are not continuous (cf. my requirement above, p. 107), and if they do occur, they depend on syntactic parallelism (e.g. rhetorical climaxes in political speeches). There are, of course, various ways in which equivalences can be established; at any given level of abstraction, we may talk in particular in terms of length (e.g. number of tone-units, or of tonic syllables, or of non-tonic pitch prominences) or structure (the distribution of non-segmental contrastivity within any one unit, e.g. the struc-

30 This underlines the need for caution in presenting *any* results in this area. Assertions that there is a 'contrast' between two phonetic effects need to be supported by statements about meaning (e.g. in terms of distribution of emphasis, segmentation, syntactic disambiguation, presuppositions, as well as the more familiar though vaguer questions of aesthetic 'appropriateness' of sound to sense); and obtaining consistent agreement here is naturally going to depend very much on the auditory and critical sensitivity of the judges (and oneself). I have not controlled for this in the present investigation, apart from having all my judges literary critics. Teachers of drama would doubtless impose finer discriminations, for instance, as would phoneticians. At least the intuitions of my judges will stand a better chance of corresponding with those of the majority of people who have contributed to the literature on this topic, and who will thus be judging the claims of the present chapter!

31 The most striking omission from the discussion so far is the extent to which the distribution of phonological features in relation to syntactic and lexical structure differs between poetry and prose. It undoubtedly does, but demonstrating this would require a separate project. Mukařovský, for instance, thought this point so important that he made it a cornerstone of his view of the poetry/prose distinction, the difference lying in 'le déplacement de la scission mélodique dans le vers par rapport a la prose' (157). He accepts that there is also a difference in phonological system; for him, this is the superimposition in poetry of two intonational schemes, one indicating semantic structure, one indicating rhythmic structure. Cf. 163: 'Il semble donc possible de définir la différence entre le rythme du vers et celui de la prose en disant que, en prose rythmée, il n'y a pas de superimposition de deux schemes mélodiques virtuels, mais seulement une suite de segments mélodiques à peu près égaux, donnés par l'intonation de la phrase.'

ture of the tone-unit, or of the head of the tone-unit). Total equivalence would
occur if lines were isomorphic in respect of all non-segmental features operating
at all levels in the hierarchy—a state of affairs unlikely to occur unless there were
considerable grammatical and lexical similarities also. And what this suggests,
of course, is that equivalence is not an all-or-none thing, but rather a scale,
running from the theoretical maximum just indicated to the theoretical minimum of non-isomorphism at any level (cf. the scale of metricality mentioned
on p. 113). Developing a set of criteria for establishing degrees of equivalence
on this scale, quantifying the amount of recurrence, and, in addition, determining whether or not there is a natural boundary between levels of perceptual
equivalence which are consistently labelled 'poetry' and those labelled 'prose'—
these are tasks for future psycholinguistic research (if my general hypothesis
is considered sufficiently acceptable to warrant the effort). Perceptual and
semantic judgments about metrical identity of different lines would have to be
correlated with controlled variations introduced into the formal features of these
lines; and this will be no small task, in view of the multivariate combinatorial
possibilities. I have hardly begun to do any experimental work along these
lines. I have not, for instance, tried to develop a technique for assigning equivalence values for lines. Impressionistically, one can see great similarities between
lines, at least in relation to the more general kinds of prosodic contrast (e.g.
tone-unit structure). And the contrast with prose is very marked. In prose, or
conversation, it is rare to find two tone-units with identical patterns of pitch-
prominence, but in poetry of *all* kinds, this is fairly normal, i.e. the prosodic
structure of any one line permits the correct prediction of the structure of the
majority of other lines in the text. I *have* however looked briefly at the extent
to which judges seem to 'expect' equivalence, independent of visual stimuli, by
asking people to assign line-boundaries to readings of texts, some poetry, some
prose, which they did not know. A set of short texts, some very regular (in the
traditional sense), some not, and some prose, were presented to informants. In
the poetic texts, there were segmental indications of line-ends (rhyme etc.).
The readings used had all previously been rated as successful. Firstly, one
group of informants was asked to judge whether the texts were poetry or prose.
As one might expect, in view of the characteristics of poetry noted above, this
was done with complete accuracy (though this does not prove very much, in the
absence of precise controls over the nature of the prosodic variability in the
readings); but it is nonetheless an interesting result, in view of the absence of
visual stimuli. A separate group was given the same texts, told that *all* were
poetry, and asked to assign line-endings. Two things emerged here. There
were hardly any errors in the poetic texts, whereas there was considerable
inconsistency among judges for the prose texts. What errors there were in the
poetry, naturally enough, clustered around the problem of the abnormally
short lines in the free verse. What is interesting, from my present point of view,
is that when a short line is missed, it is 'made up' into a long line of approxi-
mately the same length as those established previously as a prosodic norm. For
example, the sequence

And under the oppression of the silent fog
The tolling bell
Measures time not our time, rung by the unhurried
Ground swell, a time
Older than the time of chronometers, . . .

was usually transcribed as

And under the oppression of the silent fog
The tolling bell measures time not our time,
Rung by the unhurried ground swell,
A time older than the time of chronometers, . . .

This kind of response might be taken as direct evidence of a psychological expectation of equivalence; but in view of the fact that some judges did get the lineation right—presumably responding to the prosodic cues which (to my ear, at least) were certainly present in each line—I would not want to make too much of this point.

In conclusion, I should emphasize that my notion of 'prosodic contour' is not merely a terminological switch from, say, 'syllable stress pattern'. By using this term, I have tried to suggest a whole new orientation, an emphasis away from the atomistic approach of the syllable and stress phoneme—or at least (anticipating the unsympathetic), towards a different kind of atomistic approach! The term relates to a model where the basic units are perceptually and semantically meaningful, where gradation in linguistic contrastivity is an important factor, and where the notion of exponence is sufficiently flexible to permit the same abstract metrical result to be achieved in a variety of different ways. In other words, I hope that the principles which are suggested here are sufficiently general to allow us to talk of a text as being *organized* as poetry. There remain many questions—not the least being the interrelation of the phonological patterns noted with syntax. But until an adequately-unpreconceived account of the whole range of non-segmental phonological contrastivity is developed, so that we are aware of the resources which are available for the metre-constructor to tap (cf. Householder, Stankiewicz, in Sebeok, 346 and 204–5 respectively), it is unlikely that much progress will be made on this front, or any convincing typology developed.

8
Non-segmental phonology in language acquisition

Research into children's language has been almost exclusively segmental and verbal, dealing (in the early part of this century) with such matters as form-class frequency and distribution, lexical development, sentence length and phonemic inventory, and (more recently) with the system of rules which needs to be specified to account for syntactic behaviour, and the definition of semantic relations which are postulated as underlying actual utterances. The nature and development of non-segmental phenomena in children is generally ignored or referred to haphazardly, as I shall be illustrating below; and the purpose of the present chapter is therefore to argue that close account must be taken of these phenomena (particularly in relation to the study of language development in the first year), to discuss the work of those scholars who have recently begun to investigate this area, and to indicate directions for future research.

It is not difficult to see why so little attention has been paid to this area within language-acquisition studies—the reasons are largely the same as those underlying the neglect of prosodic and paralinguistic study of adult language. There is the difficulty of obtaining natural and reliable samples of speech for analysis, and of relating non-segmental characteristics to other (and even less studied) communication modalities, such as the visual and tactile—a particular problem for the study of young children, where kinesic and other cues regularly need to be taken into account for any complete interpretation of non-segmental patterns. There is the absence of a generally-agreed system of classification and transcription of the range of non-segmental contrasts: if we have had to wait until the 1960s for any remotely adequate attempts at characterizing the adult terminal behaviour involved (I exclude Pike's (1944) study from this statement, which is quite exceptional for the detail of its suggestions), then it is hardly surprising that, in the last decade, little application of these descriptions to children has been forthcoming; and next to no attempt has been made to carry out independent studies of children to avoid the danger of imposing too much adult non-segmental structure on early utterances (e.g. talking about a ten-month-old in terms of four phonemic pitch-levels). Also, there is the problem of the disproportionate amount of time it takes to process non-segmental data—checking transcriptions, carrying out acoustic analyses, and so on—which severely limits the practicability of reliable longitudinal and cross-cultural studies.

There are signs, however, that there is a growing interest on the part of many disciplines in the various aspects and implications of non-segmental studies. Most of the recent papers are to be found in journals of linguistics, social or developmental psychology, audiology, pediatrics and speech pathology. But multi-disciplinary interest in an area brings with it a host of methodological and theoretical problems, not the least of which is difficulty over terminology; and any review of the subject must begin with these, as a perspective for clear thinking.

Various terminological discrepancies emerge. One inconsistency (which may be dealt with briefly) arises in relation to the general labels used for the early stages of child development—'neonate', 'infant', 'baby', and so on. Definitions are almost entirely absent from the early literature, or use bizarre criteria (e.g. infancy as the period of childhood preceding erect posture, or the frequently cited 'etymological' definition, where 'infant' was considered to be, literally, a child 'without speech'). In recent work, a phrase such as 'infant vocalization' is sometimes used to exclude 'neonate vocalization'; sometimes it includes it; sometimes the term 'neonate' is not used at all, or is replaced by such phrases as 'the young infant'; and so on. In this chapter, *neonate* refers to a child up to and including its fourth week of life after birth; *infant* refers to a child up to and including its 104th week. One may thus talk of the neonatal period of infancy, etc.

Secondly, there are a large number of labels used to refer to the utterance of the child at any time within this period (or later)—'cry', 'vocalization', 'utterance', 'verbal gesture', 'non-verbal articulation', 'expressive noise', 'oral behaviour', 'phonation', etc. Terms from this range are hardly ever defined, and, as far as I can judge, are only occasionally used in the same way by different authors, one of the main problems being that the same label may be given a different value at different periods of development. The first two terms just listed provide the best examples of potential ambiguity. 'Cry' is regularly used to refer to *any* vocal sound pattern produced by an infant over the first few weeks of life; but some researchers state or imply a more restricted definition. For example, Blanton (1917) considers crying primarily in terms of vowel quality; for Lynip (1951: 245), the 'elements' of crying are 'intonation, cadence, rhythm, attack, duration'; Ostwald (1963: 40) requires cry to have 'tonal quality' as distinct from the 'rasp' which characterizes 'scream'. Eisenson *et al.* (1963) make a distinction between undifferentiated (reflex) crying, up to two months, differentiated crying, where there is some evidence for specific response patterns, and the subsequent stages of babbling, lallation and echolalia, from whose definition crying is specifically excluded. A cry signal, for Wasz-Höckert *et al.* (see, e.g., 1968: 9) consists of 'the total vocalization occurring during a single expiration or inspiration'. Crying as a label is not used at all by some authors, e.g. Jespersen (1922), who talks instead of 'screaming'. The term 'vocalization', similarly, is sometimes defined in an all-inclusive way, to include all patterns of sound produced by a child within a period of study; but it is sometimes narrowed in application, for example to mean a short series of cry signals indicative of a given function (Wasz-Höckert *et al.* 1968); to mean simply babbling (Dittrichová and Lapáčková 1964); to exclude grunts, cooing and singing tone (McCarthy 1946: 482–3); to include the later non-cry sounds of lalling, gurgling, laughing etc. (Wolff 1969), or to exclude them (Wasz-

Höckert *et al.* 1963); to refer to segmental features only, or to non-segmental features only, or to some combination, or to some subset of either (e.g. Ostwald (1963) restricts vocalization to sounds made when the mouth is wide, i.e. excluding lallation and babbling in his terms); to subsume both prelinguistic and linguistic utterances, or to include the former only; and so on. One could illustrate similarly from other widely-used labels; 'nonverbal' sometimes means non-vocal, sometimes non-segmental, and sometimes a specific non-segmental parameter (e.g. 'tonal' in Brooks *et al.* 1969); the 'sounds' of infant vocalization are sometimes viewed as segmental (e.g. Irwin 1941; Irwin & Chen 1943), sometimes non-segmental.

'Intonation' is another term about which there is considerable disagreement, and which, consequently, needs to be carefully watched. It is normally defined by reference to some form of pitch contrastivity alone, but other kinds of prominence are sometimes permitted under this heading, e.g. the concepts of 'accent' and 'rhythm', which require reference to loudness and duration. Tonkova-Yampolskaya (1968) uses the term to refer to the general characteristics of vocalizations; and in discussion of whispered speech in children, the term 'intonation' is sometimes used, though here the articulatory correlates are primarily pharyngeal (cf. Trim 1970). A good example of confusion arising from inconsistent definition is in the debate over Braine's theory of contextual generalization (1963; see 1967: 248). Here, intonation is 'defined' as 'the variety of phenomena referred to by such terms as stress, pitch, juncture, off-glide, on-glide, contour, superfix, intonation-pattern'. It is also 'certain specifiable properties of the speech signal', and sometimes stress is distinguished (e.g. primary stress is isolated in his fifth experiment, cf. also 1967: 278n.). In their reply, however, Bever *et al.* (1965; see 1967: 270) talk about 'pause, stress and intonation'—which makes one wonder exactly what phenomena are being discussed at all. Moreover, to define intonation in terms of pitch does not necessarily end the question, as the term 'pitch' itself has of course been taken in a number of ways, e.g. referring to fundamental frequency, to the auditory correlate of fundamental frequency, to the auditory correlate of not only fundamental frequency but also other dimensions of the speech signal (e.g. amplitude, length), and even to something separate from intonation (cf. Lewis 1936: 15), who talks of 'sounds, intonation and pitch', or Fitchen's distinction between intonation and 'tone' (1931: 325)). And Brown (1958: 202–3) implies that intonation is not a 'phonetic feature' at all. A similar range of viewpoints could be collected for many of the other central descriptive terms in this field.

In this chapter, I shall be using the term *vocalization* to refer to *any* vocal sound-pattern produced by an infant for which there is no evidence of language-specific contrastivity, i.e. the sound patterns are biologically controlled. This thus subsumes cries, cooing and other such 'pre-linguistic' phenomena, in both their segmental and non-segmental aspects. As soon as there is evidence of phonological contrastivity, segmental phonation becomes describable in terms of phonemes, distinctive features, vowels, consonants etc.; and non-segmental phonation in terms of prosodic features, intonation, paralinguistic features, etc., as described in earlier chapters. There will inevitably be occasions when it is not possible to decide clearly on the status of a sound pattern; but this of course does not invalidate the distinction. It follows from these definitions, then, that one may not consistently talk about the 'intonation of vocalizations', for this would be to use a linguistic term in a non-linguistic domain. Some alternative term (e.g. 'melody') would have to be used to refer to the auditory correlate of fundamental frequency variation in vocalization.

A crucial area of terminological difficulty in this field concerns the functional labels used in describing infant vocalization and the developing non-segmental system. Labels such as 'hunger', 'pain', 'pleasure', and the like for vocalizations are all perfectly familiar, and almost all investigators use them. But there are dangers in their uncritical use, as has been shown in connection with adult work (Kramer 1963; Crystal 1969a: Ch. 7). On the one hand, the type of descriptive label used is generally ambiguous; on the other, the interpretation which is the basis of the label need not be based on the vocalization characteristics at all. The first point may be illustrated by such terms as 'harsh', 'rasp', 'scream' and 'rhythmic', which are extremely difficult to define in any precise way; and of course terms with a strong psychological element, such as 'satisfied' or 'exhausted', are even more so. The same would apply to terms used to describe adults' responses to vocalizations (cf. Ostwald 1963). The early literature in particular makes frequent use of undefined 'imitation-labels', where the absence of controls makes it impossible to determine whether terms such as 'satisfied' are being used consistently by authors, whether there is any overlap between 'satisfied' and 'pleased', and so on (cf. Shirley 1933). More recently, there is the study by Barnard *et al.* (1961) of anxiety and verbal behaviour, where one of their 'stylistic dimensions' of description is called *voice*, for which there are three variables: 'degree of animation', comprising a 50-point scale from 'complete animation' to 'complete monotone'; 'direction of animation', comprising a 40-point scale from 'strongly positive' (i.e. 'happy', 'cheerful', 'excited' voices) to 'strongly negative' (i.e. 'sad', 'frightened', 'depressed' voices); and 'forcefulness', comprising a 30-point scale from 'forceful and persuasive' through 'undistinguished' to 'mousy'. Here, too, careful controls on the labels used are needed to render the methodology of the experiment sound.

In the majority of studies, also, it was the case that investigators believed they were identifying vocalization-types on the basis of the physical characteristics of the vocalizations, whereas in fact they were doing this on the basis of the co-occurring situational information and reading in adult situational values. This point applies *a fortiori* to the semantic description of the intonation patterns of the early years. McCarthy (1929) is aware of the problem, and Sherman (1927) has provided some evidence bearing on the issue. In this very detailed study, it was shown that judges were unable to identify vocalization types (hunger, fear, anger, pain) when the situational stimulus which gave rise to them was hidden from the judges, and concluded that knowledge of the stimulus is the deciding factor in applying a name to a vocalization-type. To be convincing, of course, this experiment needs an independent assessment of the labels used, to determine, for instance, whether the semantic generality of a label would cause it to be preferred to other labels as a matter of course, or whether individual judges had preferences for certain labels. Wasz-Höckert *et al.* (1964a, b), for example, found that when response categories were provided in advance in a multiple-choice text (and not thought up by the judges) the degree of success in identifying the various vocalizations investigated (birth, hunger, pain, pleasure) did have some correlation with the experience of the persons tested—the more experienced the judges in child-contact, the better the identification. Partanen *et al.* (1967) showed that experienced adults could discriminate three out of four cries produced by various pathological and normal children, the discrimination ability of the judges improving with practice. (See also Michelsson *et al.* 1965; Valanne *et al.* 1967.)

Determining the causes of a vocalization, as Wolff makes very clear, is an extremely complex task. One cannot assume that in any given situation what the adult sees as the obvious causative factor is in fact the real cause. This is particularly evident in the case of the so-called 'hunger cry' (cf. Wolff 1969: 82): 'The term is misleading if it implies a causal relation between hunger and a particular pattern of crying, since this is simply a "basic" pattern to which the infant sooner or later reverts from other crying, and it has no unique causal relation to hunger.' A pain cry, for example, begins distinctively, but after a while it takes on the characteristics of the basic pattern—in other words, while in one sense a pain cry is a response to a pain stimulus, it is not the case that the characteristics of the cry are constant throughout. The tendency to read meanings into infant vocalizations is common and unfortunate, particularly in the early reports on the subject; and while much less work has been done on the developing intonation system than on vocalizations, it is clear that there has been little attempt to impose careful controls on semantic labels here either. This is even more disturbing in view of the fact that as intonation contours do not have single 'meanings', but can be used in a variety of semantic contexts, the likelihood of misleading labelling is correspondingly much increased.

Underlying much of the terminological confusion, then, is a lack of attention to the demands of an explicit methodology, and also an inadequate discussion of theoretical preliminaries. The term 'non-segmental' itself provides a good example. While there has been considerable discussion of the theoretical status of non-segmental features in linguistics, it is not common to see awareness of the issues in the preamble to research reports investigating non-segmental phenomena in children. Are non-segmental features clearly linguistic (in the same sense as phonemes are said to be), marginally linguistic, or non-linguistic? Are all non-segmental contrasts of comparable status, or do some features carry a greater contrastivity than others? To what extent can intonation be seen as a single system, and isolated from other prosodic features? Can the categories and results of linguistic models set up to account for adult language be used for children? There are many such questions, and many possible positions that can be taken up. A good example of this is the first question, as applied to the concept of intonation. The early handbooks and articles (e.g. Darwin

1877), whenever they talk of intonation, seem to mean no more than the general melodic impression obtained from listening to infant cries, though sometimes only those patterns which are clearly affective are meant. Most recent approaches give intonation a clearly linguistic status, i.e. seeing it as a component of a specific language-system, and thus to be kept distinct from vocalizations; but some linguists use the term with both a linguistic and a 'pre-linguistic' reference, e.g. Lieberman (1967: 46): 'At some point in the development of speech, intonation takes on a linguistic reference.' And depending on the theoretical position adopted, so a particular pitch pattern in a child's utterance will be analysed as linguistic by some, and as non- or extra-linguistic by others. Anyone who approached the study of early language development within a Trager–Smith framework, for instance, would find that he would have to call much of the semantic contrastivity which appears towards the end of the first year non-linguistic (e.g. some of the variations in rhythm and pitch-range which contribute to the child's 'tones of voice'), for the reasons explained in Chapter 2 (pp. 47ff.). Clearly, unless one is aware of the criteria which have been used in arriving at a description, comparative study becomes impossible, and quantitative analysis largely meaningless.

Any division of this field into areas of study is inevitably arbitrary, but it is convenient to recognize three main groupings: (1) early, 'pre-scientific' investigations, largely on the first year of life; (2) recent parametric analysis of vocalizations in young infants; (3) studies of non-segmental patterning in older children, especially in relation to syntax and social role. I shall briefly review each of these groupings before concluding with some comments about the direction of future research.

Early research

A survey of the early literature on language acquisition is still very much needed. There seems to be very little reference made to infant vocalization, apart from general remarks in the standard textbooks of child psychology, and a few impressionistic comments about vowel types and affective categories; and what there is is on the whole methodologically unsatisfactory. The early biographical accounts, for instance (e.g. Taine 1877; Darwin 1877; Humphreys 1880; Champneys 1881; Hall 1891; Lukens 1896; Shinn 1900; Schäfer 1922; Hoyer and Hoyer 1924; Löwenfeld 1927; see the surveys in McCarthy 1929, Lewis 1936, and the selection in Bar-Adon and Leopold 1971), always make some mention of vocalization, and provide some suggestion of a developmental pattern, and the level is certainly more sophisticated than the passing remarks of the philosophers in the centuries preceding,[1] but the material is more valuable for its stimulus to the study of verbal and grammatical patterns. So while acknowledging the pioneer status of these scholars, it is only right to say that the occasional insight is generally obscured by the unsystematic and scattered

1 For example, Kant's comment that 'the outcry that is heard from a child scarcely born has not the note of lamentation but aroused wrath'! This kind of comment was given short shrift by Tracy (1909: 128).

observations, the absence of anything which could be called a methodology, the vague descriptions, and the flights of fancy. For example, Taine (1877: 253), after commenting on the surprising flexibility of the child's 'twitter', says: 'I am persuaded that all the shades of emotion, wonder, joy, wilfulness and sadness are expressed by differences of tone: in this she equals or even surpasses a grown up person. If I compare her to animals, even to those most gifted in this respect (dog, parrot, singing-birds), I find that with a less extended gamut of sounds she far surpasses them in the delicacy and abundance of her expressive intonations.' Then there is Blanton's (1917) 'barnyard' theory of cries (as Irwin once put it (in his 1941 paper)), comparing infant vocalizations with those of quails, goats, pigs and wild cats, amongst others. And, as a third example, there is the theorizing of Darwin (1877: 293): 'before man used articulate language, he uttered notes in a true musical scale as does the anthropoid ape Hylobates'. (Cf. also Blanton's description of a colic cry in terms of a musical scale (1917: 458–9), and Fitchen (1931: 325).)

There is more description of a functional nature, but it is extremely vague, e.g. Darwin (1877: 293) mentions interrogatory and exclamatory cries, and a 'defiant whine of refusal'; Champneys (1881) is impressed by the variability of infants' vocalization, and cites three functional differences, which he labels loneliness and fright on awakening, hunger and pain. Blanton (1917: 458) distinguishes between cries due to hunger, noxious stimuli and fatigue, and gives a fairly detailed impressionistic description of the 'rhythm' of hunger cries. The occasional theoretical digression is usually obscure, important terms not being explicitly defined, e.g. Darwin (1877: 293):

I remark in my notes that the use of these intonations seemed to have arisen instinctively, and I regret that more observations were not made on this subject . . . the wants of an infant are at first made intelligible by instinctive cries, which after a time are modified in part unconsciously, and in part, as I believe, voluntarily as a means of communication,—by the unconscious expression of the features,—by gestures and in a marked manner by different intonations, . . .

The desirable emphasis of these remarks unfortunately does not help our understanding of them. Finally in this connection, it must be pointed out that much of the discussion of articulation at this early period was in the context of correcting errors of pronunciation (see Pike 1944; Crystal 1969a: Ch. 2, for references to elocutionary manuals etc.).

Overlapping with this early period of biographically-oriented investigation, there are the larger surveys of language development: Blanton (1917) in many respects anticipates the approach of Bridges (1932), Shirley (1933) and others— see McCarthy (1929) for a good review of this early literature, and also Lynip (1951: 249ff.), Lewis (1936), McCarthy (1946), Ingram (1971) and Weir (1966), the latter for some work in Czech. Bridges, for example, provides a much fuller account of progressive differentiation of affect than hitherto: out of an initial state of 'excitement' there develops a distinction between delight, distress and excitement by three months; distress divides into fear, disgust and anger by six months; elation and affection are added to delight by twelve months; jealousy, and a distinction between affection for adults and affection for other children are added by eighteen months; and joy appears around twenty-four months. The totally personal, partial, over-simple and impressionistic nature of this account is clearly indicated when one compares the claims of other surveys of functional development: compare for example Lewis's review of various accounts (1936), or McCarthy's survey (1946: 482–3), where it emerges that discomfort, pain and hunger are said to be differentiated by two months; pleasure develops in the four months following; eagerness at about five months; satisfaction between six and seven months; and recognition between seven and eight months. Many of the criticisms which can be levelled at this kind of work were made fairly early on by Irwin (1941: 248), who pointed to the poor sampling and very restricted data, the unsystematic research methods, the general absence of statistical techniques, the lack of observer-reliability tests, the poor, alphabetic system of transcription, and the premature interpretation of few observations. I would add to this the uncritical use of semantic labels, already noted.[2]

In many ways the major difficulty in interpreting the work of this early period (and indeed of much recent work too) is the extent to which the linguistic events are automatically categorized in terms originally defined for the study of the adult language. Now while an adult-oriented approach is probably unavoidable in dealing with the semantic labelling of contrasts, there being no direct method of encountering children's intuitions at this early stage (cf. McNeill 1966: 17–18; Wasz-Höckert *et al.* 1968: 4), it is highly undesirable to allow adult considerations to interfere at the phonological level of analysis and transcription. As far as possible, the child's utterance has to be described 'in its own terms', as some would say. The point has been appreciated for some time in the context of segmental phonology; but the attitude of Lynip (1951: 226) is quite exceptional in non-segmental studies:

It is totally impractical to try and express in adult sounds an utterance of an infant prior to his speech maturation. Infant utterances are not *like* any of the well defined values of adult language. They are produced differently and they are shaped differently, their relationships with adult sounds are at first only fortuitous. Infant sounds cannot be described except in terms of themselves. There is no International Phonetic Alphabet for the utterances of a baby.

What Lynip was objecting to was the general practice of referring to infant vocalizations in terms of the vowels and consonants of adult speech. Irwin and others had earlier on objected to the habit of using ordinary orthography to

2 There are of course exceptions. As early as 1906, attempts were being made using sound recording to establish mean neonatal crying-pitch (Flatau and Gutzman 1906). And then there is the systematic approach of Bühler (e.g. 1922: 79ff.), who places great emphasis on the 'musical devices of syntax' in the early development of language— the use of intonation to distinguish sentence-types and emotional ranges of expression— and insists on its theoretical relevance for syntactic analysis.

transcribe vowel values etc.; but they failed to realize that the substitution of a phonetic alphabet developed originally to transcribe the broad phonetic categories of adult languages did not get round the basic fallacy (see, for example, Irwin and Curry (1941), who analyse the 'vowel' sounds in infant vocalization to show that [ɪ ɛ æ] and [ʌ] are the most frequent units; or Irwin (1941), who talks in terms of 'phonemes').

The adult-based procedure is fallacious for two main reasons. First, it has been shown that any such analyses are inevitably skewed due to the influence of the phonological structure of the adult language, which leads one to interpret sound qualities in terms of the adult set of distinctive features, and to ignore qualities which are functionally irrelevant in the adult language (see for example Lotz *et al*. 1960). Second, while perceptual units of infant vocalization approximate to certain adult units in some cases, the physical configuration underlying these units is by no means similar. This point has become perfectly clear since the advent of spectrographic analysis. Even the spectrograms of an adult trying his hardest to imitate an infant show major differences (see Lynip 1951; Wolff 1969: 104, for examples; and cf. Denes 1966: 338). The formant structure is different, the nature of the onset and termination of a sound is different, the transitional features between sounds differ, and so on. Lynip suggests that even approximate equivalence to adult vowels or consonants is not achieved until the end of the first year. The general point is made again by Lenneberg (1967) who, after considering spectrographic characteristics, points out that one cannot call these features 'speech sounds', neither in functional terms nor in articulatory/acoustic terms: degrees of glottalization and labialization occur which are normally absent from adult articulations, and there is a generally erratic articulation and poor coordination between the various mechanisms. A more adult-like distribution of energy does not appear until the onset of 'cooing'. See McCarthy (1946: 478) and Sheppard and Lane (1968: 94–5) for further comment, and below for details of the physical characteristics of vocalization. Cinefluorographic and other techniques likewise show considerable differences (see Bosma and Fletcher 1961). Of course it may well be that non-segmental infant patterns do show a greater similarity to adult patterns than the above spectrographic analyses suggest for segmental features. Spectrograms after all do not generally display non-segmental features as clearly as segmental ones, particularly when high fundamentals are involved. Tonkova-Yampolskaya (1968) in fact argues that there is substantial similarity between adult and early child intonations. But until there is clear evidence on the point, the wisest course of action would seem to be to develop a frame of physical reference-qualities for auditory labels in child phonetics which is as independent as possible of those used in adult classificatory systems. If this is not done, the danger is that one may find oneself studying 'pseudo-continuities' between developmental stages, i.e. continuities which are solely a function of surface similarities in the transcriptional system, and which have no basis in the physical facts of utterance.

Apart from this, the early literature talks a great deal about the development of response to adult intonation contours, though unfortunately very little information about the adult intonations used is given. For example, Schäfer (1922) states that intonation plays a large part in determining the child's response to given sound-groups, and notes that the response is facilitated whenever an exaggerated intonation ('Ammenton') is used; also that in the earlier period, the child pays more attention to non-segmental than segmental patterns. Champneys (1881: 106) notes that his child was imitating intonation from about nine months: it 'distinctly imitated the intonation of the voice when any word or sentence was repeated in the same way several times' (cf. also Darwin 1877). Further evidence for the response of children to intonation is provided by Tappolet's (1907) informal experiment, in which he switched from French to German while retaining the same intonation, without this affecting the child's response. See also Delacroix (1934), Meumann (1903), Hoyer and Hoyer (1924), Löwenfeld (1927), Guillaume (1925), Stern and Stern (1928), Bühler (1930), and Bühler and Hetzer (1928) for general agreement that early discrimination of intonation is of major importance in language acquisition, and a few details of an empirical nature. Bühler (1930) claims that the average child reacts to a change in adult tone of voice by as early as two months, and most authors cite somewhere between two and four months.

Lewis (1936) reviews most of the early literature in this respect, and refers to intonation frequently throughout his book. The effect of an intonation pattern for him may be expressive or representational (115–16), the former being 'expressive of the speaker's affective state' (115), or, more precisely, contributing to the differentiation of expressive states (23); the latter occurring when the intonation 'pictures the situation', as a 'kind of onomatopœia', as when 'tick-tack' is spoken in time with a clock (115). It is important to study intonational function, he argues, as it continues its role beyond the stage of the first word (203): 'the closer imitation of intonational patterns fosters...the instrumental use of conventional language' (95). He provides his own general analysis of the situation, distinguishing three stages in the development of a child's response to a specific sound-group (115–16):

(1) At an early stage, the child shows discrimination, in a broad way, between different patterns of expression in intonation.
(2) When the total pattern—the phonetic form together with intonational form—is made effective by training, at first the intonational rather than the phonetic form dominates the child's response.
(3) Then the phonetic pattern becomes the dominant feature in evoking the specific response; but while the function of the intonational pattern may be considerably subordinated, it certainly does not vanish.

Lewis reports many cases of intonation being imitated (in terms of number of syllables and stress as well as pitch) by seven months (94–5), and makes the point that one must distinguish between the imitation of pitch *per se* and the imitation of a pitch pattern. He considers the former rare before two years (though cf. Wolff below, and Lewis himself reports a case of a series of tones being imitated before the end of the first year), the latter beginning around eight months. More recently, Benda (1967) has found an ability to imitate intonation in the babbling of an eight-month-old girl, there being a regular correlation between the intonation and the behavioural situation. Lieberman (1967: 44–6) shows that a child's absolute fundamental frequency-range varies in terms of the relative height of the voice of the parent. Wolff (1969: 104–5) states that a baby will tend to follow adult pitch to a certain extent as early as between one and two months, but points out that this is not so much 'imitation' in his view as 'an active "accommodation" of vocal patterns which are already at the infant's disposal' (105), though it is not entirely clear what 'accommodation' refers to here. Cf. further, Fry (1966: 188), Friedlander (1968) and the references to earlier literature in Ingram (1971), especially to Lukens (1896). Kaplan and Kaplan (1970) have produced a useful summary of stages of perceptual development relating to infant vocal behaviour, as part of a general hypothesis arguing for the continuity of linguistic development in children.

It is not clear to what extent one can rely on the observations of the early work: scholars on the whole seem to underestimate the difficulty of perception and complexity of intonational patterns, and much of the terminology of description (talk of 'melody', 'descending patterns' etc.) is vague. The main weakness in this work which makes it almost impossible to use for points of detail, however, is the absence of precise information about the characteristics of the adult intonational stimulus. The nature of the 'baby-talk' is obviously an important factor in assessing response, and has to be controlled; but hardly anyone provides an account of it in this literature. Because baby-talk is so distinctive, I feel many scholars have assumed it need not be described. But the scattered evidence available suggests that it is a much more complex phenomenon than people expect, and that different languages have different kinds of baby-talk. I have come across two specific studies. Ferguson (1964) investigates baby-talk in a number of languages: with reference to English, he cites the higher overall pitch, the preference for certain pitch-contours, and labialization. Kelkar (1964), under the heading of 'para-phonology', refers to the extended pitch-loudness characteristics, and the relatively slow and regular speed of baby-talk in Marathi, and mentions certain general vocal effects, such as pouting and palatalization; Ohnesorg (cited in Weir 1966) points to the over-articulation of intonation when adults speak to children, which he says the child tends to caricature. Ohnesorg also notes a frequency of rising tones in children's early intonation, which is presumably a reflection of the kind of adult speech used. This point was also noticed by Pike (1949), who was able to train a child to replace these by falling tones for a time.

It is thus quite clear that adult intonation patterns tend to be 'picked up' (to use a neutral phrase) by the child from an extremely early age, and responded to at the expense of other linguistic features of utterance. What is now needed is an investigation of the characteristics of adult prosodic features when talking to children. It seems essential that the adult patterns should be understood, and controlled in experimental work. On the whole, however, most of the research into development at this early period fails to take any notice of non-segmental patterns at all. If an attempt is being made to elicit a response from a baby—say, reaching—I have often noticed the investigator keeping up a relatively uncontrolled flow of chatter to the baby, with frequent baby-talk, even though this could disturb the results considerably. At least the possibility of disturbance needs to be determined, and the extent to which auditory stimulation can interfere with, say, a visual experiment, tested. Braine (1963; see 1967: 245) is one who is aware of the dangers of uncontrolled non-segmental patterns; in the course of his fifth experiment, for older children, he states that 'the experimenter was careful not to give voice or gestural cues which would guide the subject to the correct response'. Here I would have liked more detail as to how this was done; but the emphasis is nonetheless welcome.

Recent analysis of vocalization

From the early studies, then, it was clear that non-segmental patterning in general, and intonation in particular, seemed to be the earliest kind of linguistic structuring in the vocalization of the child, but there was little reliable normative information, and descriptive statements stayed couched in fairly general and impressionistic terms. This state of affairs, sadly, has shown little improvement in recent work, which on the whole has concentrated on determining the onset of language-specific patterning in vocalization, the 'where does language start?' question. Most observers have concluded that the most likely period for the emergence of such features in production is six to seven months (see below, p. 147 and also Fry 1966: 191; Kaplan and Kaplan 1970; Lenneberg 1967: 279; Menyuk 1971: 56ff.; Halliday1 974; Weir 1966, and other references there). There is some suggestion of an earlier emergence in some children e.g. Raffler Engel 1966, 1970, who posited two 'intonemes' at four months in her child, one being used for desiderative and one for deictic purposes); and Nakazima's (1966) spectrographic comparison of American and Japanese infants produced no detectable difference until as late as twelve months. So the matter is by no means totally settled, as the interesting discussion of the point in Huxley and Ingram (1971: 161–4) makes very clear, and relating emergence to such factors as socio-economic family background, sex, motor development and so on has hardly begun (but see below for some references).

What happens *after* the onset of non-segmental structuring is still an open question. There has been little attempt to trace systematically the order of acquisition of the different prosodic and paralinguistic features, to study the combinations in which they occur, or their distribution in relation to syntax and lexis during the second half of the first year and thereafter. Some of the theoretical and practical reasons for this have already been mentioned in this chapter; but with fresh interest in intonation and related matters being shown by theoreticians (see Chapter 1), and with developments in computational and acoustic techniques which reduce the processing-time of data, it is quite likely that progress, once it begins, will be rapid. On the face of it, there would seem to be two possible approaches. First, one might begin with some model of adult non-segmental behaviour, and do a 'reverse longitudinal study', progressively reducing the age-level of a sample, and noting the points at which the various features of the adult system cease to be used, or take on non-adult characteristics. This approach is obviously implicit in the observations of most of the scholars referred to in the preceding paragraph, but it does not seem to have been systematically tried, presumably because of the absence, until recently, of appropriate models of adult behaviour. The second approach is the reverse of this—to study the developing characteristics of infant vocalizations to the point where they begin to be modified by language-specific characteristics, and to continue in the normal longitudinal way. This approach seems the more promising, for there are some fairly clear experimental procedures which would accumulate objective evidence about language specificity, which would not be totally dependent on one's preoccupations about the form of the terminal non-segmental system or on assumptions about the semantic function of the various patterns. For example, one could carry out cross-cultural studies which would show divergence in vocalization characteristics after a certain age: if the six to seven month hypothesis is valid, then after this point spectrograms (or other displays) of, say, Welsh and English children should begin to show regular and quantifiable differences, which could in turn be correlated with auditory judgments of informants (e.g. about the Welsh-soundingness of the children) and physiological information about the development of articulatory settings (cf. Honikman 1964). Or one could establish emergent differences between normal and deaf children after this age in a similar way. But any research along these lines presupposes that the characteristics of the infant vocalization, which provides the yardstick against which the language-specific features can be plotted, has been adequately specified. Increasing interest, therefore, is being shown by linguists in the general research which has been taking place into infant vocalization. Not only do these studies provide a wealth of descriptive information about the physical characteristics of vocalizations in the first six months in terms which tie in remarkably well with those that the linguist will need to refer to, they also lay down methodological guidelines which researchers into the later months would be foolish to ignore. An awareness of ongoing research into early vocalization is thus in my opinion an indispensable perspective for any investigation of the onset and early development of non-segmental phenomena.

This research was only able to get under way once adequate techniques of recording, analysis and measurement had been devised—developments which took place largely in the 1940s and 1950s. Sound spectrographic techniques were of particular importance: they are referred to in detail in Lynip 1951, Murai 1960, Winitz 1960, Truby 1962, Tonkova-Yampolskaya 1962 (and cf. the 'intonograms' of her 1968 paper), Wasz-Höckert *et al.* 1968 and the subsequent work by this group reviewed below, Ostwald 1963 and other work by this group reviewed below, Landtman *et al.* 1964, Wolff 1969 and Lenneberg 1967. Other techniques have involved phonophotography (e.g. Fairbanks 1942), kymography (e.g. Dittrichová and Lapáčková 1964), roentgen and cine-fluorographic study (e.g. Bosma and Smith 1961; Bosma and Fletcher 1961);

and Fisichelli and Karelitz's panoramic sonic analyser (1966). Earlier technical devices are reviewed in McCarthy 1929: 636ff.

The most important outcome of recent research involving these techniques has undoubtedly been to specify the range of parameters needed in order to describe infant vocalizations as accurately and economically as possible, and to provide precise empirical data in these terms. Most of this work has used acoustic criteria of various kinds. Early on, Fairbanks (1942) studied the fundamental frequency of hunger cries from one to nine months, finding a variation from 63 to 2631 Hz, with a mean of 556, a large and rapid rise in central tendency during the first half of the period (373—one month, 415—two months, 485—three months, 585—four months), followed by a relatively stable, consistent high level. Other potentially relevant dimensions (e.g. intensity) were not studied, however. Tonkova-Yampolskaya (1962) made an acoustic analysis of spectrograms of 18 neonates in the first six days, distinguishing a number of formant areas and describing the variations in intensity displayed. Ostwald (1963: 40) refers to glottal attack, vowel quality, fundamental frequency, pitch-range, loudness, and 'rasp' in his description of neonate cry. Other results are reported in Truby 1960, Lenneberg 1967, Kurtz (see Ostwald 1963: 18), Lieberman 1967: 41, and, much earlier, Sherman 1927, for whom cries had to be characterized by reference to intensity, duration, and type of onset and termination, as well as by tone-quality. The most precise general description of early vocalization is Wolff 1969: 82ff. For him, the 'basic' cry is rhythmical, with a fundamental frequency of between 250 and 450 Hz for either sex (concentrating between 350 and 400). A typical sequence consists of a cry (0·6 sec mean duration) followed by a silence (0·2 sec m.d.), then a short inspiratory whistle (0·1 or 0·2 sec) at a higher fundamental frequency, and then a rest period (usually shorter than the first silence). There is a slight rise in frequency at the beginning which tapers off towards the end to produce a visual 'gentle arc' on a spectrogram. Wolff also distinguishes in the first week an 'angry' cry, which has the same temporal pattern, but excess air produces a turbulence and a distinctive 'distortion' (cf. Truby's 'paraphonation' (1962)). Also in this period there is a 'pain' cry: this has a sudden onset of loud crying with no preliminary moaning, an initial long cry (4·2 sec m.d.), an extended period of breath holding in expiration (7 sec), an inspiratory gasp, and then further expiratory cries which settle down into the basic temporal pattern. In addition Wolff notes a frustration cry, which starts like pain cries but has no breath-holding, and the inspiratory whistle seems perceptually to follow the initial cry (rather than to precede the second cry); and also a cry indicating gastro-intestinal discomfort, which has a higher average frequency (450–550 Hz), is non-rhythmical and interspersed with shrill squeaks. In the third week of life he notes a 'faking' cry (where the baby is trying to get attention): this has a low pitch and intensity, a long, drawn-out 'moaning' quality (98), a more complex spectrographic shape, especially at the cry terminal (where the direction of the pitch may rise, as opposed to the characteristic falling pattern of earlier cries), and the occurrence of fundamental frequency shifts during the cry. At about this time, also, he notes the occurrence of the first non-cry vocalizations (e.g. gurgling), but finds it impossible to identify the point of transition on the spectrogram, though they are readily identifiable subjectively (98). And in his concluding section, Wolff points out that there are a number of transitional types of cry which do not fit clearly into his major threefold classification (of 'basic', 'angry' and 'pain'), and considers any final typology to be premature (86). It is clear from this work, and also that of Wasz-Höckert *et al.* (see below), that vocalization is not random, undifferentiated and non-expressive, as many earlier scholars had claimed.

The parametric identification of vocalization types, and the analysis of the conditions evoking vocalization can largely be described with reference to four groups of scholars. Firstly, there is a prolific group working largely in Scandinavia: see the introductory volume by Wasz-Höckert *et al.* (1968), which contains a recording, and associated bibliography under Bosma, Lind, Michelsson, Partanen, Valanne, Vuorenkoski and Wasz-Höckert. They have established a set of parameters, using spectrographic analysis, which they claim will adequately categorize and distinguish a number of types of normal and abnormal (pathological) vocalizations, especially of pain cries; and the results of their most recent procedures using this method are certainly impressive, as the following summary (taken from Vuorenkoski *et al.* 1971) indicates:

In order to get practical determinations of normality or degree of normality in the pain cry of an individual newborn and young infant, a new rating system, *cry score*, has been constructed. Sound spectrographic analyses were made of the pain cries obtained from 240 infants ranging in age from 0 days to 8 months. The values in 13 different cry characteristics were transformed into ratings between 0 and 4. Cry score, the sum total of the different ratings, was designated abnormal when it exceeded 3. The correspondence between diagnosis and cry score was very good: both the sensitivity and the specificity of the score exceeded 90% for groups of 120 normal infants and 120 infants in various types of serious pathological conditions and diseases. . . . Repeated measurements of cry score in three pathological cases during the newborn period showed an interesting possibility to follow the clinical development in certain rapidly changing conditions. (74)

The parameters specified in the early work (e.g. Lind *et al.* 1965; Wasz-Höckert *et al.* 1968) are: length of cry (defined as the time between the first and last vocalizations of more than 0·4 sec); voice-height (minimum, general and maximum); occurrence and height of a voice-shift (i.e. a sudden upward or downward change in frequency); latency length (time between stimulus and cry onset); voicing (whether voiced, half-voiced, or voiceless); melody type (defined as 'a change in the pitch level [*sc.* fundamental frequency], when exceeding 10 per cent of the pitch during more than 10 per cent of the length of the cry' (Wasz-Höckert *et al.* 1968: 10), and subdivided into 'rising–falling' v. other types, which subsume 'rising', 'falling', 'abrupt' and 'flat' contours); continuity of the signal (whether continuous or interrupted); presence of glottal plosives within or between cries; presence of 'vocal fry' (also called 'glottal roll' or 'creak', i.e. 'an unperiodical phonation of the vocal folds in a lower frequency range, that is below the normal pitch register' (Wasz-Höckert *et al.* 1968:13)); the occurrence of 'vibrato'; and the occurrence of 'subharmonic break'. In addition, information about head and chest voice, nasality and orality, and laxness and tenseness was obtained from auditory analysis of the tapes (voice, vocal fry and subharmonic break were also rated auditorily). One should note that some of these parameters make use of auditory labels (e.g. the melody-types), even though they are defined largely in acoustic terms (of fundamental frequency etc.). The classification, moreover, is not complete: some of the parameters are very general, and it is likely that further distinctions can be made within them. Also, the comparative importance of the parameters varies: some are considered to be more important characterizing features than others (e.g. Lind *et al.* (1966) measure cries in response to pain stimuli in terms of latency, signal length, length of second pause, and cry period only, these parameters being viewed as primary), and there is evidence of a hierarchical treatment, as in the grouping of melody-types. There is some suggestion that for the younger age-group of child, melody-form and length might suffice to discriminate the majority of signals; whereas for older children, other factors (e.g. nasality, voice shift) need to be referred to (Wasz-Höckert *et al.* 1968: 20–21).

As already indicated, much of this research has been carried out with a view to accurate diagnosis of pathological neonate cries. Thus Lind *et al.* (1965) studied brain-damaged and normal children's cries and demonstrated that while latencies were similar, the height means were doubled for the former, the pitch-pattern was rising–falling (as opposed to falling), there were 80 per cent shifts (as opposed to 30 per cent), and there was no glottal roll. For hunger cries, length, height, glottal plosives and roll were the most significant parameters. Vuorenkoski *et al.* (1966) studied the *maladie du cri du chat* syndrome in a similar manner, in terms of pitch types (rising–falling, falling, rising, falling–rising, flat and interrupted), vocal fry, subharmonic break, continuity, and expiration or inspiration, and showed that the minimum pitch-height was the optimum diagnostic parameter, with general pitch range being an important supporting factor. In 97 per cent of cases, a minimum fundamental frequency of 500 Hz was found. See also Lind *et al.* (1970) for the abnormal characteristics of Down's syndrome. This central significance of pitch-height for diagnostic purposes is supported by other scholars, e.g. Ostwald *et al.* (1968), who found in their analysis no predictability on the basis of duration alone. Variations in duration as well as interval are however considered significant by Prechtl *et al.* (1969) in their study of normal and abnormal pain cries over the first nine days.

A second group working in this same field is in New York: see the bibliography under Fisichelli and Karelitz. Their 1962 and 1963 papers, for example, showed that brain-damaged children had longer cry latencies, emitted a less sustained cry, and required more pain stimuli to produce a given level of response than normal children. Wolff (1969: 94–5) found that brain-damaged cries tend to have a fundamental frequency of between 650 and 800 Hz; and similarly high fundamentals have been noted elsewhere (e.g. for certain types of congenital heart disease). Fisichelli and Karelitz (1966) compared four normal and four mongoloid children at six months, and show that, while the frequency ranges do not differ significantly, normal cries were 'richer in spectral content', more active, less variable in sound level, and more homogeneous as a group. In another connection, it is also likely that the so-called 'deaf voice' which is developed by deaf children after an earlier period of normal babbling (cf. Sykes 1940; Fry 1966; Lenneberg *et al.* 1965; Jones 1971; Lach *et al.* 1970; Ling 1965) is ultimately correlatable with modified frequency range and direction and accompanying factors. Luchsinger and Arnold (1965: 348), for example say: 'Another sign of early deafness in children is a typical change in the crying pattern. It sounds melodically distorted, more screeching and less emotionally differentiated than in normal children.' The point is beginning to be investigated: Manolson, for instance (1972), showed that hearing-impaired infants of 12–24 months had significantly more and larger changes in fundamental frequency and amplitude, and used certain bandwidths more than normals.

A third group, also in the United States, is currently investigating abnormalities using spectrography and related techniques: see the bibliography under Ostwald and Peltzman. Ostwald *et al.* (1967) investigate the interesting possibilities of carrying out speech synthesis of cries; and other papers carry out parametrically-oriented investigations of trisomy 13–15 children and the vocalizations of twins with cephalic union. Massengill (1969) and Massengill *et al.* (1966) have studied vocalization characteristics of children with cleft palate.

The fourth area of study comprises the work of a number of experimental and social psychologists who, over the past ten years, have been investigating the nature of the conditioning that affects vocalization. They have largely used three-month-old children, and concentrated on non-crying vocalizations (as opposed to most of the work reported above). The question here is: what kind of reinforcement will affect vocalization? Rheingold *et al.* (1959) established that composite social reinforcement was an effective conditioner of vocalizations; Weisberg (1963) that only contingent social reinforcement was; see also Todd and Palmer (1968), Routh (1969), Wahler (1969), Sheppard (1969) and Kononova (1968). Tomlinson-Keasey (1972) has recently pointed out that much of this research has been on institutionalized children: upon examining reinforcement in a home context, he found that non-social reinforcement can increase rate of vocalization, *contra* many of the findings of the above. Also, much of the work so far mentioned has used complex stimuli in their experiments; recently there have been attempts to isolate the various relevant factors in the composite reinforcement that is generally presented. According to Schwarz *et al.* (1970), the various factors, either individually or in combination, can prove equally effective; and Haugan and McIntire (1972), for example, have separated food, tactile, and adult vocal stimuli (again with institutionalized children), examining the differential effect on rate, and showed that these factors can independently have a positive effect. A simple social reinforcer, especially the adult voice, can be as effective as a complex stimulus (e.g.

involving touching, lights etc.). Ramsey and Ourth (1971) have shown that immediate reinforcement is needed for a positive increase in vocalization rate. (For other work, see Beckwith 1971; Bell 1960; Chesni 1970; Cullen *et al.* 1968; Eisenson 1966; Fargo *et al.* 1968; Freedman *et al.* 1969; Gleiss and Höhn 1968; Kagan 1969; Landreth 1941; Reiber 1965; Solomon and Yaeger 1969a, b).

These are not the only research areas of relevance to language development in the first year. It is quite clear from the vast literature on audiometric testing and research, for example, that there are numerous important overlaps here with the interests of the linguist—for example, the remarks by Bench (1969) concerning the possibility of innate pitch preference in neonates in order to account for an observed (inverse) relationship between effectiveness of stimulus and frequency, or the methodological discussion in Eisenberg (1965). Nor can I do any more at the moment than refer to the potential significance of the work of the ethologists for those interested in non-segmental studies. Many of the papers in Blurton-Jones (1972), for instance, draw attention to methodological emphases which have already emerged as desirable in the course of this chapter, e.g. the need for detailed description of individual interactions, and avoidance of premature conclusions about norms, a critical attitude towards vague behavioural categories. In some respects, the movement in vocalization study is in the same direction as that recommended by the ethologists, e.g. Bateson's (1971) concept of 'proto-conversations' between parents and children of between one and four months, indicating the emergence of regular patterns of interaction involving vocalizations. But to achieve even a modicum of success in this area, better monitoring systems are needed, to encompass a wider range of potentially relevant variables (see for example Siegel and Sameroff 1971) and better systems of transcription and classification for the vocalizations are required (the attempts at transcription in Blurton-Jones need considerable refinement—interestingly, the bibliographies of the various papers in this volume show no awareness of the linguistic work going on in this field).

The existence of apparent contradictions between research findings, and the difficulty of comparing research programmes and reports, indicates that there are numerous methodological problems which still need to be sorted out before any proper evaluation of progress in the above field can be made. The central question is the standardizing of the environmental conditions for eliciting vocalizations or when describing the context of their occurrence. In the case of pain cries, for instance (upon which most research has been done), what grade of stimulus is optimal, and what aspects of the cry does variation in stimulus affect? How does one ensure that the pain stimulus has been presented consistently, especially when techniques such as pinching or flicking the sole of the foot with a rubber band are used? And when should a given stimulus be applied? The physical and physiological controls required for experimental work into vocalization, particularly when of a statistical kind, are more complex than many scholars seem to realize, and psychological factors enter in very early on (the second week, according to Wolff 1969). A selection of reports shows this clearly. The results of Karelitz and Fisichelli and Vuorenkoski *et al.* are not easy to compare for this reason: the former removed the baby's clothes and obtained the cries before feeding, whereas the latter did not remove the clothes and obtained the cries afterwards; but it has long been known that clothing- and hunger-state has a marked influence on type and quantity of vocalization—see Aldrich *et al.* (1946) for the hunger factor, Irwin and Weiss (1934b) for results indicating that clothing reduces the amount of vocalization, and Wolff (1959, 1969: 89) for results indicating that swaddling does. Irwin and Weiss (1934a) amongst others reported that increased light and heat tend to decrease vocalization; Wolff (1969: 88–9) reported that higher temperatures make children vocalize less and sleep more; Pratt (1930) also found that certain temperatures decrease vocalization, but that humidity variations had no effect. Aldrich *et al.* showed that the amount of attention that a child is used to receiving is an important factor, and certainly the method of handling the children before a stimulus is applied or during a recording session needs to be looked into. To take a simple example, arm-rocking after feeding increases the quantity of vocalization (see Smitherman 1969). Brodbeck and Irwin (1946) showed the influence of orphanage environment on reducing the amount and types of vocalization. Ostwald *et al.* (1962) pointed to the significance of weight, size, physical development and general activeness in accounting for variability in results. Greenberg *et al.* (1967) suggested that early clamped children vocalize more, both spontaneously and after stimuli, than late-clamped—this being part of a general hypothesis that they are more alert. It is important to control the nature and amount of background noise in a research situation, particularly for older neonates, where the presence of human voices could make a significant difference to the results (cf. Wolff 1969: 97). The differential effect of types of sound as stimuli has been little studied: Stubbs (1934) showed that long intense sounds inhibited vocalization more than short, soft ones; Aldrich *et al.*, in their 1945 and 1946 work, showed that continuous stimulation at mid-high intensity levels reduced vocalization intensity. Then there is the variable effect of male v. female reinforcement on vocalization: at three months there seems to be no differential effect (cf. Banikiotes *et al.* 1972), but by ten months there does (cf. Lieberman 1967: 44–6). When does this effect begin, and what are its determining factors? One possibility is that the father's voice plays an increasing role after three months as opposed to its minimal role previously (as reported by Rebelsky and Hanks 1971), providing the child with a clearer set of contrasts. Controls have to be strict here for longitudinal studies, as the vocalization pattern changes with maturation in response to any given stimulus, e.g. the 'infectious crying', or increase in vocalization on the part of a child while an adult is speaking, from between one and two months. The social importance assigned to vocalizations in the development of adult—infant interaction within a community must also be taken into account, as has been shown by Blount (1971) in his study of the Luo of Kenya. Wolff's (1969) review of infant vocalization should be referred to for other references and further discussion, in particular of those factors (e.g. visceral pain) which are not experimentally testable. He makes the important point that any of the predicted effects may vary if the 'state of the organism' varies (from the third week): a baby in an excited state will produce a different response to a given stimulus from one in a contented state, for example. (On the other hand, Lamper and Eisdorfer (1971), examining prestimulus activity level in relation to intensity of neonatal response and daily response consistency, show that while there is some interaction for mild stimuli, the activity state seems to have little relevance for more intense stimuli.) There have also been various negative findings about the determinants of vocalization patterns, which should not be ignored, e.g. the conclusion of Ostwald *et al.* (1962) that various phonetic criteria failed to predict the difference in zygoticity of 16 pairs of twins much above chance; Ruja (1948), who showed that there was no correlation between the amount of vocalization in the first eight days and the length of labour; Karelitz *et al.* (1964), who tested an expected prediction that normal high IQs would have more active cries than low IQs, finding no real correlation; Fisichelli and Karelitz (1969), who showed that, while a more intense stimulus produced a more intensive cry, latency was unaffected: and Wasz-Höckert *et al.* (1968: 3), who found that racial origin had no differential effect on vocalization. (See further, Ryan 1974, and other papers in that volume.)

There are other factors which have to be borne in mind in evaluating the results of work in this field. In particular, it is likely that a more detailed differentiation of vocalization patterns would emerge if a more sophisticated analysis of their qualities was carried out. Much of the above research has been concerned solely with amount of vocalization, and not with its qualitative characteristics, as described in terms of parameters, features etc. This is especially the case with the work on conditioning outlined above: almost all these studies examined vocalizations in terms of the number used in given time-periods, and based their conclusions on quantitative measures alone. But variables such as fundamental frequency-variation, frequency-range, rhythm, speech-register (see Weeks 1971) cannot be ignored for the three-months-plus period, in view of their demonstrated relevance for the classification of neonatal vocalizations, and their subsequent importance as part of the development of non-segmental patterns. Another factor in evaluating results is the method of carrying out the statistical part of the analysis—in particular, how the children and the vocalizations were sampled, and (for longitudinal studies) how they were divided in terms of age. For instance, Karelitz and Fisichelli have used very gross groupings of 0–3 days, 4–365 days, and 365 days plus. Vuorenkoski *et al.* on the other hand, had nine groupings in the first seven months. It is likely that statistical techniques will have to be further refined, as an increasing number of variables come to be discovered and need to be correlated (see further, Wasz-Höckert *et al.* 1964a, for suggestions on this point). A similar refinement is necessary for the spectrographic techniques. Almost all the evidence is based on spectrography, but it is well known that the amount of accurate information obtainable spectrographically when there is a high fundamental is much reduced (cf. Fant 1968: 179–81; Lindblom 1962: 192; Lenneberg 1967: 276). Also, the vast amount of time required to make even a crude analysis of a spectrogram precludes large-scale visual processing, but satisfactory longi-tudinal investigations must necessarily be committed to large-scale sampling. In a preliminary survey recently, it emerged that the full analysis of a sample of vocalization material from six to eighteen months using spectrograms would take seven research assistants working full time on a faultless machine (sic) some fourteen years! In any case, it is only possible to obtain approximate values using such a method. It is clear that the practical problems of mastering techniques of analysis and transcription have been a considerable hindrance to scholars, particularly when—as is often the case in this field—they have had little or no formal linguistic training (cf. the difficulties of Haas and Harms 1963).

The obvious solution is to automate the process, so that a fundamental frequency analyser (or some similar device) could be attached to a 'black box' which would interpret this information in digital form, and present the output to a computer. Sheppard and Lane (1968) use such a method for their research into infant vocalization: they investigate duration, intensity and fun-damental frequency as a function of age of one child of either sex. Their results largely agree with Fairbanks (1942) as regards the magnitude and general movement of frequency. Specifically, at birth, male fundamental average was 438, lowering to 411 (approx. 21–45 days), and then rising to a stable 455; female fundamental was 401 at birth, lowering to 384 (approx. 21 days), and subsequently rising to 420. The coefficient of variation in fundamental fre-quency between utterances remained nearly constant throughout, i.e. utterances did not vary much in frequency, nor did fluctuation increase with age. About two-thirds of the fundamental frequencies plotted were within 10 per cent of the mean. There was more variability in amplitude than fundamental frequency (longer utterances having greater amplitude). Average duration of the utterance became more uniform with increasing age (specific information here agreeing with Ringwall *et al.* 1965). They note a time-lag between the gradual dis-appearance of reflexive crying and the gradual appearance of motivated crying. I give these results in some detail to show that the scope and degree of specificity achieved by this survey are only really possible with the aid of a computer; it is clear that many of the practical problems which preclude large-scale research will diminish as this process is further used. For other normative data, see Ringel and Kluppel (1964), Wolff (1969), Truby and Lind (1965), Prechtl *et al.* (1969).

Other descriptions are a mixture of acoustic, auditory and articulatory characteristics. Ringwall *et al.* (1965) use distinctive features. Lynip's (1951) descriptions of early cries make use of seven partly acoustic, partly auditory parameters: pitch fundamental, attacks and terminations, time-values, rhythm, cadences, resonances and intensities. Irwin and Chen's reliability study (1941) is carried out in almost purely articulatory terms: they show a 97 per cent reliability of discrimination between 'crying' and 'whining' in terms of five parameters: breathing (regular and irregular respectively), mouth shape (wide and rectangular, and partially open respectively), tongue tip (elevated and not elevated respectively), face and lid muscle contraction (strong and slight respectively), and loudness (strong and feeble respectively).

Non-segmental patterning in older children

Despite the range of methodological questions still requiring answers in work on early vocalization, a considerable amount of empirical information and descriptive technique has been established, and it should now be possible to apply some of this to the investigation of the non-segmental patterns of language proper in the second half of the first year, and beyond. Some absolute values have been established for different periods of development, right up to the teenage range, but this research has on the whole paid little attention to relating this physical information to the properties of the developing phonological system at any given point. See for instance Fairbanks 1950, Fairbanks *et al.* (in two 1949 papers), Curry 1940, Duffy 1958, Jones 1942, Levin *et al.* 1960, 1965, 1967, Hollien 1962, Hollien and Copeland 1965, Hollien and Paul 1969, McGlone 1966, Michel *et al.* 1966, Pedrey 1945, Bergendal and Söderpalm Talo 1969, and, on the recognition of intonation patterns, Corlew 1968. There have even been few transcriptions of samples of children's speech from the non-segmental viewpoint. Albright and Albright (1956) is an exception: they transcribe the utterance of a two-year old using the Trager/Smith system, and distinguish four degrees of stress (heavy, medium, light, very light), rising, fading and sustained clause terminals, three pitch-levels, length and extralength, nasalization, rounding and raising of vowels in his speech. Weir's two-and-a-half-year-old child (1962: 28–30) cannot be used for normative data, because of interference from Swedish and Czech, but methodologically it is a most interesting study. She too distinguishes three pitch-levels, though they are not used contrastively with consistency. A fourth level, higher than any others, is used in calls and urgent requests. A sentence for her is a contour with a final fall, or rise, followed by a pause. A third, 'sustain' pitch is also possible. She summarizes the prosodic features of this age as unstable, contours being only occasionally and not reliably contrastive; pauses however are consistent. Other passing references to non-segmental features in the context of a linguistic system may be found in Benda 1967, Fargo *et al.* 1967, Tonkova-Yampolskaya 1968, Carlson and Anisfeld 1969, Leopold 1947, 1949 and Lieberman 1967. Fuller discussion of the acquisition of stress is to be found in Hornby and Hass 1970 and Atkinson-King 1973.

It is possible to suggest a sequence of development for non-segmental phenomena, based on these rather scattered observations, and incorporating some descriptive work of my own; but it should hardly be necessary to underline the tentativeness of any such progressions. Firstly, as we have seen, there is a prelinguistic stage, consisting of two periods: a period of undifferentiated, biologically determined vocalization, including for example Wolff's 'basic cry' (see Wolff 1969: 82); and a period of largely innately-determined, differentiated vocalizations with an affective interpretation only. These latter have essentially the same physical characteristics and affective function for all languages studied;

they are difficult to interpret in anything other than very vague, general, attitudinal terms, e.g. 'pleasure', 'recognition', and they display the phonetic instability characteristic of infant vocalization (and pointed out by, e.g. Lynip (1951: 226), Lenneberg (1967: 277)).

The second stage is the development of shorter and more stable, discrete vocalizations, normally between seven and ten months (cf. Luchsinger and Arnold 1965: 349; Benda 1967; Van Riper 1963), which give the impression of being more controlled, and which suggest specific interpretations, e.g. 'We think he's saying—', 'Listen to him telling us to—'. Two examples were of an [a]-type vowel with a low-mid rising tone (apparently equatable with 'ta', i.e. 'thank-you'), and a disyllabic item, roughly [ɔːdɔː] (but with varying plosive articulations) on two level pitches, the first being higher than the second (apparently equatable with 'all gone'). These 'primitive lexical items' have both a segmental and a non-segmental character, but it is the latter which is the more stable, and the more readily elicited. They are the first evidence of language-specific patterns.[3] This is a relatively short stage, and indeed it may not be essential to distinguish it from the third stage following.

At the third stage, one can point to the occurrence of 'primitive sentences' with confidence, any specific definition of 'sentence' here being identical with that required for adult grammar. In general, when a child's utterance displays some formal and functional independence, in that it can be consistently assigned a specific semantic interpretation, is no longer wholly affective in character, and has a stable phonological form, then I would call it a sentence.[4] Between stages two and three, one might hypothesize the following development. The 'primitive lexical items' are presumably the result of a process of imitation of adult forms, which the child perceives as units with a beginning, an end, and a specific phonological shape which is primarily non-segmental in character. For a while, these words are used as units with the segmental and non-segmental characteristics 'fused': the pattern on 'ta' is never used for 'all gone' and vice versa. Then, as the child becomes aware of a number of 'lexical items' of this kind, many having a similar general non-segmental phonological shape, he develops an awareness of a primitive prosodic unit, which provides a frame for any independent contrastive utterance (i.e. sentences). Initially this unit is definable quite simply as a prosodic contour surrounded by silence, the prosodic contour being expounded by any one of the patterns which the child has been able to produce in a babbling way for some months as part of his infant vocaliz-

3 Lenneberg (1967: 279): 'The first feature of natural language to be discernible in a child's babbling is contour of intonation. Short sound sequences are produced that may have neither any determinable meaning nor definable phoneme structure, but they can be proffered with recognizable intonation such as occurs in questions, exclamations or affirmations. The linguistic development of utterance does not seem to begin with a composition of individual, independently movable items but as a whole total pattern. With further development, this whole becomes differentiated into component parts. . . .'
4 For further discussion of the notion of sentence applied to this early period, see Bloom 1973 and Dore 1975.

ation—and which may of course include other vocal effects as well as pitch (e.g. huskiness), though a pitch feature is usually the dominant one.

Simultaneously, the child begins to develop the range of non-segmental contrasts which can operate as exponents of the prosodic contour, and his phonemic oppositions. The phonemic character of his various 'words' clarifies, along lines which are fairly familiar. The range of exponents of the prosodic unit fairly rapidly extends to include contrasts in loudness, pitch-range, duration, tension and rhythmicality. Between nine and twelve months, I have noted contrasts between high- and low-pitched, loud and soft, drawled and short, tense and lax, and rhythmic and arhythmic sentences. Contrastivity involving two or more non-segmental parameters simultaneously (e.g. an opposition between a high long and a low short utterance) and most paralinguistic effect does not develop until later, as more 'sophisticated' attitudes develop, e.g. the low, tense, soft, husky voice associated with a 'dirty snigger'.[5] Before long (details are unclear), some of the parameters split, e.g. there develop two forms of pitch-range contrast, wide v. narrow, and high v. low; pitch-direction as a system begins with an initial contrast between falling and rising-type tones (i.e. falling subsumes high fall, low fall, rise-fall etc.), the opposition usually distinguishing statement from query.

Four things should be noted during this period (say, 9–18 months). First, some of these vocal effects may be superficially similar to the vocalizations of the earlier periods, but there is a distinct acoustic and usually auditory difference between, say, the rising tone of query, when this develops, and the rising vocalizations common in the babbling stage. Secondly, some of the parameters relevant for the study of neonate vocalizations have ceased to be used by this period, e.g. nasalization in British English. Thirdly, some non-segmental effects are used around this time which are not retained by adults (unless adopting baby-talk), e.g. marked labialization, use of falsetto voice for whole utterances, some spasmodic articulations (lip trills, raspberries etc). Fourthly, during this period of simultaneous development of phonemic and non-segmental systems, the child may at times be uncertain as to what the basis of word identification is, whether segmental or non-segmental. (Presumably tone-language children make a different set of decisions at this stage from those in atonal languages.) The uncertainty rapidly disappears, as the number of phonemic contrasts increases, and the importance of communicating referential meanings becomes apparent; but one should note that the function of non-segmental features may be misinterpreted, even quite late on, as being the dominant cue. I have come across a case in English, for example, where the child (in this case of 18 months) referred consistently to all four-wheeled vehicles that made an engine noise as 'bus', with a low falling tone; but when a real bus went by, he would say 'bus', with a wide rising-falling tone. Granted the original reason for the distinction

5 See further below, p. 155. It is important to stress at this point that the notion of 'contrast' is extremely subjective, for this stage of language development; more than at any other stage, there is the danger of attributing adult semantic 'knowledge' to the child; cf. p. 132.

is probably ultimately affective in character, the fact remains that for a period of some two months, this child was using English as a tone-language, in this single respect.

The next stage covers the period (around 18 months) when a child begins to group together his primitive sentences, to produce the first evidence of form-classes. (This is the point at which most studies of grammatical development begin, but even if the above hypothesis is wildly incorrect, it should be clear that a great deal of grammatical relevance has taken place hitherto.) Each sentence still has its phonological character, and at this time there is evidence of the child playing intonational 'substitution-games'.[6]

As sentences get more complex syntagmatically, and develop into the so-called 'two-word' sentences, two things happen non-segmentally. The first and most important development is the use of tonicity to control the distribution of emphasis.[7] Secondly, the range of sequential non-segmental patterns increases, e.g. rhythmic contrasts, pause contrasts, speed contrasts (though it should be pointed out that some reduplicative effects are heard from earlier on with monosyllabic 'lexical items', e.g. a rhythmic glissando effect on an [o] type vowel was used by one child when asking to be tickled, at nine months). Then, as the range of sentence-types increases, and the amount of functional load for any one prosodic feature increases, there develops the situation of grammatical structure selecting specific prosodic interpretations; e.g. a rising tone, originally only a query-indicator, but later usable as an indication of grammatical subordination, or as a calling intonation, is interpreted accordingly in the light of the grammatical structure with which it co-occurs. The affective information of the prosodic patterns also becomes influenced by other factors, e.g. the vocabulary, the kinesics, and the environment in general. At this stage, normally arrived at between the age of two and two-and-a-half for British English children, the non-segmental system seems sufficiently close to the adult system to pose no further major problem for the researcher. Subsequent patterns of development, such as the extent to which intonations are appropriately used in increasingly complex syntactic constructions (e.g. apposition, types of relative clause, and subordinate clauses) do not seem to require the definition of additional non-segmental categories. The issue is largely an empirical one, and is dependent on the prior study of syntactic development in older children in its own terms.

The relationship between non-segmental phonology and syntax in language acquisition has attracted a number of scattered observations, but remains

6 Carlson and Anisfeld (1969) note this at about 22 months; they distinguish listing, question and statement intonations, loud and soft tones, staccato and drawled articulation, as well as a number of 'styles of speaking' (see 118). Eisenson *et al.* (1963) refer to frequent experiments in pitch at 18 months, and note the variety of the child's 'vocal overflow'.

7 The importance of intonation as a criterion for distinguishing sequences of independent one-word utterances from two-word utterances is well recognized (e.g. Brown 1973, Bloom 1973), but the details of the transition have received little empirical study, and only a few of the relevant prosodic features have been discussed.

almost totally unexplored. This is partly a reflection of the theoretical position adopted by linguists, which often dismisses non-segmental phenomena as marginally linguistic, or 'mere performance' (see Chapters 1 and 2). But any reference at all to grammar is fairly unusual in this context, as most of the literature that recognized the existence of non-segmental patterns assumed that the earliest patterns should be given an interpretation wholly in terms of attitudinal or 'affective' meaning (see above, p. 131). I am not now concerned with general criticisms which might be made of these approaches, but rather with the specific issue of the inadequacy of such work when viewed in the context of grammatical development. The point may be introduced with a quotation from Fry (1966), who states (after mentioning that the reproduction of intonation patterns is learned early) that this is 'not because rises and falls in pitch are particularly easy to imitate but rather because intonation is closely linked with the affective side of speech; its use grows naturally out of the expressive sounds the child has been making . . .' (191). Now this position—and it is a fairly typical one—does contain a certain amount of truth, and I would obviously not wish to deny that there are close links between intonation and affect; but this account is quite inadequate as a view about the place of intonation in language acquisition, for two reasons. It is an oversimplified account of intonational form, considering pitch-direction only (cf. 'rises and falls' above), and ignoring other parameters; and it is by no means clear on what grounds intonational phenomena have been singled out from the totality of prosodic and paralinguistic features. It takes very little observation (as noted above) to show that pitch contrastivity itself is quite complex in character in this early period, involving features of range as well as direction, and that other variables than pitch expound contrasts (loudness, tempo and pause in particular). There is also evidence that, if a more comprehensive study of non-segmental features is made, the patterns which emerge in this earliest period of language acquisition can be shown to have a major grammatical function, i.e. the substitution of one non-segmental pattern for another would cause one to assign a different structural description to the utterance, the terms of the description being provided by some already available grammatical model.

The interesting theoretical question concerns the implied relationship between the non-segmental features and syntax. To what extent can these features be studied independently of, and be said to contribute to, the development of a grammatical framework? Two theoretical positions seem to be taken regarding this point in the recent literature. First, there is a view which sees intonation, and presumably other prosodic features, as being ontogenetically prior to any period of grammatical acquisition. Weir, for example, (1966: 153) argues that 'early' intonation patterns (it is not clear how early) are the means of 'segmenting utterance into sentencelike chunks, regardless of the intelligibility of the utterance to an adult listener', and in her 1962 book, she makes use of a phonological sentence defined with reference to pitch-direction and pause. See also Kaplan & Kaplan (1970), and Moskowitz (1970: 14–17), which sees intonation as a possible discovery procedure, not solely for sentence-units, but for subordinate syntactic units as well. Similarly, Braine (1963; see 1967: 252), in his discussion of how a child learns segmentation, claims that intonation is one means of indicating phrase boundaries. He cites Trager and Smith, claiming that the progressive segmentation of an utterance is almost completely specified by intonation, i.e. the utterance contains boundary information, though he is not sure exactly how much help intonation is in assigning grammatical structure. As evidence for this, he describes an experiment with a 5-word nonsense sentence, in which the 'primary stress' was varied from 12345 to 12345, which showed that the boundary assigned followed the stress on each occasion (248). There is insufficient information given about the other prosodic variables to allow proper interpretation of this experiment, but it is clear that his general position, and that of many other scholars, is that intonation is the vehicle on which children arrive at the rudiments of syntax (cf. McNeill 1966: 53).

Bever *et al.* (1963) take a generally opposite position, though they attribute more to Braine in this matter than he claimed. The grounds for their reply are not wholly clear, partly because they take a different definition of intonation from Braine (see p. 127 above), and partly because they confuse issues which should be kept apart;[8] but the following points emerge. They admit that intonation can induce structure in a random sequence, but argue that this is not the issue: 'the correct interpretation may not be that the perceived location of pause, stress and intonation are the child's clue to the analysis of structure, but rather that the prior analysis of structure is what determines where the child learns to hear pause, stress and intonation. Nor is the possibility of some intermediate position excluded' (270). On the face of it, this is rather unlikely, at least for the earliest period of language acquisition, in view of the large amount of evidence already accumulated showing that children respond to prosodic parameters from a very early age at the expense of structural information (cf. Tappolet 1907: Schäfer 1922; and the literature reviewed in Lewis 1936 including his own position (115–16); or, more recently, Benda 1967 and Kaplan 1970).[9] But the main reason why the position of Bever *et al.* is not very convincing is because the only evidence they cite in favour of the argument that one

---

8 They argue at one point that the physical cues for non-segmental contrasts are ambiguous, saying for example that physical intensity is relevant to the specification of stress only in cases of special emphasis. This is in any case an overstatement (cf. Fry 1958, for example), but it is by no means clear how the absence of any one-for-one correlation between attribute and dimension of sound affects the argument. There may be a point here for a theory of perceptual development in relation to learning, but this is quite irrelevant to the syntactic argument, where the precise constitution of the physical cues is beside the point. Intonation is a linguistic category, not a physical one, and the question which has to be answered is whether there are intonational cues for structure (whatever their physical basis) in utterances.

9 It should be pointed out, however, that recent work using habituation tests has not made a systematic distinction between language-specific and non-linguistic features of the prosodic stimuli used. Children are shown to discriminate between broad types of pitch movement, but how far this ability relates specifically to their mother-tongue, and is more than just a general, non-linguistic response to pitch, is unclear.

needs prior knowledge of syntactic structure in order to analyse intonation is derived from Lieberman's experiment (1965). A great deal of significance has been placed on this experiment in this context, by other scholars also. McNeill (1966: 53), for example, cites it in support of the same view, that syntactic information is prior to intonation in language acquisition, and it is considered an important issue in the discussion which follows Weir's paper at this conference (see Smith and Miller 1966: 170ff.). McNeill's summary will suffice as a basis for comment.

Lieberman (1965) compared the ability of linguists to transcribe the intonation contours of real speech with their ability to transcribe physically identical contours of simulated speech that consisted of a single prolonged vowel sound. He found that linguists' transcriptions matched the actual physical contour only of the simulated speech. When the linguists transcribed real speech, the actual and the perceived intonation contours often differed strikingly, which suggests that structure is an important source of information about perceived intonation but not vice versa. A prelingual child listening to adult speech is in a position comparable to Lieberman's linguists transcribing a simulated vowel. He is not comparable to Lieberman's linguists transcribing real speech. Infants could note only the physical contour in parental speech, not the perceived contour that is correlated with grammatical structure. It is difficult, therefore, to see how intonation could guide a child to syntax; for no matter how strong the tendency is for children to imitate speech they receive from their parents, they will not imitate the appropriate feature unless important parts of the syntax have already been acquired.

But it is fallacious to apply the results of Lieberman's experiment to child language in this way. Lieberman's experiment was an extremely specific one: it was designed 'to ascertain what aspects of the acoustic signal linguists actually note when they make *Trager/Smith* transcriptions' (1965: 40, my italics). It shows quite conclusively that the Trager/Smith system conditions linguists to react to real speech in the way McNeill outlines, but what must be pointed out is that the Trager/Smith system is an extremely restrictive one—the number of intonational contrasts permitted to appear (as Bolinger pointed out years ago) is relatively small, and omits a great deal. If Lieberman's linguists had been trained exclusively in a system which recognized more contrasts and avoided a phonemic orientation, then it could be argued that there would have been better results. Lieberman does in fact bring a tonetic transcriptional system into the experiment, and finds that the results were much more consistent (the linguist changing only 25 per cent of his notation, compared with the 60 per cent changed when Trager/Smith was used). This suggests that Lieberman's conclusions are only relevant for those people who have mastered a specific transcriptional system of intonation—or, one might generalize, for people who have mastered some transcriptional system. Now there is no evidence whatsoever that the prelingual child has mastered a Trageremic transcriptional system, or any other; consequently Lieberman's conclusions do not apply, and his experiment should not be cited.[10]

10 An identical conclusion on this point has been reached independently in a very useful thesis by Kaplan (1969: 16) as part of a more general argument that 'the prior

What seems to have happened in recent discussions of this problem is that a pseudo-problem has been created, i.e. a problem which is solely an artefact of some specific linguistic model, which vanishes when an alternative model is used. In the present case, children's utterances have been studied in the light of a model which requires a clear formal and functional distinction to be made between intonation and syntax, as such phrases as 'intonation guiding one to syntax' implies. But while the analyst may find it convenient to describe the speech-signal presented to the child in terms of functionally distinct segmental and non-segmental components, there are no grounds at all for assuming that the child perceives this in any other way than as a single functionally un-differentiated event. Whether a particular syntactic category or meaning-relation is expounded phonologically by segmental-verbal or by prosodic markers is a language-specific question, and clearly the child cannot know this in advance. Consequently, it is misleading to say that syntax guides a child to the use of intonation. But it is also misleading to say the reverse, without careful qualification. All one can say is that there is evidence that the dominant per-ceptual component of the speech signal is non-segmental, and that some non-segmental patterns are understood and produced prior to anything conven-tionally syntactic. The details of this process (outlined above), suggest, if they suggest anything, that the child's ability to discriminate non-segmental con-trasts at the expense of segmental, in the earliest period, allows him to develop a prosodic frame which organizes his utterance into—as Weir put it—sentence-like chunks. But this is not enough to substantiate a hypothesis that 'intonation guides a child to syntax', as the notion of intonation implicit in this phrase is very much an oversimplification. The implication is that 'intonation' is a single 'feature' (or 'parameter') which is 'acquired' all at once, and, once acquired, retains the same function while the rest of language develops. But (a) intonation is not a single feature, but a complex of features; (b) these features are not acquired simultaneously; and (c) their function is complex, involving gram-matical, attitudinal, and social factors, the relative importance of which varies considerably with increasing complexity of the rest of language: and while some aspects of intonation presuppose syntactic competence, other aspects do not.

Concerning the first point, the various systems underlying intonation have been outlined above (e.g. pp. 11ff.), but a highly relevant aspect of this ap-proach needs to be stated here, namely the point that the adult prosodic system —and to a lesser extent that of the child—is hierarchical in character (e.g. Rossi 1970). A hierarchical approach is implicit in most models of intonation, and experimental evidence for it is presented in Quirk and Crystal 1966. There is also some evidence of a hierarchical ordering of prosodic features and cate-gories in children. It is clear that some types of prosodic contrasts are more important for comprehension than others. Tonicity is a particularly clear case. For example, there are the phenomena noted by Brown and Bellugi (1964: 141-2),

---

detection of supra-segmental information by the child can lead to the discovery of more basic kinds of language patterns (4).

amongst others, that differential stress may be the cause of the child's reduction of adult language in his telegraphic speech, and that children tend to delete the initial unstressed element of polysyllables (e.g. 'tend' for 'pretend'). Also, such notions as 'pivot word' only make sense when seen in connection with intonational emphasis. If this point is considered, along with the view that intonation is not to be considered as a single feature of speech, but rather a complex of parameters and systems, then it immediately becomes apparent that a 'compromise' position (cf. Bever *et al.* above) is not only feasible but probably the only realistic way of resolving the controversy within the terms of the model people have been using. Some aspects of intonation (and other prosodic features) help one to assign structure, *especially in the early period*; other aspects require grammatical cues (of the conventional kind) in order to be analysed, *especially in the later period.* (Cf. Fodor, in Smith and Miller 1966 (171), who argues in favour of a simultaneity of cues.) Such a theory would be quite compatible with a theory required for the adult system. Here too one finds many examples of a 'grammatical' function of intonation, i.e. cases where one has to be aware of the intonation before one can assign a complete structural description to a sentence, such as the distinction between restrictive and nonrestrictive relative clauses, or the use of tonicity to control the nature of the 'presuppositions' which would be part of the complete semantic analysis of a sentence (see Chapter 1); and there are also many cases where one is unable to analyse the intonation without some reference to grammatical boundaries (e.g. when unstressed syllables at the end of one tone-unit and at the beginning of the next are at the same pitch-level and not separated by any pause).

Apart from this general discussion, references to the use of intonation in relation to specific syntactic patterns are quite sporadic, and are usually couched in relatively vague terms (e.g. talking about 'rising contours' on a given structure, without reference to such matters as the extent of the rise in pitch, whether alternative contours are possible, and so on). Structures which have been noticed as requiring some intonational exponence include questions, negation, holophrasis and presuppositions (see for example McNeill 1966: 55; Gruber 1967; Ingram 1971; Menyuk and Bernholtz 1969; many of the papers in Fillmore and Langendoen 1971; Menyuk 1969; and the chapters on syntax in Menyuk 1971). But there are very many structures, which require intonational exponence in adult language, which have not been studied at all from the point of view of acquisition (e.g. relative clauses, appositional patterns, types of coordination). Blasdell (1969) and others are trying to provide a framework of analysis for the gestural, segmental and suprasegmental signs in the first language between 15 and 30 months; they aim to provide, *inter alia,* an acoustic specification of the types of contours which appear to be equivalent to adult 'statement', 'question' and 'command' contours. I have not come across comparable projects for other syntactic structures of a more specific kind. (See further, Leroy 1973; Cruttenden 1974; Wode 1975.)

Despite the absence of any reasonably complete descriptions of the nonsegmental system at given stages of development, a certain amount of work has

gone ahead looking at the way older children develop stylistically- or socio-
linguistically-restricted linguistic behaviour using intonation and other features.
Intonation is obviously an important mediating factor in many interaction
situations: for example, in a three-element pattern of (a) child's utterance (a
question, perhaps), (b) parent's response, and (c) child's further response, the
nature of (c) will be very dependent on the intonation of (b), whatever the syntax
of the various utterances. The point does not seem to have been much investigated (cf. Brown 1958; Campbell and Wales 1970), though there are a number of
relevant comments in the literature, e.g. Lewis's (1936: 151) distinction between
declarative and manipulative functions of intonation (i.e. intonation which
expresses moods, and intonation which draws attention to situations). Flavell
(1968: 149) cites intonation, stress, loudness and rate as relevant for the description of role-playing, and this is supported by other observations, e.g.
Ervin-Tripp (1964) on children's play intonations, and Burling (1966) on the
metrics of children's verse. Carlson and Anisfeld (1969) note a joking tone of
voice in their two-year-old subject, which was seldom used in imaginative play;
and they refer to a style of speech which the child developed in situations in
which he knew he was not allowed to do something but still wanted to, which
they describe as 'fuzzy enunciation, very soft voice, and twisting of the head'
(p. 575). I have recorded a clear case of role-play in a child of 13 months (in
this case a switch to falsetto register when talking as he supposed—under an
older brother's influence—a rabbit did). Barnard *et al.* (1961) distinguish 'voice'
as one of their 'stylistic dimensions' in this study of anxiety correlates. Weeks
(1971) makes a strong case in support of the hypothesis that children learn a
number of speech-registers (or styles) from a very early age, these being identified primarily in terms of non-segmental parameters; the detail of this analysis
is welcome. Brooks *et al.* 1969 is a large-scale programme of research designed
to establish social determinants involving the use of the non-segmental system.
Working within the theoretical framework of Wiener and Mehrabian 1968,
they study the responses of children from middle and low socio-economic
groups to verbal reinforcers communicated with and without tonal inflection.
Positive reinforcement words (e.g. 'fine', 'good') and negative words (e.g. 'bad')
were presented with a congruent inflection (a 3–1 glide in the Trager/Smith
system) and uninflected (a level tone on 2); it was found that the low socio-
economic class responded more to verbal reinforcers which included inflection
than to the same reinforcers when they did not; but the middle class did not
show such a preference. A similar experiment using a negative tone ('characterized more by a rasping tone-timbre than by uniformity of pitch contour')
produced similar results: the middle class showed no difference in response;
the lower class responded only to inflected conditions—and more to positive
words said with positive tone than negative words with negative tone. After
some discussion of possible interpretations of these results, they conclude that
the function of tone 'serves primarily as a language marker and then as an
information bearer; that is, tone "directs" the child to the message carried in the
semantic component, and in the absence of a marker, no response need be

made to the word alone' (469). See also Kashinsky and Wiener 1969. Finally, in the context of plotting the linguistic identity of social groups, Becker and McArdle (1967) examine what they call 'nonlexical speech similarities' in non-clinical families as an index of intrafamilial identification: average length and frequency of pause in wives and husbands, children and mother, and children and father provides some support for their hypothesis. Friedlander (1968) finds a preference among children between 11 and 15 months for mothers over strangers or music, one of the bases for the preference being variation in 'inflection'. Gedda *et al.* (1960) present some evidence in favour of the hypothesis that monozygotic twins sound more alike as adults than dizygotic. Cameron *et al.* (1967), developing earlier work by Bayley (1932), suggest that the age at which babbling begins (in girls) is predictive of later intelligence scores. Phillis (1970) presents some evidence suggesting that younger (junior high) children are more sensitive than older children or adults to nonlinguistic vocal cues (voice-quality) in judging personality on the basis of voice types; but a contrary result is found by Solomon and Ali (1972) in relation to the judgment of affect.

Lastly, the innateness issue has of course been raised in relation to intonation, but the discussion which has ensued has produced no clearer answers than for any other area of language. Whether non-segmental features have an innate basis or are learned is very much an open question. Most of the early scholars (e.g. Darwin (1877)) felt that such patterns were instinctive, and there is some support for an explanation in similar terms still. The clearest arguments in support of innateness are in Lieberman 1967 (Ch. 3), who maintains that there is an innate physiological basis for the 'shape' of the normal breath-group, which occurs in very many languages. (His 'archetypal normal breath group' refers to a postulated pattern of articulatory activity which produces 'a prosodic pattern that is characteristic of the ones that are used to delimit the boundaries of unemphatic, declarative sentences in normal speech. . . . We shall use the term "breath group" to encompass all the intonational signals that are acoustically or perceptually equivalent to the archetypal breath group' (27). 'The presence of a basic synchronization between the laryngeal muscles and the chest muscles to form a basic intonation contour for a language, of course, explains how children acquire a "native accent" so quickly' (29).) According to Lieberman, 'It is a universal of human speech that, except for certain predictable cases, the fundamental frequency of phonation and the acoustic amplitude fall at the end of a sentence' (26). This is an attractive hypothesis, but the fundamental concept of the 'hypothetical innate referential breath-group' requires considerable further substantiation and clarification before it can be accepted. There is some counter-evidence to the claim that short, normal declarative sentences end with a falling contour for all languages—it is not true for some dialects of Welsh or German, for instance (cf. Hlubík 1968)—and such terms as 'characteristic', 'unemphatic' and 'normal' in the first sentence of the above quotation need amplification. Supporting evidence is provided by Painter (1971). Lewis (1936: 49) took up a compromise position between innateness and learning hypotheses. Having noted that the child discriminates pleasant

and unpleasant adult voice at three months, he states that this 'may in part be
due to maturation of an innate tendency to respond to expression; but it is also
likely to be due to training by the conditions in which the speech is heard' (e.g.
the kinesics). Trojan (1957: 438) and Bolinger (1949: 249) have also argued that
intonation is in some way tied to nervous tension; e.g. the latter states that
'intonation contains a few arbitrary uses, but they are embedded in a matrix of
instinctive reactions . . . even the arbitrary uses may generally be assigned
values consistent with the nervous interpretation.' I would however argue that
most of the central 'core' of the intonation system of a language (and most of the
prosodic system in general) bears no relation to nervous tension, e.g. the
splitting up of an utterance into tone-units, most of the contrasts in tonicity, the
main oppositions of tone (falling, rising etc.), and the less extreme contrasts of
the pitch-range and loudness prosodic subsystems. It is when one considers
the formal extremes of articulation of a given feature (e.g. very high or loud
speech) that one becomes aware of a partial physiological determination in the
production of the effects (though this of course does not necessarily deny them
a conventional role, as obviously the perception and interpretation of a finite
number of contrasts along a parameter is something which may take place
without reference to one's physiological resources). While one allows that there
may well be an innate predisposition for the acquisition of prosodic features, as
for the rest of language, then, there is no evidence to suggest that the features
themselves are innate.

From all this discussion, it should be clear that the two main tasks facing the
language-acquisition scholar in this area are descriptive and methodological in
character. Normative descriptive data is needed about many matters: the
physical properties of infant vocalizations and non-segmental patterns, for any
given 'state of the organism'; the changes in vocal behaviour between any given
pair of states; the individual differences between children; the socio-economic
and dialect variations between children; the range of determinants (physical,
psychological, physiological, environmental) which affect vocal behaviour; the
norms of adult speech which elicit vocal behaviour (especially the non-segmental
characteristics of 'baby-talk'); and the emergence of the affective, syntactic and
social functions of the various vocal patterns. Particular attention has to be
paid to the period between six and twelve months, and to the need for comparative analysis of the progressive differentiation of vocalization in different
languages. From the methodological point of view, the primary task seems to be
the development of more adequate descriptive frameworks, incorporating
articulatory, acoustic and auditory dimensions of classification and transcription.
Also, for infant vocalization, an acoustic specification seems the most satisfactory technique of all, at the present stage of study, as the information it
provides is fairly conveniently obtainable and precise (as compared with the
articulatory approach) and to a very great extent avoids the dangers arising
from the subjectivity inherent in the auditory approach (cf. p. 128 above). But
it is desirable as soon as possible to correlate acoustic/articulatory and auditory
information, so that the onset of non-segmental linguistic contrastivity can be

studied in terms which are capable of correlation with the results of research upon older children and adults. At the moment it is not at all clear which method of description would provide the most accurate and consistent correlates of the various labels used in specifying the meanings of a non-segmental pattern. To label a pattern as 'happy', for instance, might best be correlated with acoustic data, or with articulatory data, or with auditory data. To avoid prejudging the issue, then, it would seem most satisfactory to make use of an approach in which all three kinds of information would be obtained to produce a complex specification of a label, until such time as one or other of the phonetic techniques turns out to be the most reliable diagnostic. In any event, research which does not make the basis of its descriptive techniques absolutely explicit (e.g. in using auditory labels in description of acoustic events) should be carefully avoided.

As Lewis (1936: 95) said: 'The whole question of intonation in children's speech is . . . extremely obscure.' It is depressing, nearly forty years later, still to have to agree with him.

Bibliography

ABE, I. 1967. On bio-phonetics. *Bull. Tokyo Inst. Tech.* **79**, 53–7.
— 1972. The rise-fall question tune. *Bull. Phon. Soc. Japan* **140**, 13–16.
— 1973. The intonation of the expression 'I beg your pardon'. *Study of Sounds* **16**, 315–28.
ABERCROMBIE, D. 1965. A phonetician's view of verse structure. In D. Abercrombie (ed.), *Studies in Phonetics and Linguistics* (London), 16–25.
— 1967. *Elements of general phonetics* (Edinburgh).
— 1968. Paralanguage. *B. J. Dis. Comm.* **3**, 55–9.
— 1971. Some functions of silent stress. In Aitken, A. J., McIntosh, A. and Pálsson, H. (eds.), *Edinburgh studies in English and Scots* (London), 147–56.
ADAMS, C. M. 1969. A survey of Australian English intonation. *Phon.* **20**, 81–130.
ADAMS, J. B. 1957. Culture and conflict in an Egyptian village. *Am. Anth.* **59**, 225–35.
AKIYAMA, K. and YUMOTO, K. 1966. A study of voice identification using Japanese speech. *Study of Sounds* **12**, 209–23.
ALBERT, E. M. 1964. 'Rhetoric', 'logic', and 'poetics' in Burundi: culture patterning of speech behavior. *Am. Anth.* **66**, 35–54.
ALBRIGHT, R. W. and ALBRIGHT, J. B. 1956. The phonology of a two-year old child. *Word* **12**, 382–90.
ALDRICH, C. A., NORVAL, M. A., KNOP, C. and VENEGAS, F. 1946. The crying of newly born babies: (IV) a follow-up study after additional nursing care had been provided. *J. Pediat.* **28**, 665–70.
ALDRICH, C. A., SUNG, C. and KNOP, C. 1945a. The crying of newly born babies: (II) the individual phase. *J. Pediat.* **27**, 89–96.
— 1945b. The crying of newly born babies: (III) the early period at home. *J. Pediat.* **27**, 428–35.
ALDRICH, C. A., SUNG, C., KNOP, C., STEVENS, G. and BURCHELL, M. 1945. The crying of newly born babies: (I) the community phase. *J. Pediat.* **26**, 313–26.
ALLEN, G. D. 1971. Acoustic level and vocal effort as cues for the loudness of speech. *J. Ac. Soc. Am.* **49**, 1831–41.
— 1972. The location of rhythmic stress beats in English: an experimental study. *Lg. and Sp.* **15**, 72–100, 179–95.
ALLERTON, D. J. and CRUTTENDEN, A. 1974. English sentence adverbials: their syntax and their intonation in British English. *Lingua* **34**, 1–30.
ALLPORT, G. W. and CANTRIL, H. 1934. Judging personality from voice. *J. Soc. Psychol.* **5**, 37–55.
ALTMANN, S. A. 1967. The structure of primate social communication. In Altmann, S. A. (ed.), *Social communication among primates* (Chicago), 325–62.
— 1968. Primates. In Sebeok 1968, 466–522.
ANDRÉ, E. 1965. Notes on 'Systems of prosodic and paralinguistic features in English'. *Rev. Phon. App.* **1**, 7–13.

160 *The English tone of voice*

ANDRÉ, E. 1966. Le statut linguistique des traits prosodiques et paralinguistiques (mimeo, École d'Interprètes, Mons).
— 1974. Studies in the correspondence between English intonation and the noun-phrase in English grammar, with special reference to the tone-unit (PhD thesis, University of Liège).
ARTEMOV, V. A. 1972. Intonatsiya, intonatsionnyi variant, intonatsionnyi invariant i intonema. *Jazykovedný Časopis* **23**, 3–12.
— 1973. The unity of analysis and synthesis in structure-functional study of speech intonation. *Study of Sounds* **16**, 83–100.
ATKINSON-KING, K. 1973. Children's acquisition of phonological stress contrasts (*UCLA Working Papers in Phonetics* **25**).
AUSTIN, W. M. 1965. Some social aspects of paralanguage. *Can. J. L.* **11**, 31–9.
— 1972. Nonverbal communication. In Davis, A. L. et al. (eds.), *Culture, class, and language variety* (Urbana), 140–69.

BAGMUT, A. J. 1970. *Intonatsiya budova prostogo rozpovidnogo recennya u slovjankix movax* (Kiev).
BAILEY, C.-J. N. 1970a. A new intonation theory to account for Pan-English and idiom-particular patterns. *Papers in Linguistics* **2**, 522–604.
— 1970b. New thoughts on accent and intonation. *Working Papers in Linguistics* **2** (University of Hawaii), 25–32.
— 1971a. Tempo and phrasing. *Working Papers in Linguistics* **3**, ii (University of Hawaii), 105–14.
— 1971b. Intonation. *Working Papers in Linguistics* **3**, v (University of Hawaii), 43–118.
BANIKIOTES, F. G., MONTGOMERY, A. A. and BANIKIOTES, P. G. 1972. Male and female auditory reinforcement of infant vocalizations. *Dev. Psychol.* **6**, 476–8.
BAR-ADON, A. and LEOPOLD, W. 1971. *Child language: a book of readings* (Englewood Cliffs).
BARBARA, D. A. 1963. Nonverbal communication. *J. Comm.* **13**, 166–73.
BARHAM, T. 1860. On metrical time, or, the rhythm of verse, ancient and modern, *Tr. Phil. Soc.* 45–62.
BARIK, H. C. 1968. On defining juncture pauses. A note on Boomer's 'Hesitation and grammatical encoding'. *Lg. and Sp.* **11**, 156–9.
BARNARD, J. W., ZIMBARDO, P. G. and SARASON, S. B. 1961. Anxiety and verbal behavior in children. *Ch. Dev.* **32**, 379–92.
BARYSNIKOVA, K. A. and GAJDUCIK, S. M. 1969. O prosodemax voprosa i utverzdeniya. *ZPSK* **22**, 321–4.
BASTIAN, J. 1964. The biological background of man's languages. In Stuart, C. I. J. M. (ed.), *Georgetown Round Table on language and linguistics* **15** (Washington), 141–8.
BATESON, G. (in press). Communication. In McQuown.
BATESON, M. C. 1971. Speech communication. The interpersonal context of infant vocalization. *MIT QPR, MIT Electronics Laboratory* **100**, 170–76.
BAYLEY, N. 1932. A study of the crying of infants during mental and physical tests. *J. Genet. Psychol.* **40**, 306–29.
BAZELL, C. E. 1954. Choice of criteria in structural linguistics. *Word* **10**, 126–35.

BECKER, J. and MCARDLE, J. 1967. Nonlexical speech similarities as an index of intrafamilial identification. *J. Ab. Psychol.* **72**, 408–14.

BECKWITH, L. 1971. Relationships between infants' vocalizations and their mothers' behaviors. *Merrill-Palmer Quart.* **17**, 211–26.

BEIER, E. G. 1969. The accuracy of the interpretation of emotional meaning as a function of audiovisual and neutral content cues. *Language Research in Progress Abstract* **819C.**

BELL, R. Q. 1960. Relations between behavior manifestations in the human neonate. *Ch. Dev.* **31**, 463–77.

BENCH, J. 1969. Some effects of audio-frequency stimulation on the crying baby. *J. Aud. Res.* **9**, 122–8.

BENDA, R. 1967. The significance of babbling to language development. A study of the intonation patterns of an eight-month-old child (*ERIC Abstract*).

BENYON, A. J. 1969. A study of the prosodic and paralinguistic features in a corpus of academic lectures in present-day English (M.Phil. thesis, University of London).

BERGENDAL, B.-I. and SÖDERPALM TALO, E. 1969. The responses of children with reduced phonemic systems to the Seashore measures of musical talents: a preliminary study of their ability to discriminate between differences in pitch, loudness, rhythm, time, timbre and tonal memory. *F. Phon.* **21**, 20–38.

BERGER, K. W. 1964. Some factors in the recognition of timbre. *J. Ac. Soc. Am.* **36**, 1888–91.

BERMAN, A. and SZAMOSI, M. 1972. Observations on sentential stress. *Lg.* **48**, 304–25.

BERNSTEIN, B. 1962. Linguistic codes, hesitation phenomena and intelligence. *Lg. and Sp.* **5**, 31–46.

— 1964. Elaborated and restricted codes: their social origins and some consequences. *Am. Anth.* **66**, 55–69.

BEVER, T. G., FODOR, J. A. and WESKEL, W. 1965. On the acquisition of syntax: a critique of 'contextual generalization'. *Psychol. Rev.* **72**, 467–82; page references to the reprint, in Jakobovits, L. A. and Miron, M. S. (eds.), *Readings in the psychology of language* (Englewood Cliffs, 1967), 257–73.

BIERWISCH, M. 1968. Two critical problems in accent rules. *JL* **4**, 173–8.

BIERWISCH, M. and HEIDOLPH, K. G. (eds.) 1970. *Progress in linguistics* (The Hague).

BIRDWHISTELL, R. L. 1959. The frames in the communication process. Paper presented to the American Society of Clinical Hypnosis (mimeo).

— 1961. Paralanguage—25 years after Sapir. In Brosin, H. (ed.), *Lectures on experimental psychiatry* (Pittsburgh).

— 1966. Some relationships between American kinesics and spoken American English. In Smith, A. (ed.), *Communication and culture* (New York), 182–189.

— 1970. *Kinesics and context: essays on body-motion communication* (Philadelphia).

BLACK, J. W. 1950. The effect of room characteristics upon vocal intensity and rate. *J. Ac. Soc. Am.* **22**, 174–6.

— 1961. Relationships among fundamental frequency, vocal sound pressure, and rate of speaking. *Lg. and Sp.* **4**, 196–9.

— 1970. The magnitude of pitch inflection. In Hála *et al.*, 177–81.

BLACK, J. W., TOSI, O., SINGH, S. and TAKEFUTA, Y. 1966. A study of pauses in oral reading of one's native language and English. *Lg. and Sp.* **9**, 237–41.

BLANKENSHIP, J. and KAY, C. 1964. Hesitation phenomena in English speech. *Word* **20**, 360–72.

BLANTON, M. G. 1917. The behavior of the human infant during the first thirty days of life. *Psychol. Rev.* **24**, 456–83.

BLASDELL, R. and ARAM, D. 1969. Kinesic, phonetic and prosodic communicative systems of the first-language learner (*ERIC Abstract*).

BLASDELL, R. and JENSEN, P. 1970. Stress and word position as determinants of imitation in first-language learners. *J. Sp. H. Res.* **13**, 193–202.

BLOOM, L. 1973. *One word at a time* (The Hague).

BLOUNT, B. G. 1970. The pre-linguistic system of Luo children. *Anth. Ling.* **12**, 326–42.

— 1971. Socialization and pre-linguistic development among the Luo of Kenya. *Southwest J. Anth.* **27**, 41–50.

BLUHME, T. 1971. L'identification de différentes attitudes émotionelles par l'intonation. *Trav. Inst. Phon. Strasbourg* **3**, 248–60.

BLURTON-JONES, N. (ed.) 1972. *Ethological studies of child behaviour* (London).

BOLINGER, D. L. 1949. Intonation and analysis. *Word* **5**, 248–54.

— 1951. Intonation—levels v. configurations. *Word* **7**, 199–210.

— 1958. A theory of pitch accent in English. *Word* **14**, 109–49.

— 1970. Relative height. In Léon 1970, 109–25.

— (ed.) 1972a. *Intonation* (Harmondsworth).

— 1972b. Accent is predictable (if you're a mind-reader). *Lg.* **48**, 633–44.

BOOMER, D. S. 1963. Speech disturbance and body movement in interviews. *J. Nerv. Ment. Dis.* **136**, 263–6.

— 1965. Hesitation and grammatical encoding. *Lg. and Sp.* **8**, 148–58.

BOOMER, D. S. and DITTMAN, A. T. 1962. Hesitation pauses and juncture pauses in speech. *Lg. and Sp.* **5**, 215–20.

— 1964. Speech rate, filled pause, and body movement in interviews. *J. Nerv. Ment. Dis.* **139**, 324–7.

BOOMER, D. S. and LAVER, J. 1968. Slips of the tongue. *B. J. Dis. Comm.* **3**, 2–12.

BOSMA, J. F. and FLETCHER, S. G. 1961. Comparison of pharyngeal action in infant cry and mature phonation. *Logos* **4**, 100–117.

BOSMA, J. F. and LIND, J. 1962. Upper respiratory mechanisms of newborn infants. *Acta Paed. Scand., Supp.* **135**, 32–44.

BOSMA, J. F., LIND. J. and TRUBY, H. M. 1964. Respiratory motion patterns of the newborn infant in cry. In Kay, J. L. (ed.), *Physical diagnosis of the newly born* (Columbus), 103–16.

BOSMA, J. F. and SMITH, C. C. 1961. Infant cry: a preliminary study. *Logos* **4**, 10–18.

BOSMA, J. F., TRUBY, H. M. and LIND, J. 1965. Cry motions of the newborn infant. *Acta Paed. Scand., Supp.* **163**, 61.

BOWLER, N. W. 1964. A fundamental frequency analysis of harsh vocal quality. *Sp. Monogs.* **31**, 128–34.

BRAINE, M. D. S. 1963. On learning the grammatical order of words. *Psychol. Rev.* **70**, 323–48; page references to the reprint, in Jakobovitz, L. A. and Miron, M. S. (eds.), *Readings in the psychology of language* (Englewood Cliffs, 1967), 232–56.

— 1965. On the basis of phrase structure: a reply to Bever, Fodor and Weksel. *Psychol. Rev.* **72**, 483–92; page references to the reprint, in Jakobovitz and Miron, *op. cit.*, 274–84.

BRANDT, J. F., RUDER, K. F. and SHIPP, T. 1969. Vocal loudness and effort in continuous speech. *J. Ac. Soc. Am.* **46**, 1543–8.

BRAZELTON, T. B. 1962. Crying in infancy. *Pediat.* **29**, 579.

BRESNAN, J. W. 1971. Sentence stress and syntactic transformations. *Lg.* **47**, 257–81.

— 1972. Stress and syntax: a reply. *Lg.* **48**, 326–42.

BRIDGES, K. M. B. 1932. Emotional development in early infancy. *Ch. Dev.* **4**, 324–41.

BRIGHT, W. (ed.) 1966. *Sociolinguistics* (The Hague).

BROADBENT, D. E. and GREGORY, M. 1967. Perception of emotionally toned words. *Nature* **215**, 581–4.

BRODBECK, A. J. and IRWIN, O. C. 1946. The speech behavior of infants without families. *Ch. Dev.* **17**, 145–56.

BRODNITZ, F. S. 1962. The holistic study of the voice. *QJS* **48**, 280–84.

BRONSTEIN, A. J. and JACOBY, B. F. 1967. *Your speech and voice* (New York).

BROOK, S. 1965. *The language of the Book of Common Prayer* (London).

BROOKS, R., BRANDT, L. and WIENER, M. 1969. Differential response to two communication channels: socioeconomic class differences in response to verbal reinforcers communicated with and without tonal inflection. *Ch. Dev.* **40**, 453–70.

BROWN, E. and MIRON, M. S. 1971. Lexical and syntactic predictors of the distribution of pause time in reading. *JVLVB* **10**, 658–67.

BROWN, R. 1958. *Words and things* (New York).

— 1973. *A first language* (Harvard).

BROWN, R. and BELLUGI, U. 1964. Three processes in the child's acquisition of syntax. *Harvard Educ. Rev.* **34**, 133–51.

BÜHLER, C. 1930. *The first year of life*; tr. P. Greenberg and R. Ripkin (New York).

BÜHLER, C. and HETZER, H. 1928. Das erste Verständnis von Ausdruck im ersten Lebensjahr. *Z. Psychol.* **107**, 50–61.

BÜHLER, K. 1922. Vom Wesen der Syntax. In V. Klemperer and E. Lerch (eds.), *Idealistische Neuphilologie, Festschrift für Karl Vossler* (Heidelberg), 54–84.

BURGESS, O. N. 1973. Intonation patterns in Australian English. *Lg. and Sp.* **16**, 314–26.

BURLING, R. 1966. The metrics of children's verse: a cross-linguistic study. *Am. Anth.* **68**, 1418–41.

BUSNEL, R.-G. (ed.) 1963. *Acoustic behaviour of animals* (Amsterdam).

CAMERON, J., LIVSON, N. and BAYLEY, N. 1967. Infant vocalizations and their relationship to mature intelligence. *Science* **157**, 331–3.

CAMMACK, F. M. and VAN BUREN, H. 1967. Paralanguage across cultures: some comparisons between Japanese and English. *ELEC Bulletin* **22**, 7–10, 47.

CAMPBELL, R. and WALES, R. 1970. The study of language acquisition. In Lyons, J. (ed.), *New horizons in linguistics* (Harmondsworth), 242–60.

CAPELL, A. 1966. *Studies in socio-linguistics* (The Hague).

CARLSON, P. and ANISFELD, M. 1969. Some observations on the linguistic competence of a two-year-old child. *Ch. Dev.* **40,** 569–75.

CARRELL, J. and TIFFANY, W. R. 1960. *Phonetics: theory and application to speech improvement* (New York).

CATFORD, J. C. 1964. Phonation types: the classification of some laryngeal components of speech production. In Abercrombie, D. *et al.* (eds.), *In honour of Daniel Jones* (London), 26–37.

CHAMPNEYS, F. H. 1881. Notes on an infant. *Mind* **6,** 104–7.

CHAO, Y. R. 1962. Models in linguistics and models in general. In Nagel, E. *et al.* (eds.), *Logic, methodology and philosophy of science* (Stanford), 558–66.

CHARLESTON, B. M. 1960. *Studies on the emotional and affective means of expression in modern English* (Berne).

CHATMAN, S. 1956. Robert Frost's 'Mowing': an inquiry into prosodic structure. *Kenyon Rev.* **18,** 421–38.

— 1957. Linguistics, poetics, and interpretation: the phonemic dimension. *QJS* **43,** 248–56.

— 1965. *A theory of meter* (The Hague).

CHATMAN, S. and LEVIN, S. R. (eds.) 1967. *Essays on the language of literature* (New York).

CHESNI, Y. 1970. Sur le cri et quelques autres comportements mimiques innés examinés pendant les premiers jours de la vie. *Rev. Laryng. Bordeaux* **91,** 339–57.

CHEYNE, W. M. 1970. Stereotyped reactions to speakers with Scottish and English regional accents. *B. J. Soc. Clin. Psychol.* **9,** 77–9.

CHOMSKY, N. 1969. Deep structure, surface structure and semantic interpretation (Indiana Linguistics Club); reprinted in Jakobson, R. and Kawamoto, S. (eds.), *Studies in general and oriental linguistics* (Tokyo 1970), 52–91.

CHOMSKY, N. and HALLE, M. 1968. *The sound pattern of English* (New York).

CHOMSKY, N. and LUKOFF, F. 1956. On accent and juncture in English. In Halle, M. *et al.* (eds.), *For Roman Jakobson* (The Hague), 65–80.

CHREIST, F. M. 1964. *Foreign accent* (Englewood Cliffs).

CLAY, M. M. and IMLACH, R. H. 1971. Juncture, pitch and stress as reading behavior variables', *JVLVB* **10,** 133–9.

COHEN, A., SCHOUTEN, J. F. and 'T HART, J. 1962. Contribution of the time parameter to the perception of speech. *Proc. 4th Int. Cong. Phon. Sci.* (The Hague), 555–60.

COHEN, A. and STARKWEATHER, J. 1961. Vocal cues to language identification. *Am. J. Psychol.* **74,** 90–93.

COHEN, A. and 'T HART, J. 1970. Comparison of Dutch and English intonation contours in spoken news bulletins. *IPO Annual Progress Report* **5,** 78–82.

COLLIER, R. 1971. A grammar of pitch movements in Dutch intonation. *IPO Annual Progress Report* **6,** 17–21.

— 1971. From pitch to intonation (PhD thesis, University of Louvain).

COLLIER, R. and 'T HART, J. 1970. Basic patterns in Dutch intonation. *IPO Annual Progress Report* **5,** 73–8.

— 1972. Perceptual experiments in Dutch intonation. *Proc. 7th Int. Cong. Phon. Sci.* (The Hague), 880–84.

CONKLIN, H. C. 1959. Linguistic play in its cultural context. *Lg.* **35,** 631–6.

CONWELL, M. J. and JUILLAND, A. 1963. *Louisiana French grammar: 1, Phonology, morphology, and syntax* (The Hague).

COOK, M. 1969. Transition probabilities and the incidence of filled pauses. *Psychonom. Sci.* **16**, 191–2.

— 1971. The incidence of filled pauses in relation to part of speech. *Lg. and Sp.* **14**, 135–9.

COOK, M. and LALLJEE, M. G. 1970. The interpretation of pauses by the listener. *B. J. Soc. Clin. Psychol.* **9**, 375–6.

COOK, M., SMITH, J. and LALLJEE, M. G. 1974. Filled pauses and syntactic complexity. *Lg. and Sp.* **17**, 11–16.

COOPER, M. and YANAGIHARA, N. 1971. A study of the basal pitch level variations found in the normal speaking voices of males and females. *J. Comm. Dis.* **3**, 261–6.

COPCEAG, D. and ROCERIC-ALEXANDRESCU, A. 1968. Intonation et structure logique. *Rev. Roum. Ling.* **13**, 499–502.

CORLEW, M. M. 1968. A developmental study of intonation recognition. *J. Sp. H. Res.* **11**, 825–32.

COSTANZO, F. S., MARKEL, N. and COSTANZO, P. R. 1969. Voice quality profile and perceived emotion. *J. Counsel. Psychol.* **16**, 267–70.

CRUTTENDEN, A. 1970. On the so-called grammatical function of intonation. *Phon.* **21**, 129–37.

— 1974. An experiment involving comprehension of intonation in children from 7 to 10. *J. Ch. Lang.* **1**, 221–31.

CRYSTAL, D. 1963. A perspective for paralanguage. *M. Phon.* **120**, 25–9.

— 1964. An approach to a reply. *M. Phon.* **122**, 23–4.

— 1966a. The linguistic status of prosodic and paralinguistic features in English. *Proceedings of the University of Newcastle-upon-Tyne Philosophical Society*, Series B (Arts), **1**, 93–108.

— 1966b. Word classes in English. In *Word classes* (Amsterdam, special volume of *Lingua*), 24–56.

— 1969a. *Prosodic systems and intonation in English* (London).

— 1969b. Review of Halliday 1967. In *Lg.* **45**, 378–94.

— 1969c. A forgotten English tone: an alternative analysis. *M. Phon.* **132**, 34–7.

— 1971. Intonation and semantic structure. In *Actes 10e Cong. Int. Ling.* (Bucharest), 415–22.

— 1972. Objective and subjective in stylistic analysis. In Kachru, B. B. and Stahlke, H. (eds.), *Current trends in stylistics* (Edmonton), 103–14.

CRYSTAL, D. and DAVY, D. 1969. *Investigating English style* (London).

— 1975. *Advanced conversational English* (London).

CRYSTAL, D. and QUIRK, R. 1964. *Systems of prosodic and paralinguistic features in English* (The Hague).

CULLEN, J. K., FARGO, N. L. and BAKER, P. 1968. The development of auditory feedback monitoring: (III) delayed auditory feedback studies of infant cry using several delay times. *Neurocommunications Laboratory Annual Reports* (Johns Hopkins University), 77–93.

CULLEN, J. K., FARGO, N. L., CHASE, R. A. and BAKER, P. 1968. The development of auditory feedback monitoring: (I) delayed auditory feedback studies of infant cry. *J. Sp. H. Res.* **11**, 85–93.

CULLEN, J. M. 1972. Some principles of animal communication. In Hinde, 101–122.

CURRY, E. T. 1940. The pitch characteristics of the adolescent male voice. *Sp. Monogs.* 7, 48–62.

DABROWSKA, J. 1969. Message linguistique et intonation. *Kwartalnik Neofilologiczny* 16, 165–9.
— 1970. Le rôle de l'intonation dans la langue parlée. *Biuletyn Fonograficzny* 11, 147–52.

DARWIN, C. 1877. A biographical sketch of an infant. *Mind* 2, 285–94.

DAVITZ, J. R. (ed.) 1964. *The communication of emotional meaning* (New York).

DAVY, D. 1968. A study of intonation and analogous features as exponents of stylistic variation, with special reference to a comparison of conversation with written English read aloud (MA thesis, University of London).

DAVY, D. and QUIRK, R. 1969. An acceptability experiment with spoken output. *JL* 5, 109–20.

DEBRECZENI, Á. 1972. The problem of relationship between intonation and sentence stress in Hindi. *Acta Ling.* 22, 309–15.

DE GROOT, A. W. 1968. Phonetics in its relation to aesthetics. In Malmberg 1968, 533–49.

DELACK, J. B. 1971. Analysis of infant speech sound production and development (mimeo, University of British Columbia).

DELACROIX, H. 1934. *L'enfant et le langage* (Paris).

DELATTRE, P. 1969. L'intonation par les oppositions. *Français dans le monde* 64, 6–13.
— 1970. Syntax and intonation: a study in disagreement. *MLJ* 54, 3–9.

DE MARTINO, G. 1972. L'intonazione e l'insegnamento della lingua straniera. *Rassegna Italiana di Linguistica Applicata* 4, 41–61.

DENES, P. B. 1966. Comments on 'Preparations for discussing behaviorism with chimpanzee'. In Smith and Miller, 337–8.

DEVEREUX, G. 1949. Mohave voice and speech mannerisms. *Word* 5, 268–72.

DIEBOLD, A. R. 1965. A survey of psycholinguistic research, 1954–64. In Osgood, C. E. and Sebeok, T. A. (eds.), *Psycholinguistics* (Bloomington), 205–291.
— 1968. Anthropological perspectives. In Sebeok 1968, 525–71.

DITTMAN, A. T. and LLEWELLYN, L. G. 1967. The phonemic clause as a unit of speech decoding. *J. Pers. Soc. Psychol.* 6, 341–9.
— 1968. Relationship between vocalizations and head nods as listener responses. *J. Pers. Soc. Psychol.* 9, 79–84.

DITTMAN, A. T. and WYNNE, L. C. 1961. Linguistic techniques and the analysis of emotionality in interviews. *J. Ab. Soc. Psychol.* 63, 201–4.

DITTRICHOVÁ, J. and LAPÁČKOVÁ, V. 1964. Development of the waking state in young infants. *Ch. Dev.* 35, 365–70.

DORE, J. 1975. Holophrases, speech acts and language universals. *J. Ch. L.* 2, 21–40.

DRIVER, H. E. and DRIVER, W. 1963. *Ethnography and acculturation of the Chichimeca-Jonaz of northeast Mexico* (The Hague).

DROMMEL, R., GERŠIĆ, S. and HINTZENBERG, D. 1973. Eine Methode zur numerischen Erfassung der Suprasegmentalia. *Phon.* 27, 1–20.

DU FEU, V. 1970. Word prosody and sentence prosody. *Phon.* **21**, 31–9.

DUFFY, R. 1958. The vocal pitch characteristics of 11, 13 and 15 year old female speakers (PhD thesis, University of Iowa).

DUNCAN, S. D. 1965. Paralinguistic behaviors in client-therapist communication in psychotherapy (PhD dissertation, University of Chicago).

— 1969. Nonverbal communication. *Psychol. Bull.* **72**, 118–37.

DUNCAN, S. D., RICE, L. N. and BUTLER, J. M. 1968. Therapists' paralanguage in peak and poor psychotherapy hours. *J. Ab. Psychol.* **73**, 566–70.

DUNCAN, S. D., ROSENBERG, J. and FINKELSTEIN, J. 1969. The paralanguage of experimenter bias. *Sociometry* **32**, 207–19.

DUNCAN, S. D. and ROSENTHAL, R. 1968. Vocal emphasis in experimenters' instruction reading as unintended determinant of subjects' responses. *Lg. and Sp.* **11**, 20–36.

EGOROV, G. G. 1967. *Suprasegmental phonology* (Moscow).

EISENBERG, R. B. 1964. Auditory behavior in the human neonate: a preliminary report. *J. Sp. H. Res.* **7**, 245–69.

— 1965. Auditory behaviour in the human neonate: methodological problems and the logical design of research procedures. *J. Aud. Res.* **5**, 159–77.

EISENSON, J. 1966. Developmental patterns of non-verbal children and some therapeutic implications. *J. Neurol. Sci.* **3**, 313–20.

EISENSON, J., AUER, T. and IRWIN, J. 1963. *The psychology of communication* (New York).

EKMAN, P. 1965. Communication through nonverbal behavior: a source of information about an interpersonal relationship. In Tomkins, S. S. and Izard, C. E. (eds.), *Affect, cognition and personality* (New York), 390–442.

ELERT, C.-C. 1970. *Ljud och ord i svenskan* (Uppsala).

ENGLER, L. F. and HILYER, R. G. 1971. Once again: American and British intonation systems. *Acta Ling. Hafn.* **13**, 99–108.

EPSTEIN, E. L. and HAWKES, T. 1959. *Linguistics and English prosody* (Buffalo).

ERVIN-TRIPP, S. 1964. An analysis of the interaction of language, topic, and listener. *Am. Anth.* **66**, 86–102.

FAIRBANKS, G. 1942. An acoustical study of the pitch of infant hunger wails. *Ch. Dev.* **13**, 227–32.

— 1950. An acoustical comparison of vocal pitch in seven- and eight-year-old children. *Ch. Dev.* **21**, 121–9.

FAIRBANKS, G., HERBERT, E. L. and HAMMOND, J. M. 1949. An acoustical study of vocal pitch in seven- and eight-year-old girls. *Ch. Dev.* **20**, 71–8.

FAIRBANKS, G., WILEY, J. H. and LASSMAN, F. M. 1949. An acoustical study of vocal pitch in seven- and eight-year-old boys. *Ch. Dev.* **20**, 63–9.

FANT, G. 1968. Analysis and synthesis of speech processes. In Malmberg 1968, 173–277.

FARGO, N. *et al.* 1967. Prosodies and phone types in the vocalizations of young children (mimeo, Johns Hopkins University).

FARGO, N., PORT, D. K., MOBLEY, R. L. and GOODMAN, V. E. 1968. The development of auditory feedback monitoring: (IV) delayed auditory feedback studies on the vocalizations of children between six and nineteen months. *Neurocommunications Laboratory Annual Report* (Johns Hopkins University), 95–118.

FAURE, G. 1970. *Les éléments du rythme poétique en anglais moderne* (The Hague).

— 1971. La description phonologique des systèmes prosodiques. *ZPSK* **24**, 347–59.

FELDMAN, D. M. 1973. Measuring auditory discrimination of suprasegmental features in Spanish. *IRAL* **11**, 195–210.

FERGUSON, C. 1964. Baby talk in six languages. *Am. Anth.* **66**, 103–14.

FICHTNER, E. G. 1972. The Trager-Smith stress levels of English: a reinterpretation. *IRAL* **10**, 21–34.

FILLMORE, C. J. 1968a. The case for case. In Bach, E. and Harms, R. T. (eds.), *Universals in linguistic theory* (New York), 1–88.

— 1968b. Types of lexical information. In Fillmore, C. J. and Lehiste, I. (eds.), *Working papers in linguistics* 2 (Columbus), 65–103.

FILLMORE, C. J. and LANGENDOEN, D. T. (eds.) 1971. *Studies in linguistic semantics* (New York).

FIRBAS, J. 1968. On the prosodic features of the modern English finite verb as means of functional sentence perspective. *Brno Studies in English* **7**, 11–48.

FIRTH, J. R. 1948. Sounds and prosodies. *Tr. Phil. Soc.* 127–52.

FISCHER, J. L. 1966. Syntax and social structure: Truk and Ponape. In Bright, 168–83.

FISICHELLI, V. R., HABER, A., DAVIES, J. and KARELITZ, S. 1966. Audible characteristics of the cries of normal infants and those with Down's Syndrome. *Percept. Mot. Skills* **23**, 744–6.

FISICHELLI, V. R. and KARELITZ, S. 1963. The cry latencies of normal infants and those with brain damage. *J. Pediat.* **62**, 724–34.

— 1966. Frequency spectra of the cries of normal infants and those with Down's Syndrome. *Psychonom. Sci.* **16**, 195–6.

— 1969. The effect of stimulus intensity on induced crying activity in the neonate. *Psychonom. Sci.* **16**, 327–8.

FISICHELLI, V. R., KARELITZ, S., EICHBAUER, J. and ROSENFELD, L. S. 1961. Volume-unit graphs: their production and applicability in studies of infants cries. *J. Psychol.* **52**, 423–9.

FISICHELLI, V. R., KARELITZ, S. and HABER, A. 1969. The course of induced crying activity in the neonate. *J. Psychol.* **73**, 183–9.

FITCHEN, M. 1931. Speech and music development of a one-year-old child. *Ch. Dev.* **2**, 324–6.

FITZGERALD, D. K. 1970. Prophetic speech in Gã spirit mediumship. *Working Paper* **20** (Language Behavior Research Laboratory, University of California, Berkeley).

FLATAU, T. S. and GUTZMANN, H. 1906. Die Stimme des Säuglings. *Archiv Laryngol. Rhino.* **18**, 139–51.

FLAVELL, J. H. 1968. *The development of role-taking and communication skills in children* (New York).

FLINT, E. H. 1970. The influence of prosodic patterns upon the mutual intelligibility of Aboriginal and General Australian English. In Wurm, S. A. and Laycock, D. C. (eds.), *Pacific Linguistics studies in honour of Arthur Capell* (Canberra), 717–40.

FLOYD, W. 1964. *Voice identification techniques* (Washington, US Dept Comm., A.D-606 634).

FÓNAGY, I. 1969a. Accent et intonation dans la parole chuchotée. *Phon.* **20**, 177–192.

— 1969b. Métaphores d'intonation et changements d'intonation. *Bull. Soc. Ling. Paris* **64**, 22–42.

FÓNAGY, I. and MAGDICS, K. 1960. Speed of utterance in phrases of different lengths. *Lg. and Sp.* **3**, 179–92.

— 1963. Emotional patterns in intonation and music. *Z. Phon.* **16**, 293–326.

FORMBY, D. 1967. Maternal recognition of infant's cry. *Dev. Med. Ch. Neurol.* **9**, 293.

FOWLER, R. 1968. What is metrical analysis? *Anglia* **86**, 280–320.

FOX, A. 1969. A forgotten English tone. *M. Phon.* **131**, 13–14.

— 1973. Tone-sequences in English. *Arch. Ling.* **4** (new series), 17–26.

FRAKE, C. O. 1964. How to ask for a drink in Subanun. *Am. Anth.* **66**, 127–32.

FREEDMAN, D. A., FOX-KOLENDA, B. J., MARGILETH, D. A. and MILLER, D. H. 1969. The development of the use of sound as a guide to affective and cognitive behavior—a 2-phase process. *Ch. Dev.* **40**, 1099–1105.

FREEMAN, D. C. (ed.) 1970. *Linguistics and literary style* (New York).

FRIEDLANDER, B. Z. 1968. The effect of speaker identity, voice inflection, vocabulary, and message redundancy on infants' selection of vocal reinforcement. *J. Exp. Ch. Psychol.* **6**, 443–59.

FRY, D. B. 1958. Experiments in the perception of stress. *Lg. and Sp.* **1**, 126–52.

— 1966. The development of the phonological system in the normal and deaf child. In Smith, F. and Miller, G. A. (eds.), *The genesis of language* (Cambridge, Mass.), 187–206.

FUSSELL, P. 1965. *Poetic meter and poetic form* (New York).

GARBELL, I. 1965. *The Jewish neo-Aramaic dialect of Persian Azerbaijan* (The Hague).

GARDE, P. 1969. Contraste accentuel et contraste intonationnel. In Juilland, A. (ed.), *Linguistic studies presented to A. Martinet* I (New York), 187–95.

GARDINER, W. 1839. *The music of nature* (Boston).

GARVIN, P. L. and LADEFOGED, P. 1963. Speaker identification and message identification in speech recognition. *Phon.* **9**, 193–9.

GEDDA, L., FIORI-RATTI, L. and BRUNO, G. 1960. La voix chez les jumeaux monozygotiques. *F. Phon.* **12**, 81–94.

GILES, H. 1970. Evaluative reactions to accents. *Educ. Rev.* **22**, 211–27.

— 1971a. Ethnocentrism and the evaluation of accented speech. *B. J. Soc. Clin. Psychol.* **10**, 187–8.

— 1971b. Patterns of evaluation to RP, South Welsh and Somerset accented speech. *B. J. Soc. Clin. Psychol.* **10**, 280–81.

— 1972. The effect of stimulus mildness-broadness in the evaluation of accents. *Lg. and Sp.* **15**, 262–9.

GLEASON, H. A. 1961. *An introduction to descriptive linguistics* (New York).

GLEISS, J. and HÖHN, W. 1968. Das Verhalten beim Schreiben nach konstanter Schmerzreizung atemgesunder und atemgestörter Neugeborener. *Deut. Z. Nervenheilk.* **194**, 311–17.

GOFFMAN, E. 1964. The neglected situation. *Am. Anth.* **66**, 133–7.
GOLDMAN-EISLER, F. 1961a. A comparative study of two hesitation phenomena. *Lg. and Sp.* **4**, 18–26.
— 1961b. The significance of changes in the rate of articulation. *Lg. and Sp.* 4 171–4.
— 1961c. Continuity of speech utterance, its determinants and its significance. *Lg. and Sp.* **4**, 220–31.
— 1961d. The distribution of pause durations in speech. *Lg. and Sp.* **4**, 232–7.
— 1961e. Hesitation and information in speech. In Cherry, C. (ed.), *Proceedings of the 4th London Symposium of Information Theory* (Washington and London), 162–73.
— 1964. Hesitation, information and levels of speech production. In de Reuck, A. V. S. and O'Connor, M. (eds.), *Disorders of language* (London).
— 1967. Sequential temporal patterns and cognitive processes in speech. *Lg. and Sp.* **10**, 122–32.
— 1968. *Psycholinguistics: experiments in spontaneous speech* (New York).
— 1972. Pauses, clauses, sentences. *Lg. and Sp.* **15**, 103–13.
GONZALEZ, A. 1970. Acoustic correlates of accent, rhythm and intonation in Tagalog. *Phon.* **22**, 11–44.
GOODMAN, F. D. 1969. Phonetic analysis of glossolalia in four cultural settings. *J. Sci. Stud. Relig.* **8**, 227–39.
GREENBERG, N., VUORENKOSKI, V., PARTANEN, T. J. and LIND, J. 1967. Behavior and cry patterns in the first two years of life in early and late clamped newborn. *Ann. Paediat. Fenn.* **13**, 64–70.
GREENBERG, S. R. 1970. An experimental study of certain intonational contrasts in American English. *Diss. Abs. Int.* **30**, 4964A–65A.
GRÉGOIRE, A. 1937, 1947. *L'apprentissage du langage* I, II (Gembloux).
GRIŠINA, O. 1969. Hesitation phenomena in English and Russian from a phonetic, phonological and sociolinguistic point of view (thesis, Moscow University).
GROSS, H. (ed.) 1966. *The structure of verse: modern essays on prosody* (Greenwich, Conn.).
GRUBER, J. S. 1967. Topicalization in child language. *FL* **3**, 37–65.
GRUNDSTROM, A. and LÉON, P. (eds.) 1973. *Interrogation et intonation* (Montreal).
GUENTHERODT, I. 1969. Der Melodieverlauf bei Fragesätzen in zwei Lothringer Mundarten. *Phon.* **19**, 156–69.
GUILLAUME, P. 1925. *L'imitation chez l'enfant* (Paris).
GUMPERZ, J. J. 1964. Linguistic and social interaction in two communities. *Am. Anth.* **66**, 137–54.
— 1966. On the ethnology of linguistic change. In Bright, 27–38, discussion 39–49.
GUMPERZ, J. J. and HERASIMCHUK, E. 1972. The conversational analysis of social meaning. In Shuy, R. (ed.), *23rd Annual Round Table* (Georgetown), 99–134.
GUMPERZ, J. J. and HYMES, D. (eds.) 1964. *The ethnology of communication*, special volume of *Am. Anth.* **66**, 6, pt. ii.
— (eds.) 1972. *Directions in sociolinguistics* (New York).

HAAS, M. R. 1944. Men's and women's speech in Koasati. *Lg.* **20**, 142–9.

Bibliography 171

HAAS, M. B. and HARMS, L. E. 1963. Social interaction between infants. *Ch. Dev.* **64,** 79–97.

HAAS, W. 1957. The identification and description of phonetic elements. *Tr. Phil. Soc.* 118–59.

— 1973. Meanings and rules. *Proc. Arist. Soc.* 135–55.

HADDING, K. and STUDDERT-KENNEDY, M. 1974. Are you asking me, telling me, or talking to yourself? *J. Phon.* **2,** 7–14.

HÁLA, B., ROMPORTL, M. and JANOTA, P. (eds.) 1970. *Proceedings of the 6th International Congress of Phonetic Sciences* (Prague).

HALIM, A. 1970. Intonation in relation to syntax in Bahasa Indonesia. *Diss. Abs. Int.* **30,** 3927A–28A.

HALL, R. A. 1964. *Introductory linguistics* (Philadelphia).

HALL, R. S. 1891. Notes on the study of infants. *Ped. Sem.* **1,** 127–38.

HALLE, M. 1970. On meter and prosody. In Bierwisch, M. and Heidolph, K. G. (eds.), *Progress in linguistics* (The Hague).

HALLIDAY, M. A. K. 1961. Categories of the theory of grammar. *Word* **17,** 241–92.

— 1967. *Intonation and grammar in British English* (The Hague).

— 1970. *A course in spoken English: intonation* (London).

— 1974. A sociolinguistic perspective on language development. *Bull. SOAS* **37,** 98–118.

HALLIDAY, M. A. K., MCINTOSH, A. and STREVENS, P. D. 1964. *The linguistic sciences and language teaching* (London).

HAMMARSTRÖM, U. G. E. 1963. Prosodeme und Kontureme. *Phon.* **10,** 194–202.

— 1971. On linguistic terminology. *Actes 10ᵉ Cong. Int. Ling.* 321–5.

HAN, M. S. 1966. Acoustic-phonetic study on speech tempo. *Study of Sounds* **12,** 70–83.

HARGREAVES, W. A. and STARKWEATHER, J. A. 1963. Recognition of speaker identity. *Lg. and Sp.* **6,** 63–7.

HARRIS, D. P. 1971. The intonation of English 'yes-no' questions: two studies compared and synthesized. *TESOL Quart.* **5,** 123–7.

HARRIS, R. M. 1971. Paralinguistics. *Lang. Sci.* **19,** 8–11.

HARTVIGSON, H. H. 1969. *On the intonation and position of the so-called sentence modifiers in present-day English* (Odense).

HARWEG, R. 1971. Die textologische Rolle der Betonung. In Stempel, W.-D. (ed.), *Beiträge zur Textlinguistik* (Munich), 123–59.

HAUGAN, G. M. and MCINTIRE, R. W. 1972. Comparisons of vocal imitation, tactile stimulation, and food as reinforcers for infant vocalizations. *Dev. Psychol.* **6,** 201–9.

HAWKES, T. 1962a. The problem of prosody. *REL* **3,** 32–49.

— 1962b. The matter of metre. *Ess. Crit.* **12,** 413–21.

HAWKINS, P. R. 1971. The syntactic location of hesitation pauses. *Lg. and Sp.* **14,** 277–88.

HAYES, A. S. 1964. Paralinguistics and kinesics. In Sebeok *et al.*, 145–72.

HEBB, D. O. and THOMPSON, W. R. 1954. The social significance of animal studies. In Lindzey, G. (ed.), *Handbook of social psychology* (Reading, Mass.), 532–61.

HEIKE, G. 1969. *Suprasegmentale Analyse* (Marburg).

HENDERSON, A., GOLDMAN-EISLER, F. and SKARBEK, A. 1965a. Temporal patterns of cognitive activity and breath-control in speech. *Lg. and Sp.* **8,** 236–42.

HENDERSON, A., GOLDMAN-EISLER, F. and SKARBEK, A. 1965b. The common value of pausing time in spontaneous speech. *Q. J. Exp. Psychol.* **17**, 343–5.

HENDREN, J. W. 1961. A word for rhythm and a word for meter. *PMLA* **76**, 300–305.

HENRY, J. 1936. The linguistic expression of emotion. *Am. Anth.* **38**, 250–56.

HERRIOT, P. 1970. *An introduction to the psychology of language* (London).

HERZOG, G. 1934. Speech melody and primitive music. *Mus. Q.* **20**, 452–66.

HEWITT, E. K. 1971. Prosody: a structuralist approach. *Style* **6**, 229–59.

HIGGINS, J. J. and WINDSOR LEWIS, J. 1969. Teaching intonation in the language laboratory. *ELT* **24**, 46–8.

HILDEBRANDT, B. 1963. Effektives Sprechtempo, reflexives Sprechtempo und Lautzahlminderung. *Z. Phon.* **16**, 63–76.

HILL, A. A. 1958. *Introduction to linguistic structures* (New York).

HINDE, R. A. (ed.) 1972. *Non-verbal communication* (London).

HIRVONEN, P. 1970. *Finnish and English communicative intonation* (Phonetics Dept, University of Turku).

HLUBÍK, T. 1968. Some observations on the sound system of the subdialect of the town of Laupen, near Berne, Switzerland. *University of Leeds Phonetics Dept. Report* **1**, 28–40.

HOCKETT, C. F. 1958. *A course in modern linguistics* (New York).

— 1960. The origin of speech. *Sci. Am.* **203**, 89–96.

— (in press). Vocal activity. In McQuown.

HOCKETT, C. F. and ALTMANN, S. 1968. A note on design features. In Sebeok 1968, 61–72.

HOENIGSWALD, H. M. 1966. A proposal for the study of folk-linguistics. In Bright, 16–20.

HOLLIEN, H. 1962. Selected vocal characteristics and physical size measurements of pre-adolescent males. *NIH Progress Report*, Grant NB.02813.

— 1974. On vocal registers. *J. Phon.* **2**, 125–43.

HOLLIEN, H. and COPELAND, R. H. 1965. Speaking fundamental frequency (SFF) characteristics of mongoloid girls. *J. Sp. H. Dis.* **30**, 344–9.

HOLLIEN, H. and PAUL, P. 1969. A second evaluation of the speaking fundamental frequency characteristics of post-adolescent girls. *Lg. and Sp.* **12**, 119–124.

HONIKMAN, B. 1964. Articulatory settings. In Abercrombie, D. *et al.* (eds.), *In honour of Daniel Jones* (London), 73–84.

HORNBY, P. A. 1971. Surface structure and the topic comment distinction. *Ch. Dev.* **42**, 1975–88.

HORNBY, P. A. and HASS, W. A. 1970. Use of contrastive stress by preschool children. *J. Sp. H. Res.* **13**, 395–9.

HOYER, A. and HOYER, I. 1924. Über die Lallsprache eines Kindes. *Z. Angew. Psychol.* **24**, 363–84.

HUBERS, G. A. C. 1971. Review of Crystal 1969a. In *Lingua* **26**, 370–82.

HUMPHREYS, W. 1880. A contribution to infantile linguistics. *Tr. Am. Phil. Soc.* 5–17.

HUXLEY, R. and INGRAM, E. (eds.) 1971. *Language acquisition: models and methods* (London).

HYMES, D. H. 1961. On typology of cognitive styles in language. *Anth. Ling.* **3**, 22–54.

ILLINGWORTH, R. S. 1955. Crying in infants and children. *Biomed. J.* 1, 75–8.

IMAZU, T. 1973. A comparative study of stress-tone contours in Spanish, English, and Russian. *Study of Sounds* 16, 169–80.

INGRAM, D. 1971. Transitivity in child language. *Lg.* 47, 888–910.

IRWIN, O. C. 1941. Research on speech sounds for the first six months of life. *Psychol. Bull.* 38, 277–85.

— 1960. Language and communication. In Mussen, P. H. (ed.), *Handbook of research methods in child development* (New York).

IRWIN, O. C. and CHEN, H. P. 1941. A reliability study of speech sounds observed in the crying of newborn infants. *Ch. Dev.* 12, 351–68.

— 1943. Speech sound elements during the first years of life: a review of the literature. *J. Sp. Dis.* 8, 109–21.

IRWIN, O. C. and CURRY, T. 1941. Vowel elements in the crying vocalization of infants under ten days of age. *Ch. Dev.* 12, 99–109.

IRWIN, O. C. and WEISS, L. 1934a. Differential variations in the activity and crying of the newborn infant under different intensities of light: a comparison of observational with polygraph findings. *Univ. Iowa Stud. Ch. Welf.* 9, 137–47.

— 1934b. The effect of clothing on the general and vocal activity of the newborn infant. *Univ. Iowa Stud. Ch. Welf.* 9, 149–62.

ISAČENKO, A. V. and SCHÄDLICH, H.-J. 1970. *A model of standard German intonation* (The Hague).

IVIČ, P. 1970. Prosodic possibilities in phonology and morphology. In Jakobson, R. and Kawamoto, S. (eds.), *Studies in general and oriental linguistics* (Tokyo), 287–301.

JACOBS, M. 1956. Thoughts on methodology for comprehension of an oral literature. In Wallace, A. F. C. (ed.), *Men and cultures* (Pittsburgh), 123–30.

JANOTA, P. 1967. Personal characteristics of speech. *Tr. Czech. Acad. Sci.*, Social Science Series 77, 1.

JASSEM, W. 1972. The question-phrase fall-rise in British English. In Valdman, A. (ed.), *Papers in linguistics and phonetics to the memory of Pierre Delattre* (The Hague), 241–52.

JESPERSEN, O. 1922. *Language: its nature, development and origin* (London).

JOHNSON, C. D. 1970. Unbounded expressions in rules of stress and accent. *Glossa* 4, 185–96.

JONES, C. M. 1971. Diagnostic implications of acoustic cry features. *J. Comm. Dis.* 4, 310–16.

JONES, H. E. 1942. The adolescent growth study: (VI) the analysis of voice records. *J. Consult. Psychol.* 6, 255–6.

JOOS, M. 1962. *The five clocks* (The Hague).

KAGAN, J. 1969. On the meaning of behavior: illustrations from the infant. *Ch. Dev.* 40, 1121–34.

KAPLAN, E. L. 1969. The role of intonation in the acquisition of language (PhD thesis, Cornell University).

— 1970. Intonation and language acquisition. *Papers and Reports on Child Language Development* 1 (Stanford University), 1–21.

KAPLAN, E. L. and KAPLAN, G. A. 1970. Is there any such thing as a prelinguistic child? In Eliot, J. (ed.), *Human development and cognitive processes* (New York).

KARELITZ, S. (recording). Infant vocalizations. *Rec. C1 2669A* (Long Island Jewish Hospital).

KARELITZ, S. and FISCIHELLI, V. 1962. The cry thresholds of normal infants and those with brain damage. *J. Pediat.* **61**, 679–85.

— 1969. Infants' vocalizations and their significance. *Clin. Proc. Child. Hosp.* **25** (Washington, DC), 345–61.

KARELITZ, S., FISICHELLI, V., COSTA, J., KARELITZ, R. and ROSENFELD, L. 1964. Relations of crying activity in early infancy to speech and intellectual development at age three years. *Ch. Dev.* **35**, 769–77.

KARELITZ, S., KARELITZ, R. and ROSENFELD, L. S. 1960. Infants' vocalizations and their significance. In Bowman, P. W. and Mautner, H. V. (eds.), *Mental retardation* (New York), 439–46.

KASHINSKY, M. and WIENER, M. 1969. Tone in communication and the performance of children from two socioeconomic groups. *Ch. Dev.* **40**, 1193–1202.

KEITEL, H. G., COHN, R. and HARNISH, D. 1960. Diaper rash, self-inflicted excoriations, and crying in full-term newborn infants kept in the prone or supine position. *J. Pediat.* **57**, 884–6.

KELKAR, A. 1964. Marathi baby-talk. *Word* **20**, 40–54.

KEMPSON, R. M. 1969. A transcription and prosodic analysis of an approved selection of spoken English used in an interview (MA thesis, University of London).

KERSTA, L. G. 1962. Voiceprint identification. *Nature* **196**, 1253–7.

KEY, H. 1967. *Morphology of Cayuvava* (The Hague).

KEY, M. R. 1970. Preliminary remarks on paralanguage and kinesics in human communication. *Linguistique* **6**, 17–36.

KIRK, L. 1973. An analysis of speech imitations by Gã children. *Anth. Ling.* **15**, 267–75.

KNAPP, P. (ed.) 1963. *Expression of the emotions in man* (New York).

KOLSHANSKII, G. V. 1973. Funktsii paralingvisticheskikh sredstv v yazykovoi kommunikatsii. *Vop. Yazyk.* **1**, 16–25.

KONONOVA, I. M. 1968. Vocal responses in children in the first year of life and their relation to various patterns of behaviour. Trans. from *Vopr. Psikhol.* **5**, 119–27 (in *LLBA*, 1969, 669).

KOPCZYŃSKA, Z. and PSZCZOŁOWSKA, L. 1961. Le rôle de l'intonation dans la versification. In D. Davie *et al.* (eds.), *Poetics* (The Hague), 215–24.

KRAMER, E. 1963. Judgment of personal characteristics and emotions from non-verbal properties of speech. *Psychol. Bull.* **60**, 408–20.

— 1964. Elimination of verbal cues in judgment of emotion from voice. *J. Ab. Soc. Psych.* **68**, 390–96.

KUMAR, A. and OJAMNA, K. 1970. Pitch and sentence intonation. *J. Ac. Soc. Am.* **50**, 48–84.

KUNIHURA, S. 1971. Effects of the expressive voice on phonetic symbolism. *JVLVB* **10**, 427–9.

KURYŁOWICZ, J. 1966. Accent and quantity as elements of rhythm. In Jakobson, R. *et al.* (eds.), *Poetics II* (The Hague), 163–72.

KURTZ, J. H. (recording). The sounds of a day-old baby (Langley Porter Neuropsychiatric Institute, San Fransisco).

KVAVIK, K. H. and OLSEN, C. L. 1972. A survey and bibliography of Spanish intonation (mimeo).

LA BARRE, W. 1964. Paralinguistics, kinesics and cultural anthropology. In Sebeok *et al.*, 191–220.

LABOV, W. 1964. Phonological correlates of social stratification. *Am. Anth.* **66**, 164–76.

— 1967. The effect of social mobility on linguistic behavior. In Lieberson, 58–75.

LACH, R., LING, D., LING, A. H. and SHIP, N. 1970. Early speech development in deaf infants. *Am. Ann. Deaf* **115**, 522–6.

LAKOFF, G. 1972. The global nature of the Nuclear Stress Rule. *Lg.* **48**, 285–303.

LAMBERT, W. E. 1967. A social psychology of bilingualism. *J. Soc. Issues* **23**, 91–109.

LAMPER, C. and EISDORFER, C. 1971. Prestimulus activity level and responsivity in the neonate. *Ch. Dev.* **42**, 465–73.

LANDRETH, C. 1941. Factors associated with crying in young children in the nursery school and home. *Ch. Dev.* **12**, 81–97.

LANDTMAN, B., WASZ-HÖCKERT, O. and VUORENKOSKI, V. 1964. The use of sound spectrography in pediatric cardiology. *Ann. Pediat. Fenn.* **10**, 122.

LANGACKER, R. W. 1970. English question intonation. In *Studies presented to R. B. Lees* (Papers in Linguistics **1**, Edmonton), 139–61.

LAVER, J. 1964. *The synthesis of voice quality.* Edinburgh University Dept of Phonetics PAT Report.

— 1967. The synthesis of components in voice quality. In Hála *et al.*, 523–5.

— 1968. Voice quality and indexical information. *B. J. Dis. Comm.* **3**, 43–54.

— 1970. The production of speech. In Lyons, J. (ed.), *New horizons in linguistics* (Harmondsworth), 53–75.

LAVER, J. and HUTCHESON, S. (eds.) 1972. *Communication in face-to-face interaction* (Harmondsworth).

LAWENDOWSKI, B. 1970. Some observations concerning emphasis. *Stud. Ang. Posnan.* **2**, 73–83.

LAWRENCE, T. Z. 1971. Regional speech of Texas: a description of certain paralinguistic features. *Actes 10e Cong. Int. Ling.* 125–30.

LAY, C. H. and BURRON, B. F. 1968. Perception of the personality of the hesitant speaker. *Percept. Mot. Skills* **26**, 951–6.

LEECH, G. N. 1969. *A linguistic guide to English poetry* (London).

LEHISTE, I. 1970. *Suprasegmentals* (Cambridge, Mass.).

LEHTO, L. 1969. *English stress and its modification by intonation* (Helsinki).

LENNEBERG, E. H. 1964. Language disorders in childhood. *Harvard Educ. Rev.* **34**, 152–77.

— 1967. *Biological foundations of language* (New York).

LENNEBERG, E. H., NICHOLAS, I. A. and ROSENBERGR, E. F. 1964. Primitive stages of language development in mongolism. *Dis. Comm.* **42**, 119–37.

LENNEBERG, E. H., REBELSKY, F. F. and NICHOLS, I. A. 1965. The vocalizations of infants born to deaf and to hearing parents. *Hum. Dev.* **8**, 23–37.

LÉON, P. (ed.) 1970. *Prosodic feature analysis* (Montreal).

LÉON, P. 1972. Patrons expressifs de l'intonation. *Acta Univ. Carol.*, *Phon. Prag.* 3, 149–56.

— 1972. Où en sont les études sur l'intonation. *Proc. 7th Int. Cong. Phon. Sci.* (The Hague), 113–56.

— 1973. Réflexions idiomatologiques sur l'accent en tant que métaphore sociolinguistique. *The French Review* 46, 783–9.

LÉON, P. and MARTIN, P. 1970 *Prolégomènes à l'étude des structures intonatives* (Montreal).

LEONARD, L. B. 1973. The role of intonation in recall of various linguistic stimuli. *Lg. and Sp.* 16, 327–35.

LEOPOLD, W. F. 1947, 1949. *Speech development of a bilingual child* 1, 2 (Evanston).

LEPSCHY, G. C. 1968. Note su accento e intonazione con riferimento all' Italiano. *Word* 24, 270–85.

LERMAN, J. W. and DAMSTÉ, P. H. 1969. Voice pitch of homosexuals. *F. Phon.* 21, 340–46.

LEROY, C. 1973. Àpropos du rôle de l'intonation dans l'acquisition des structures syntaxiques. *Études de Ling. App.* 9, 67–75.

LEVIN, H., BALDWIN, A. L., GALLWEY, M. and PAIVIO, A. 1960. Audience stress, personality, and speech. *J. Ab. Soc. Psychol.* 61, 469–73.

LEVIN, H. and SILVERMAN, I. 1965. Hesitation phenomena in children's speech. *Lg. and Sp.* 8, 67–85.

LEVIN, H., SILVERMAN, I. and FORD, B. L. 1967. Hesitations in children's speech during explanation and description. *JVLVB* 6, 560–64.

LEVIN, S. R. 1962. Suprasegmentals and the performance of poetry. *QJS* 48, 366–72.

LEWIS, M. M. 1936. *Infant speech: a study of the beginnings of language* (New York).

LIEBERMAN, P. 1965. On the acoustic basis of the perception of intonation by linguists. *Word* 21, 40–54.

— 1967. *Intonation, perception and language* (Cambridge, Mass.).

— 1970. A study of prosodic features. *Haskins Status Report on Speech Research* 23, 179–208, also in *Current Trends in Linguistics* 12 (The Hague, 1974).

— 1973. Linguistic and paralinguistic interchange. *Haskins Status Report on Speech Research* 33, 167–72.

LIEBERMAN, P., HARRIS, K. S. and WOLFF, P. 1968. Newborn infant cry in relation to nonhuman primate vocalization. *J. Ac. Soc. Am.* 44, 365.

LIEBERMAN, P. HARRIS, K. S., WOLFF, P. and RUSSELL, L. H. 1971. Newborn infant cry and nonhuman primate vocalization. *J. Sp. H. Res.* 14, 718–27.

LIEBERMAN, P. and MICHAELS, S. B. 1962. Some aspects of fundamental frequency and envelope amplitude as related to the emotional content of speech. *J. Ac. Soc. Am.* 34, 922–7.

LIEBERSON, S. (ed.) 1967. *Explorations in sociolinguistics* (The Hague).

LIND, J. (ed.) 1965. Newborn infant cry. *Acta Paediat. Scand.*, Supp. 163.

— 1971. The infant cry. *Proc. Roy. Soc. Med.* 64, 468–71.

LIND, J., VUORENKOSKI, V., ROSBERG, G., PARTANEN, T. J. and WASZ-HÖCKERT, O. 1970. Spectrographic analysis of vocal response to pain stimuli in infants with Down's Syndrome. *Dev. Med. Ch. Neurol.* 12, 478–86.

LIND, J., WASZ-HÖCKERT, O., VUORENKOSKI, V. and VALANNE, E. 1965. The vocalization of a newborn, brain-damaged child. *Ann. Paediat. Fenn.* **13,** 56–63.

LIND, J., WASZ-HÖCKERT, O., VUORENKOSKI, V., PARTANEN, T. J., THEORELL, K. and VALANNE, E. 1966. Vocal response to painful stimuli in newborn and young infants. *Ann. Paediat. Fenn.* **12,** 55–63.

LINDBLOM, B. 1962. Accuracy and limitations of Sona-graph measurements. In Sovijärvi, A. and Aalto, P. (eds.), *Proc. 4th Int. Cong. Phon. Sci.* (The Hague), 188–200.

LINDSTRÖM, O. 1973. Review of Crystal 1969a. In *Eng. Stud.* **54,** 249–59.

LING, A. H. 1965. Early stages in the development of speech in hearing and deaf babies. *Voice* **8,** 12–18.

LIPKA, L. 1973. Review of Crystal 1969a. In *Anglia* **91,** 378–82.

LIVANT, W. P. 1963. Antagonistic functions of verbal pauses: filled and unfilled pauses in the solution of additions. *Lg. and Sp.* **6,** 1–4.

LOMAX, A. (ed.) 1968. *Folk song style and culture: a staff report on cantometrics* (Washington, AAAS).

LONGACRE, R. E. 1957. *Proto-Mixtecan* (Bloomington).

LOTZ, J. 1963. On the linguistic structure of speech. *Logos* **6,** 13–23.

LOTZ, J., ABRAMSON, A. S., GERSTMAN, L., INGEMANN, F. and NEMSER, W. J. 1960. The perception of English stops by speakers of English, Spanish, Hungarian and Thai. *Lg. and Sp.* **3,** 71–7.

LÖWENFELD, B. 1927. Systematisches Studium der Reaktionen der Säuglinge auf Klänge und Geräusche. *Z. Psychol.* **105,** 62–96.

LUCHSINGER, R. and ARNOLD, G. E. 1965. *Voice—speech—language*; tr. G. E. Arnold and E. R. Finkbeiner (Belmont and London).

LUCHSINGER, R., DUBOIS, C., VASSELLA, F., JOSS, E., GLOOR, R. and WEISMANN, U. 1967. Spektralanalyse des 'miauens' bei Cri-du-Chat Syndrome. *F. Phon.* **19,** 27–33.

LUKENS, H. 1896. Preliminary report on the learning of language. *Ped. Sem.* **3,** 424–60.

LYNCH, J. J. 1953. The tonality of lyric poetry: an experiment in method. *Word* **9,** 211–24.

LYNIP, A. W. 1951. The use of magnetic devices in the collection and analysis of the preverbal utterances of an infant. *Genet. Psychol. Monog.* **44,** 221–262.

LYONS, J. 1968. *An introduction to theoretical linguistics* (London).
— 1970. *Chomsky* (London).
— 1972. Human language. In Hinde, 49–85.

MAHL, G. F. 1963. The lexical and linguistic levels in the expression of the emotions. In Knapp, P. (ed.), *Expression of the emotions in man* (New York), 77–105.

MAHL, G. F. and SCHULZE, G. 1964. Psychological research in the extralinguistic area. In Sebeok *et al.*, 51–124.

MAJEWSKI, W. and BLASDELL, R. 1969. Influence of fundamental frequency cues on the perception of some synthetic intonation contours. *J. Ac. Soc. Am.* **45,** 450–57.

MALMBERG, B. (ed.) 1968. *Manual of phonetics* (Amsterdam).

MALMBERG, B. 1971. Analyse des faits prosodiques: problèmes et méthodes. In Malmberg, B. (ed.), *Phonétique générale et romane* (The Hague), 222–30.

MANDELBAUM, D. G. (ed.) 1949. *Selected writings of Edward Sapir* (Berkeley).

MANOLSON, A. 1972. Comparative study of intonation patterns in normal hearing and hearing-impaired infants. *Proc. 7th Int. Cong. Phon. Sci.* 962–5.

MARKEL, N. N. 1965. The reliability of coding paralanguage: pitch, loudness and tempo. *JVLVB* 4, 306–8.

— 1969a. Relationship between voice-quality profiles and MMPI profiles in psychiatric patients. *J. Ab. Psychol.* 74, 61–6.

— (ed.) 1969b. *Psycholinguistics: an introduction to the study of speech and personality* (Homewood, Ill.).

— 1970. Review of Crystal 1969a. In *Contemp. Psychol.* 15, 547–8.

MARKEL, N. N., BEIN, M. F. and PHILLIS, J. A. 1973. The relationship between words and tone-of-voice. *Lg. and Sp.* 16, 15–21.

MARKEL, N. N., EISLER, R. M. and REESE, H. W. 1967. Judging personality from dialect. *JVLVB* 6, 33–5.

MARKEL, N. N., MEISELS, M. and HOUCK, J. E. 1964. Judging personality from voice quality. *J. Ab. Soc. Psychol.* 69, 458–63.

MARKS, M. 1972. Afro-American gospel music (paper given to Sociolinguistics of Religion section, Georgetown Round Table on Linguistics, Washington, March 1972).

MARLER, P. 1961. The logical analysis of animal communication. *J. Theor. Biol.* 1, 295–317.

MARTIN, J. G. 1967. Hesitations in the speaker's production and listener's re-production of sentences. *JVLVB* 6, 903–9.

— 1970. On judging pauses in spontaneous speech. *JVLVB* 9, 75–8.

MARTIN, J. G. and STRANGE, W. 1968a. Determinants of hesitations in spontaneous speech. *J. Exp. Psychol.* 76, 474–9.

— 1968b. The perception of hesitation in spontaneous speech. *Percept. Psychophys.* 3, 427–38.

MASSENGILL, R. M. 1969. Cry characteristics in cleft-palate neonates. *J. Ac. Soc. Am.* 45, 782–4.

MASSENGILL, R. M., QUINN, G. W. and BRYSON, M. R. 1966. Judging of cleft-palate and normal neonatal cries. *Percept. Mot. Skills* 22, 963–6.

MATARAZZO, J. D., WIENS, A. N., MATARAZZO, R. G. and SASLOW, G. 1968. Speech and silence behavior in clinical psychotherapy and its laboratory cor-relates. In Shlien, J. (ed.), *Research in psychotherapy* 3 (Washington), 347–394.

MCCARTHY, D. 1929. The vocalizations of infants. *Psychol. Bull.* 26, 625–51.

— 1946. Language development in children. In Carmichael, L. (ed.), *A manual of child psychology* (New York), 476–581.

— 1952. Organismic interpretations of infant vocalization. *Ch. Dev.* 23, 273–80.

MCCLEAN, M. D. and TIFFANY, W. R. 1973. The acoustic parameters of stress in relation to syllable position, speech loudness and rate. *Lg. and Sp.* 16, 283–91.

MCGLONE, R. E. 1966. Vocal pitch characteristics of children aged one to two years. *Sp. Monogs.* 33, 178–81.

MCNEILL, D. 1966. Developmental psycholinguistics. In Smith and Miller, 15–84.

MCQUOWN, N. A. (ed.) in press. *Natural history of an interview* (New York).

Bibliography 179

MEESE, E. A. 1968. The art of the tale teller: a study of suprasegmental phonemes in a folktale. *Kentucky Folklore Record* **14**, 25–37.

MENYUK, P. 1969. Prosodic features and children's language production. *MIT, QPR* **93**, 216–19.

MENYUK, P. 1971. *The acquisition and development of language* (Englewood Cliffs).

MENYUK, P. and BERNHOLTZ, N. 1969. Prosodic features and children's language production. (*MIT, QPR, Research Lab. of Electronics* **93**).

METTAS, O. 1971. *Les techniques de la phonétique instrumentale et l'intonation* (Brussels).

MEUMANN, E. 1903. *Die Sprache des Kindes* (Zürich).

MICHEL, J. F., HOLLIEN, H. and MOORE, P. 1966. Speaking fundamental frequency characteristics of 15, 16 and 17-year-old girls. *Lg. and Sp.* **9**, 46–51.

MICHELSSON, K., VUORENKOSKI, V., PARTANEN, T., VALANNE, E. and WASZ-HÖCKERT, O. 1965. Identifikation av spädbarnets preverbal a kommunikation. *Finska Läkaresällsk. Handl.* **109**, 43.

MIGLIAZZA, E. and GRIMES, J. E. 1961. Shiriana phonology. *Anth. Ling.* **3**, 31–41.

MILLER, R. L. 1970. Performance characteristics of an experimental Harmonic Identification Pitch Extraction (HIPEX) system. *J. Ac. Soc. Am.* **47**, 1593–1601.

MILLER, W. B. 1956. A system for describing and analysing the regulation of coordinated activity. In Wallace, 175–82.

MITCHELL, T. F. 1969. Review of Abercrombie 1967. In *JL* **5**, 153–64.

MORAIS-BARBOSA, J. DE, 1966. O problema linguístico da entoação: (I) Théorie de l'intonation; (II) Intonation port. *Rev. Lab. Fon. Exp.* **6** (Coimbra), 107–255.

MOREY, E. and KOENIG, F. 1970. Paralinguistic and kinesic cues in a word association game. *Lg. and Sp.* **13**, 279–84.

MOSKOWITZ, A. L. 1970. The acquisition of phonology. *Language Behavior Research Laboratory Working Paper* **34** (University of California, Berkeley).

MUKAŘOVSKÝ, J. 1933. Intonation comme facteur de rythme poétique. *Arch. Néer. Phon. Exp.* **8–9**, 153–65.

MURAI, J. I. 1960. Speech development of infants: analysis of speech sounds by sona-graph. *Psychologia* **3**, 27–35.

MURPHY, A. 1964. *Functional voice disorders* (Englewood Cliffs).

NAKAZIMA, S. 1962. A comparative study of the speech developments of Japanese and American English in childhood: (I) a comparison of the developments of voices at the prelinguistic period. *Stud. Phonol.* **2**, 27–39.

— 1966. A comparative study of the speech developments of Japanese and American English in childhood: (II) the acquisition of speech. *Stud. Phonol.* **4**, 38–55.

NASH, R. 1970. John likes Mary more than Bill. An experiment in disambiguation using synthesised intonation contours. *Phon.* **20**, 170–88.

— 1973. *Turkish intonation: an instrumental study* (The Hague).

NEELLEY, J. N., EDSON, S. K. and CARLILE, L. 1968. Speaking voice fundamental frequency of mentally retarded adults and normal adults. *Am. J. Ment. Defic.* **72**, 944–7.

NEWMAN, S. S. 1946. On the stress system of English. *Word* 2, 171–87.

NIKOLAEVA, T. M. 1968. O sootnošenii segmentnyx ukazatclej i supersegmentnyx jazykovyx sredstv. *Vop. Jazyk.* 17, 49–57.

— 1969. *Intonatsiya slozhnogo predlozheniya v slavyanskikh yazykakh* (Moscow).

NIST, J. 1964. The word-group cadence: basis of English metrics. *Lings.* 6, 73–82.

NORK, O. A. 1970. Izučenie intonacii na sovremennom ètape i nekotorye zadači intonacionnyx issledovanij. *Inostrannye Jazyki v Škole* 4, 11–19.

NOSS, R. B. 1972. The ungrounded transformer. *Lang. Sci.* 23, 8–14.

O'CONNELL, D. C., TURNER, E. A. and ONUSKA, L. A. 1968. Intonation, grammatical structure, and contextual association in immediate recall. *JVLVB* 7, 110–16.

O'CONNOR, J. D. 1970. Review of Crystal 1969a. In *M. Phon.* 133, 13–16.

OSMERS, E. 1967. A study of the present-day spoken English of church sermons (MPhil thesis, University of London).

OSTWALD, P. F. 1963. *Soundmaking: the acoustic communication of emotion* (Springfield, Ill.).

— 1964. How the patient communicates about disease with the doctor. In Sebeok *et al.* 1964, 11–34.

OSTWALD, P. F., FREEDMAN, D. G. and KURTZ, J. H. 1962. Vocalization of infant twins. *F. Phoniat.* 14, 37–50.

OSTWALD, P. F., PELTZMAN, P., GREENBERG, M. and MEYER, J. 1970. Cries of a Trisomy 13–15 infant. *Dev. Med. Ch. Neurol.* 12, 472–7.

OSTWALD, P. F., PHIBBS, R. and FOX, S. 1968. Diagnostic use of infant cry. *Biol. Neonat.* 13, 68–82.

OSTWALD, P. F., SLIS, I. H. and WILLEMS, L. F. 1967. Synthesis of human infant cries. *IPO Annual Progress Report* 2, 109–14.

PACE, G. B. 1961. The two domains: meter and rhythm. *PMLA* 76, 413–20.

PAINTER, C. 1971. Archetypal breath-groups and the motor theory of speech perception: evidence from a register tone language. *Anth. Ling.* 13, 349–60.

PARMELEE, A. H. 1955. Infant speech development: a report of a study of one child by magnetic tape recordings. *J. Pediat.* 46, 447–50.

PARRISH, W. M. 1962. The rhythm of oratorical prose. In Drummond, A. M. *et al.* (eds.), *Studies in rhetoric and public speaking in honor of James Albert Winans* (New York), 217–31.

PARTANEN, T. J., WASZ-HÖCKERT, O., VUORENKOSKI, V., THEORELL, K., VALANNE, E. H. and LIND, J. 1967. Auditory identification of pain cry signals of young infants in pathological conditions and its sound spectrographic basis. *Ann. Paediat. Fenn.* 13, 56–63.

PECK, C. W. 1969. *An acoustic investigation of the intonation of American English* (Ann Arbor).

PEDREY, C. P. 1945. A study of voice change in boys between the ages of eleven and sixteen. *Sp. Monogs.* 12, 30–36.

PELLOWE, J. 1970. Establishing some prosodic criteria for a classification of speech varieties (mimeo, University of Newcastle).

PELTZMAN, P., OSTWALD, P. F., YEAGER, C. L. and MANCHESTER, D. 1970. Sensory-vocal studies of a twin pair with cephalic union. *Neuropädiatrie* 2, 79–97.

PENDERGRAFT, E. D. and ZIEHE, T. W. 1967. Research in semiotic systems (*Language Research in Progress*, Abstract 701).

PENGE, H. R. 1970: A study of the distribution of pauses in a specimen of live drama (MA thesis, University of London).

PETŘIKOVA-RYNDOVÁ, L. 1941. Melodie čteni. *Časopis pro Moderni Filologii* 27, 322-7.

— 1942. Intonace hovoru dospělých dětem. *Slovo a Slovesnost* 8, 27-9.

— 1943. K melodie děstské mluvy. *Slovo a Slovesnost* 9, 19-25.

PHILLIS, J. A. 1970. Children's judgments of personality on the basis of voice quality. *Dev. Psychol.* 3, 411.

PIKE, E. G. 1949. Controlled infant intonation. *Lang. Learning* 2, 21-4.

PIKE, K. L. 1944. *The intonation of American English* (Ann Arbor).

— 1948. *Tone languages* (Ann Arbor).

— 1963. The hierarchical and social matrix of suprasegmentals. *Prace Filologiczne* 18, 95-104.

PILCH, H. 1970. Pike-Scott's analysis of Fore suprasegmentals. *Kivung* 3, 133-42.

PITTENGER, R. E. and SMITH, H. L. 1957. A basis for some contributions of linguistics to psychiatry. *Psychiatry* 20, 61-78.

PLANCHON, F. 1968. La recherche linguistique et l'enseignement des langues vivantes: les éléments prosodiques du langage parlé. *Linguistica Antverpiensia* 2, 353-67.

POPE, E. 1971. Answers to yes-no questions. *LI* 2, 69-82.

POTAPOVA, R. K. and BLOXINA, L. P. 1970. *Prosodiceskie xarakteristiki reci* (Moscow).

POYATOS, F. 1970. Lección de paralenguaje. *Fil. Mod.* 39, 265-300.

PRATT, K. C. 1930. Note on the relation of temperature and humidity to the activity of young infants. *Ped. Sem.* 38, 480-84.

PRECHTL, H. F. R., THEORELL, K., GRAMSBERGEN, A. and LIND, J. 1969. A statistical analysis of cry patterns in normal and abnormal new born infants. *Dev. Med. Ch. Neurol.* 11, 142-52.

PREYER, W. 1882. *Die Seele des Kindes* (Leipzig); trans. W. Brown, *The mind of the child* (New York, 1889.)

PRONOVOST, W. 1942. An experimental study of methods for determining natural and habitual pitch. *Sp. Monogs.* 9, 111-23.

PTACEK, P. H. and SANDER, E. K. 1966. Age recognition from voice. *J. Sp. H. Res.* 9, 273-7.

QUIRK, R. and CRYSTAL, D. 1966. On scales of contrast in English connected speech. In Bazell, C. E. *et al.* (eds)., *In memory of J. R. Firth* (London), 359-69.

QUIRK, R., GREENBAUM, S., LEECH, G. N. and SVARTVIK, J. 1972. *A grammar of contemporary English* (London).

RABINER, L. R., LEVITT, H. and ROSENBERG, A. E. 1969. Investigation of stress patterns for speech synthesis by rule. *J. Ac. Soc. Am.* 45, 92-101.

RAFFLER ENGEL, W. von, 1966. L'intonazione come prima espressione linguistica dell'infante. *Il Lattante* 37, 29-36.

RAFFLER ENGEL, W. von, 1970. The relationship of intonation to first vowel articulation in infants (paper given to a symposium on Intonology, Prague).
— 1972. Intonational and vowel correlates in contrasting dialects. *Proc. 7th Int. Cong. Phon. Sci.* 768–73.

RAMSAY, R. W. and LAW, L. N. 1966. The measurement of duration of speech. *Lg. and Sp.* 9, 96–102.

RAMSEY, C. T. and OURTH, L. 1971. Delayed reinforcement and vocalization rates in infants. *Ch. Dev.* 42, 291–7.

REBELSKY, F. and HANKS, C. 1971. Fathers' verbal interaction with infants in the first three months of life. *Ch. Dev.* 42, 63–8.

REBELSKY, F., STARR, R. H. and LURIA, Z. 1967. Language development: the first four years. In Brackbill, Y. (ed.), *Infancy and early childhood* (New York), 289–357.

REIBER, M. 1965. The effect of music on the activity level of children. *Psychonom. Sci.* 3, 325–6.

RENSKY, M. 1966. The systematics of paralanguage. *TLP* 2, 97–102.

REVILL, P. M. 1970. Preliminary report on para-linguistics in Mbembe (E. Nigeria). In Pike, K. L. (ed.), *Tagmemic and matrix linguistics applied to selected African languages* (Santa Ana, Calif.).

REVTOVA, L. D. 1970. Intonacija obraščenija. In Hála, 755–7.

RHEINGOLD, H. L., GEWIRTZ, J. L. and ROSS, H. W. 1959. Social conditioning of vocalizations in the infant. *J. Comp. Physiol. Psychol.* 52, 68–73.

RINGEL, R. L. and KLUPPEL, D. D. 1964. Neonatal crying: a normative study. *F. Phoniat.* 16, 1–9.

RINGWALL, E. A., REECE, H. W. and MARKEL, N. M. 1965. A distinctive-feature analysis of prelinguistic infant vocalization. In Riegel, K. F. (ed.), *The development of language functions* (Ann Arbor).

ROBINS, R. H. 1964. *General linguistics: an introductory survey* (London).

ROBINSON, W. P. 1972. *Language and social behaviour* (Harmondsworth).

ROCERIC-ALEXANDRESCU, A. 1970. Intonation and predictability. In Hála, 771–772.

RODÓN, E. 1970. On the grammatical relevance of prosodemes. *Actes 10ᵉ Cong. Int. Ling.* 721–4.

ROSENBERG, B. A. 1970. The formulaic quality of spontaneous sermons. *J. Am. Folk.* 83, 3–20.

ROSSI, M. 1970. Sur la hiérarchie des paramètres de l'accent. In Hála, 779–85.
— 1973. L'intonation prédicative dans les phrases transformées par permutation. *Lings.* 103, 64–94.

ROUBAUD, J. 1971. Mètre et vers: deux applications de la métrique générative de Halle-Keyser. *Poétique* 7, 366–87.

ROUNTREE, S. C. 1972. Saramaccan tone in relation to intonation and grammar. *Lingua* 29, 308–25.

ROUTH, D. K. 1969. Conditioning of vocal response differentiation in infants. *Dev. Psychol.* 1, 219–26.

RUBENSTEIN, H. and ABORN, M. 1960. Psycholinguistics. *Ann. Rev. Psychol.* 11, 291–322.

RUJA, H. 1948. The relation between neonate crying and length of labor. *J. Genet. Psychol.* 73, 53–5.

RUSH, J. 1827. *The philosophy of the human voice* (Philadelphia).

RYAN, J. 1974. Early language development: towards a communicational analysis. In Richards, M. P. M. (ed.), *The integration of a child into a social world* (London), 185–213.

SACK, F. L. 1969. English word-stress. *ELT* 23, 141–4.
SAMARIN, W. J. 1968. The art of Gbeya insults (African Studies Association, California).
— 1972. *Tongues of men and angels* (New York).
SAPIR, F. 1910. Song recitative in Paiute mythology. In Mandelbaum, 463–7.
— 1915. Abnormal types of speech in Nootka. In Mandelbaum, 179–96.
— 1929. Male and female forms of speech in Yana. In Mandelbaum, 206–12.
SCHÄFER, P. 1922. Beobachtungen und Versuche an einem Kinde in der Entwicklungsperiode des reinen Sprachverständnisses *Z. Päd. Psychol.* 23, 269–89.
SCHMERLING, S. F. 1974. A re-examination of 'normal stress'. *Lg.* 50, 66–73.
SCHVEIGER, P. 1968. Sur la pathologie de la dérivation et de l'intonation. *Cah. Ling. Théor. App.* 5, 219–20.
SCHWARTZ, M. F. and RINE, H. E. 1968a. Identification of speaker sex from isolated voiceless fricatives. *J. Ac. Soc. Am.* 43, 1178–9.
— 1968b. Identification of speaker sex from isolated, whispered vowels. *J. Ac. Soc. Am.* 44, 1736–7.
SCHWARZ, A., ROSENBERG, D. and BRACKBILL, Y. 1970. Analysis of the components of social reinforcement of infant vocalization. *Psychonom. Sci.* 20, 323–5.
SEBEOK, T. A. (ed.) 1960. *Style in language* (Cambridge, Mass.).
— 1962. Coding in the evolution of signalling behavior. *Behav. Sci.* 7, 430–442.
— (ed.) 1968. *Animal communication: techniques of study and results of research* (Bloomington).
SEBEOK, T. A., HAYES, A. S. and BATESON, M. C. 1964. *Approaches to semiotics* (The Hague).
SEDLÁČKOVÁ, E. 1964. Analyses acoustiques de la voix des nouveaux nés. *F. Phoniat.* 16, 44–58.
— 1967. *Development of the acoustic pattern of the voice and speech in the newborn and infant* (Prague).
SELIGMAN, C. R., TUCKER, G. R. and LAMBERT, W. E. 1970. The effects of speech style on teachers attitudes toward pupils (mimeo, McGill University).
SETHI, J. 1971. *Intonation of statements and questions in Panjabi* (Hyderabad).
SHAPIRO, J. G. 1968. Variability in the communication of affect. *J. Soc. Psychol.* 76, 181–8.
SHAPIRO, K. and BEUM, R. 1965. *A prosody handbook* (New York).
SHAPIRO, M. 1968. *Russian phonetic variants and phonostylistics* (Berkeley).
SHARPE, M. C. 1970. Voice quality: a suggested framework for description and some observations. In Wurm, S. A. and Laycock, D. C. (eds.), *Pacific linguistics studies in honour of Arthur Capell* (Canberra), 115–34.
SHEN, Y. 1969. Two intonations in eight types of English questions. *J. Eng. Ling.* 3, 66–81.
SHEPARD, R. N. 1964. Circularity in judgments of relative pitch. *J. Ac. Soc. Am.* 36, 2346–53.

SHEPPARD, W. C. 1969. Operant control of infant vocal and motor behavior. *J. Exp. Ch. Psychol.* **7,** 36–51.

SHEPPARD, W. C. and LANE, H. L. 1968. Prosodic features of infant vocalizing. *J. Sp. H. Res.* **11,** 94–108.

SHERMAN, M. 1927. The differentiation of emotional responses in infants: (I) judgments of emotional responses from motion picture views and from actual observation; (II) the ability of observers to judge emotional characteristics of the crying infants and of the voice of an adult. *J. Comp. Psychol.* **7,** 265–84, 335–51.

SHEVCHENKO, T. I. 1972. Ob odnom opyte sintagmaticheskogo issledovaniya intonatsii: analiz posledovatelnostei melodicheskikh konturov v trekh tipakh angliiskikh predlozhenii *loose, balanced, periodic. Inostrannye Yazyki v Škole* **1,** 18–23.

SHINN, M. W. 1900. *The biography of a baby* (New York).

SHIRLEY, M. M. 1933. The first two years: a study of 25 babies: (II) intellectual development. *Inst. Ch. Welf. Monogr. Series* 7 (University of Minnesota).

SIEGEL, L. and SAMEROFF, A. 1971. Monitoring system for infant movement, vocalization, and nurse interaction. *Behav. Res. Meth. Instr.* **3,** 305–6.

SIERTSEMA, B. 1962. Timbre, pitch and intonation. *Lingua* **11,** 388–98.

SIMKINS, L. 1963. Modification of pausing behavior. *JVLVB* **2,** 462–9.

SKEAT, W. W. 1898. On the scansion of English poetry. *Tr. Phil. Soc.* 484–503.

SMITH, F. and GOODENOUGH, C. 1971. Effects of context, intonation and voice on the reaction time to sentences. *Lg. and Sp.* **14,** 241–50.

SMITH, F. and MILLER, G. A. (eds.) 1966. *The genesis of language* (Cambridge, Mass.).

SMITH, H. L. 1952. The communication situation (Washington, US Dept of State, Foreign Service Institute).

— 1959. Toward redefining English prosody. *SIL* **14,** 68–76.

— 1969. Language and the total system of communication. In Hill, A. A. (ed.), *Linguistics today* (New York), 89–102.

SMITHERMAN, C. 1969. The vocal behavior of infants as related to the nursing procedure of rocking. *Nursing Res.* **18,** 256–8.

SOLOMON, D. and ALI, F. A. 1972. Age trends in the perception of verbal reinforcers. *Dev. Psychol.* **7,** 238–43.

SOLOMON, D. and YAEGER, J. 1969a. Effects of content and intonation on perceptions of verbal reinforcers. *Percept. Mot. Skills* **28,** 319–27.

— 1969b. Determinants of boys' perceptions of verbal reinforcers. *Dev. Psychol.* **1,** 637–45.

SOSKIN, W. F. and KAUFFMAN, P. 1961. Judgment of emotion in word-free voice samples. *J. Comm.* **11,** 73–80.

SOTKIS, Y. A. 1972. K voprosu o ritmiko-intonatsionnoi strukture sverkhfrazovogo edinstva. *Filologicheskie Nauki* **15,** 67–73.

STAGEBERG, N. C. 1971. Structural ambiguity and the suprasegmentals. *English Record* **21,** 64–8.

STANKIEWICZ, E. 1964. Problems of emotive language. In Sebeok *et al.,* 239–264.

STARKWEATHER, J. 1961. Vocal communication of personality and human feelings. *J. Comm.* **11,** 63–72.

STERN, C. and STERN, W. 1928. *Die Kindersprache* (Leipzig, 4th edn).

STERN, T. 1956. Some sources of variability in Klamath mythology: (3) style and elements of the myth. *J. Am. Folk.* **69**, 377–86.

STEVENS, S. S. and DAVIS, H. 1938. *Hearing, its psychology and physiology* (London).

STEWART, A. *et al.* 1954. Excessive infant crying (colic) in relation to parent behavior. *Am. J. Psychiat.* **110**, 687–94.

STOCKWELL, R. P. 1960. The place of intonation in a generative grammar of English. *Lg.* **36**, 360–67.

— 1972. The role of intonation: reconsiderations and other considerations. In Bolinger 1972a, 87–109.

STRONGMAN, K. T. and WOOSLEY, J. 1967. Stereotyped reactions to regional accents. *B. J. Soc. Clin. Psychol.* **6**, 164–7.

STUBBS, E. M. 1934. The effect of the factors of duration, intensity, and pitch of sound stimuli on the responses of newborn infants. *Univ. Iowa Stud. Child Welf.* (University of Iowa), **9**, 4.

STUDDERT-KENNEDY, M. and HADDING, K. 1973. Auditory and linguistic processes in the perception of intonation contours. *Lg. and Sp.* **16**, 293–313.

STURTEVANT, E. H. 1947. *An introduction to linguistic science* (New Haven).

SUCI, G. J. 1967. The validity of pause as an index of units in language. *JVLVB* **6**, 26–32.

SVENSSON, S.-G. 1971. A preliminary study of the role of prosodic parameters in speech perception. *Speech Transmission Laboratory Quarterly* (Royal Institute of Technology, Stockholm, PSR, KTH, 2/3), 24–42.

SYCHRA, A. 1962. Kapitola z experimentalniko vyzkumu vyrazu v hubde a reci. *Acta Univ. Carol.* **2**, 49–85.

SYPHER, W. E. 1970. Prosodic aspects of memory for verbal material (PhD thesis, University of Pittsburgh).

SYKES, J. L. 1940. A study of the spontaneous vocalizations of young deaf children. *Psychol. Monogs.* **52**, 104–23.

TAGLICHT, J. 1969. The function of intonation in English verse. *Language and Style* **4**, 116–22.

TAINE, H. 1877. M. Taine on the acquisition of language by children. Trans. from *Rev. Philos.* **1** in *Mind* **2**, 252–9.

TANNENBAUM, P. H., WILLIAMS, F. and HILLIER, C. S. 1965. Word predictability in the environments of hesitations. *JVLVB* **4**, 134–40.

TANNENBAUM, P. H., WILLIAMS, F. and WOOD, B. S. 1967. Hesitation phenomena and related encoding characteristics in speech and typewriting. *Lg. and Sp.* **10**, 203–15.

TAPPOLET, E. 1907. *Die Sprache des Kindes* (Basle).

TEMBROCK, G. 1968. Land mammals. In Sebeok 1968, 338–404.

TERANGO, L. 1966. Pitch and duration characteristics of the oral reading of males on a masculinity-femininity dimension. *J. Sp. H. Res.* **9**, 590–95.

THORPE, W. H. 1961. *Bird song: the biology of vocal communication and expression in birds* (London).

— 1972. The comparison of vocal communication in animals and man. In Hinde, 27–47.

'T HART, J. 1971. Concatenation of intonational blocks. *IPO Annual Progress Report* **6**, 21–4.

— 1972. Intonational rhyme. *Acta Univ. Carol. Phil. I, Phon. Prag.* **3**, 105–9.

'T HART, J. and COHEN, A. 1973. Intonation by rule: a perceptual quest. *J. Phon.* **1**, 309–27.

TODD, G. A. and PALMER, B. 1968. Social reinforcement of infant babbling. *Ch. Dev.* **39**, 591–6.

TOMLINSON-KEASEY, C. 1972. Conditioning of infant vocalizations in the home environment. *J. Genet. Psychol.* **120**, 75–82.

TONKOVA-YAMPOLSKAYA, R. V. 1962. On the question of studying physiological mechanisms of speech. *Pavlov. J. Higher Nerv. Activ.* **12**, 82–7.

— 1968. Razvitie rechevoi intonatsii u detei pervykh dvukh let zhizni. *Vop. Psikh.* **14**, 94–101; trans. in Ferguson, C. and Slobin, D. I. (eds.), *Studies of child language development* (New York 1973), 128–38.

TRACY, F. 1909. *The psychology of childhood* (Boston, 7th edn).

TRAGER, G. L. 1949. *The field of linguistics* (Norman, Okla.)

— 1958. Paralanguage: a first approximation. *SIL* **13**, 1–12.

— 1960. Taos III, paralanguage. *Anth. Ling.* **2**, 24–30.

— 1961. The typology of paralanguage. *Anth. Ling.* **3**, 17–21.

— 1964. Paralanguage and other things. *M. Phon.* **122**, 21–3.

TRAGER, G. L. and SMITH, H. L. 1951. *An outline of English structure* (Norman, Okla.).

TRIM, J. L. M. 1970. Cues to the recognition of some linguistic features of whispered speech in English. In Hála *et al.*, 919–23.

— 1971. Some continuously variable features in British English intonation. *Actes 10ᵉ Cong. Int. Ling.* (The Hague), 267–72.

TROJAN, F. 1957. General semantics (a comparison between linguistic and sublinguistic phonic expression). In Kaiser, L. (ed.), *Manual of phonetics* (Amsterdam), 437–9.

TRUBY, H. M. 1960. Some aspects of acoustical and cineradiographic analysis of newborn-infant and adult phonation and associated vocal tract activity. *J. Ac. Soc. Am.* **32**, 1518.

— 1962. A technique for visual-acoustic analysis of the sounds of infant cry. *J. Ac. Soc. Am.* **34**, 996.

TRUBY, H. M. and LIND, J. 1965. Cry sounds of the newborn infant. In Lind, J. (ed.), *Newborn infant cry* (*Acta Paediat. Scand.*, Supp. **163**), 8–54.

URBAIN, M. 1969. The investigation of some extra-semantic features of English intonation. *Rev. Phon. App.* **10**, 45–63.

VALANNE, E. H., VUORENKOSKI, V., PARTANEN, T. J., LIND, J. and WASZ-HÖCKERT, O. 1967. The ability of human mothers to identify the hunger cry signals of their own new-born infants during the lying-in period. *Experientia* **23**, 768.

VANDERSLICE, R. 1970a. Occam's razor and the so-called stress cycle. *Lang. Sci.* **13**, 9–15.

— 1970b. Prosodic model for orthographic-to-phonetic conversion of English. *J. Ac. Soc. Am.* **48**, 84.

VANDERSLICE, R. and LADEFOGED, P. 1972. Binary suprasegmental features and transformational word-accentuation rules. *Lg.* **48**, 819–38.

VANDERSLICE, R. and PIERSON, L. S. 1967. Prosodic features of Hawaiian English. *Q. J. Sp.* 53, 156–66.

VAN KATWIJK, A. 1972. On the perception of stress. *Acta Univ. Carol. Phil. I, Phon. Prag.* 3, 127–35.

— 1974. Accentuation in Dutch: an experimental linguistic study (PhD thesis, University of Utrecht).

VAN LANCKER, D. and FROMKIN, V. A. 1973. Hemispheric specialization for pitch and 'tone': evidence from Thai. *J. Phon.* 1, 101–9.

VAN RIPER, C. 1963. *Speech correction: principles and methods* (Englewood Cliffs, 4th edn).

VENDE, K. 1969. O roli intonacii v opoznavanii voprosa v èstonskom jazyke. *Sovetskoe Finno-Ugrovedenie* 1, 161–5.

VETTER, H. J. 1969. *Language, behavior and communication* (Ithaca).

VOIERS, W. D. 1964. Perceptual bases of speaker identity. *J. Ac. Soc. Am.* 36, 1065–73.

VUORENKOSKI, V., KAUNISTO, M., TJERNLUND, P. and VESA, L. 1970. Cry detector: a clinical apparatus for surveillance of pitch and activity of a newborn infant. *Acta Paediat. Scand.* 59, Supp. 206, 103–4.

VUORENKOSKI, V., LIND, J., PARTANEN, T. J., LEJEUNE, J., LAFOURCADE, J. and WASZ-HÖCKERT, O. 1966. Spectrographic analysis of cries from children with maladie du cri du chat. *Ann. Paediat. Fenn.* 12, 174–80.

VUORENKOSKI, V., LIND, J., WASZ-HÖCKERT, O. and PARTANEN, T. J. 1971. Cry score: a method of evaluating the degree of abnormality in the pain cry response of the newborn and young infant. *QPSR* (Dept of Speech Comm., Royal Inst. of Technology, Stockholm), 68–75.

VUORENKOSKI, V., WASZ-HÖCKERT, O., KOIVISTO, E. and LIND, J. 1969. The effect of cry stimulus on the temperature of the lactating breast of primapara: a thermographic study. *Experientia* 25, 1286–7.

WAHLER, R. G. 1969. Infant social development: some experimental analyses of an infant-mother interaction during the first year of life. *J. Exp. Ch. Psychol.* 7, 101–13.

WALCH, M. L. 1973. Stress rules and performance. *Lg. and Sp.* 15, 279–87.

WALLACE, A. F. C. (ed.) 1956. *Men and cultures* (Philadelphia).

WASZ-HÖCKERT, O., KOIVISTO, M., VUORENKOSKI, V., PARTANEN, T. J. and LIND, J. 1971. Spectrographic analysis of pain cry in hyperbilirubinemia. *Biol. Neonate* 17, 260–71.

WASZ-HÖCKERT, O., LIND, J., VUORENKOSKI, V., PARTANEN, T. J. and VALANNE, E. 1967. The spectrographic and auditive identification of the cry of the normal newborn and young infant. *Dev. Med. Child. Neurol.* 9, 66–8.

— 1968. *The infant cry: a spectrographic and auditory analysis* (accompanied by a recording) (London).

WASZ-HÖCKERT, O., PARTANEN, T. J., VUORENKOSKI, V., VALANNE, E. and MICHELS-SON, K. 1964a. The identification of some specific meanings in infant vocalization. *Experientia* 20, 154.

— 1964b. Effect of training on ability to identify preverbal vocalization. *Dev. Med. Ch. Neurol.* 6, 393–6.

WASZ-HÖCKERT, O., SIMILÄ, S., ROSBERG, G., VUORENKOSKI, V. and LIND, J. 1969.

El sindrome de Smith-Lemli-Opitz en dos niñas, con especial atención a los patrones de sus gritos de dolor. *Rev. Mex. Pediat.* **38**, 63–8.

WASZ-HÖCKERT, O. VALANNE, E., VUORENKOSKI, V., MICHELSSON, K. and SOVIJÄRVI, A. 1963. Analysis of some types of vocalization in the newborn and in early infancy. *Ann. Paediat. Fenn.* **9**, 1–5.

WASZ-HÖCKERT, O., VUORENKOSKI, V., VALANNE, E., MICHELSSON, K. and LIND, J. 1964. Estudios espectrographicos de los gritos de hambre en los recién nacidos e infantes. *Rev. Mex. Pediat.* **33**, 98–103.

WATANABE, K. 1972. The intonation of *wh*-questions in English. *Bull. Phon. Soc. Japan* **140**, 4–6.

WEAKLAND, J. H. 1967. Communication and behavior—an introduction. *Am. Behav. Sci.* **10**, 1–4.

WEBSTER, W. G. and KRAMER, E. 1968. Attitudes and evaluational reactions to accented English speech. *J. Soc. Psychol.* **75**, 231–40.

WEEKS, T. 1971. Speech registers in young children. *Ch. Dev.* **42**, 1119–31.

WEINBERG, M. B. F. DE, 1970. Review of Crystal 1969a. In *Eng. Lang. J.* **1**, 399–406.

— 1971. La entonación del español de Córdoba (Argentina). *Bol. Inst. Caro y Cuervo* **26**, 11–21.

WEIR, R. 1962. *Language in the crib* (The Hague).

— 1966. Some questions on the child's learning of phonology. In Smith and Miller, 153–68.

WEISBERG, P. 1963. Social and nonsocial conditioning of infant vocalizations. *Ch. Dev.* **34**, 377–88.

WENDAHL, R. W. 1966. Some parameters of auditory roughness. *F. Phon.* **18**, 26–32.

WENDLER, J. 1970. Zur auditiven Steuerung der Sprechintonation. In Hála, 1009–1013.

WERNER, M. S. 1969. Alterations in the duration, pitch, and intensity of spoken passages successively heard and repeated several times. *J. Ac. Soc. Am.* **46**, 1051–2.

WEST, J. D. 1962. Phonology of Mikasuki. *SIL* **16**, 77–91.

WHITEHALL, H. 1956. From linguistics to criticism. *Kenyon Review* **13**, 710–14; reprinted in **18**, 411–21.

WIENER, M. and MEHRABIAN, A. 1968. *Language within language: immediacy, a channel in verbal communication* (New York).

WINDSOR LEWIS, J. 1969. The tonal system of remote speech. *M. Phon.* **132**, 31–6.

— 1970. English intonation: (I) before the sixties; (II) comments on 'Intonation of colloquial English' (mimeo, University of Leeds).

WINITZ, H. 1960. Spectrographic analysis of infant vowels. *J. Genet. Psychol.* **96**, 171–81.

WITTMAN, H. 1970. The prosodic formatives of modern German. *Phon.* **22**, 1–10.

WODARZ-MAGDICS, K. 1973. Review of Crystal 1969a. In *Lings.* 117–19.

WODE, H. 1972a. Zur Erzeugung der Tonhöhe englischer Syntagmata. *Acta Univ. Carol. Phil. I, Phon. Prag.* **3**, 271–80.

— 1972b. The intonation of replies to *wh*-questions in English. In Rigault, A. and Charbonneau, R. (eds.), *Proc. 7th Int. Cong. Phon. Sci.* (The Hague), 1058–63.

— 1975. Grammatical intonation in child language: a case from German and some complaints. In Sangster, L. and Van Schooneveld, C. H. (eds.), *Intonation and prosodic analysis* (The Hague).

WOLFF, P. H. 1959. Observations on newborn infants. *Psychosom. Med.* 21, 110–118.

— 1969. The natural history of crying and other vocalizations in early infancy. In Foss, B. (ed.), *Determinants of infant behaviour* 4 (London), 81–109.

YORIO, C. A. 1973. The generative process in intonation. *Lings.* 97, 111–25.

ZACHARIAS, C. 1970. Form-Funktionsbestimmung der Intonation einer Interferenzvariante des Fragesatzes. In Hála, 1051–3.

ZACHER, O. 1970. Zur phonologischen Wertung der Intonatsionsmittel. In Hála, 1055–6.

ZHIRMUNSKI, V. 1966. The versification of Majakowski. In Jakobson, R. *et al.* (eds.), *Poetics II* (The Hague), 211–42.

ZURIF, E. B. and MENDELSOHN, M. 1972. Hemispheric specialization for the perception of speech sounds: the influence of intonation and structure. *Percep. Psychophys.* 11, 329–32.

Person Index

194 *Person Index*

Subject Index

accent 5–6, 9, 94, 108, 117, 127
acceptability 7–9, 24, 29, 56
acoustics 61, 75–6, 133, 136, 138–41, 144–6, 157–8
affect 1, 12–15, 21–2, 49, 116, 130–32, 134
age 56, 58, 79, 84, 86–7, 125–58
ambiguity 9, 18, 20, 30, 50, 59, 115–16, 122
Anglo-Saxon 108
animal communication 51–2, 56, 65–72, 131
anthropology 2, 49, 50, 56, 84–5, 92–3, 110
Approaches to Semiotics 47
Arabic 86
arbitrariness 67, 71, 73
articulatory setting 52–3, 104, 137
Aspects of the Theory of Syntax 4
assimilation 14
attitude 6–7, 24, 26, 29–32, 36–41, 51, 55–62, 65, 71, 79, 81, 146–50, 156–7
audiology 125, 142
authority role 89

babbling 15, 126–7, 135, 141, 147–8, 156
baby-talk 86, 135–7, 157
Bible 98
Book of Common Prayer 78
breath group 156
broadcast transmission 66
Burundi 84, 86–7

cadence 117, 126, 145
caesura 116, 120
cantometrics 56
case grammar 48
Cayuvava 87, 92
channel 67, 70
Chichimeca 86
choreometrics 56
clause 15–22, 28, 35, 43, 46, 99, 115, 146, 154
code-switching 103
cognitive 12–13, 59, 71, 116
collocation 99, 117
common core 63
community quality 62–3
competence 10, 48, 106

—, communicative 2
computing 136, 145
connected speech 29, 33–4, 46, 75, 82, 94, 113
context 6–8, 24, 29–34, 37, 46, 68, 72, 79, 96, 115, 128–9, 143–4
contextual generalization 127
conversation 3, 12, 50, 76, 90–91, 116, 121, 123
—, proto- 142
cooing 133
corpus 9–10, 15, 17, 23, 43, 46
criteria 30, 33, 37, 50, 54–5, 58–61, 69, 78, 96, 130
cry 126–32, 138–46
    score 139
Czech 107, 111, 131, 146

Darkhat Mongol 86
deaf 137, 141
dialect 8, 42–3, 57, 62–3, 79, 87, 157
diglossia 104
discourse 32–4, 48, 97, 115
discreteness 49, 52, 59–60, 67, 71–3, 113, 147
displacement 32, 67, 71
double articulation 67
Down's syndrome 140
duality 67, 73
duration 52, 109, 120, 138, 140, 145–6, 148

elision 14
elocution 88, 89, 131
emic 48, 58
endogenous 71
English dialects 42–3, 56
enjambement 116, 120
equivalence 41–2, 46, 123
Essays in Criticism 118
ethnography 2, 84
ethology viii, 142
expansion 16–21
extralinguistic 48, 55, 60, 89, 109, 151

fading 66
feedback 67, 70–71
Field of Linguistics, The 48
focus 11, 27, 30, 36
foot 90, 107, 117–18

specialization   67
spectrography   133, 136–41, 144
speech style   84–5, 91, 149, 155
speech surrogate   92
speech synthesis   75
statistics   9, 33, 104, 132, 142, 144
status   56, 79, 87–9
stereotype   viii, 15, 57, 63–4, 75, 79–80, 87, 89–90, 98
stress   4–12, 94, 107–24, 146, 151
stylistics   viii, 17, 21, 45, 69, 71, 79, 87, 90, 128, 155
subordination (grammar)   18, 28, 149–150
subordination (prosodic)   25–7, 116, 120–21
surface structure   4–5, 11
Swedish   146
syllable   11, 15, 22, 26, 28, 68, 76, 94–5, 107, 110–24
syntax   1–46, 60, 93, 97, 99, 115, 122, 149–54
system   29, 33–41, 49, 59–60, 94–5, 112–13, 121–2

tempo   11, 14, 87, 94–5, 120–21
tension   95, 102, 140, 148
timbre   53, 77
Theory of Meter, A   108
tonal paragraph   121
tonal reduplication   33
tone   6–7, 11–13, 15, 28–45, 72, 82, 86, 94, 113, 120, 157
— lexical   12, 14, 71, 148
— of voice   vii, 57, 65, 84, 88, 90, 130, 134
tone-unit   6–23, 43–6, 68, 81, 94, 112–123, 154, 157
toneme   75
tonetic   78, 152

tonicity   4–15, 21–8, 44–5, 112–16, 121–122, 149, 153–4, 157
— compound   8, 23, 26–8
tongue-slip   15
Tracor   56
tradition   67
trait   89
transcription   1, 20–21, 61, 101, 121, 125, 132–3, 142, 152, 157
transformation   4–5
Truk   91
Twi   71
twins   144, 156

Uchucklesit   90
universals   45–6, 71
Urmi   86

valeur   113
variety   55–6, 58, 62, 79, 97–104, 116
verse   86, 111–23
vocabulary   2, 84, 87, 93, 99
vocal identifiers   52
vocal segregates   52–3
vocalization   65–73, 93, 126–33, 136–49, 157
voice disorder   79, 81
voice qualifications   68
voice quality   2, 21, 53–4, 57, 60–62, 75, 79, 82, 89–93, 113, 156
voice type   75, 79, 82, 156

weight   108, 118
Welsh   91, 108, 137
writing   1, 9, 14, 115–16

Yana   86

zoösemiotics   65